THE
MICHELIN
GUIDE

SAN FRANCISCO
BAY AREA & WINE COUNTRY

2018

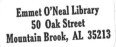

MICHELIN

THE MICHELIN GUIDE'S COMMITMENTS

Whether they are in Japan, the USA, China or Europe, our inspectors apply the same criteria to judge the quality of each and every establishment that they visit. The MICHELIN guide commands a **worldwide reputation** thanks to the commitments we make to our readers—and we reiterate these below:

Our inspectors make **anonymous visits** to restaurants to gauge the quality of cuisine offered to the everyday customer. They pay their own bill and make no indication of their presence. These visits are supplemented by comprehensive monitoring of information—our readers' comments are one valuable source, and are always taken into consideration.

Our choice of establishments is a completely **independent** one, made for the benefit of our readers alone. Decisions are discussed by the inspectors and editor, with the most important considered at the global level. Inclusion in the Guide is always free of charge.

The Guide offers a **selection** of the best restaurants in each category of comfort and price. A recommendation in the Guide is an honor in itself, and defines the establishment among the "best of the best."

All practical information, the classifications, and awards are revised and updated every year to ensure the most **reliable information** possible.

The standards and criteria for the classifications are the same in all countries covered by the MICHELIN guides. Our system is used worldwide and easy to apply when selecting a restaurant.

As part of Michelin's ongoing commitment to improving **travel and mobility**, we do everything possible to make vacations and eating out a pleasure.

THE MICHELIN GUIDE'S SYMBOLS

AVERAGE PRICES

⊛	Under $25
$$	$25 to $50
$$$	$50 to $75
$$$$	Over $75

FACILITIES & SERVICES

	Notable wine list
	Notable cocktail list
	Notable beer list
	Notable sake list
	Wheelchair accessible
	Outdoor dining
	Private dining room
	Breakfast
	Brunch
	Dim sum
	Valet parking
	Cash only

RESTAURANT CLASSIFICATIONS BY COMFORT
More pleasant if in red

	Small plates
	Comfortable
	Quite comfortable
	Very comfortable
	Top class comfortable
	Luxury in the traditional style

THE MICHELIN DISTINCTIONS FOR GOOD CUISINE

STARS

Our famous one ❀, two ❀❀ and three ❀❀❀ stars
identify establishments serving the highest quality
cuisine – taking into account the quality of ingredients,
the mastery of techniques and flavors, the levels of
creativity and, of course, consistency.

❀❀❀ Exceptional cuisine, worth a special journey
❀❀ Excellent cuisine, worth a detour
❀ High quality cooking, worth a stop

BIB GOURMAND

Inspectors' favorites for good value.

MICHELIN PLATE

Good cooking.
Fresh ingredients, carefully
prepared: simply a good meal.

DEAR READER,

It's been an exciting year for the entire team at the MICHELIN guides in North America, and it is with great pride that we present you with our 2018 edition to San Francisco. Over the past year our inspectors have extended their reach to include a variety of establishments and multiplied their anonymous visits to restaurants in our selection in order to accurately reflect the rich culinary diversity this great city has to offer.

As part of the Guide's highly confidential and meticulous evaluation process, our inspectors have methodically eaten their way through the entire city with a mission to marshal the finest in each category for your enjoyment. While they are expertly trained professionals in the food industry, the Guides remain consumer-driven and provide comprehensive choices to accommodate your every comfort, taste, and budget. By dining and drinking as "everyday" customers, they are able to experience and evaluate the same level of service and cuisine as any other guest. This past year has seen some unique advancements in San Francisco's dining scene. Some of these can be found in each neighborhood introduction, complete with photography depicting our favored choices.

Our company's founders, Édouard and André Michelin, published the first MICHELIN guide in 1900, to provide motorists with useful information about where they could service and repair their cars as well as find a good quality meal. In 1926, the star-rating system was introduced, whereby outstanding establishments are awarded for excellence in cuisine. Over the decades we have made many new enhancements to the Guide, and the local team here in San Francisco eagerly carries on these traditions.

As we take consumer feedback seriously, please feel free to contact us at: michelin.guides@michelin.com. You may also follow our Inspectors on Twitter (@MichelinGuideSF) and Instagram (@michelininspectors) as they chow their way around town. We thank you for your patronage and truly hope that the MICHELIN guide will remain your preferred reference to San Francisco's restaurants.

CONTENTS

■ INDEXES

SAN FRANCISCO

CASTRO

COLE VALLEY · HAIGHT-ASHBURY · NOE VALLEY

The Castro, once a cluster of farmland, is today a pulsating community punctuated by chic boutiques, hopping bars, and handsomely restored Victorians. In fact, it's a perpetual party here, with everybody waiting to sample the area's range of shabby to sleek bars, and dance clubs that spin tunes from multi-platinum pop icons. To feed its buzzing population of gym bunnies, leather daddies, and out-of-towners on tour to this mecca, the Castro teems with cool cafeterias. Start your day right at **Kitchen Story**, where the mascarpone-stuffed, deep-fried French toast has a following as large as the district's diversity. Then, stop in at **Thorough Bread & Pastry** if only to watch their bakers craft the best almond croissant in town. Linger at **Café Flore**, where the quaint patio is more evocative of its Parisian namesake than the simple continental fare. And primo for a quick lunch, the original **Rosamunde Sausage Grill** serves a variety of sandwiches like those stuffed with links of wild boar, cheddar brat, and chicken habanero. Counter seats are limited, so grab your sausage and head next door to enjoy it with a pint at **Toronado**. While

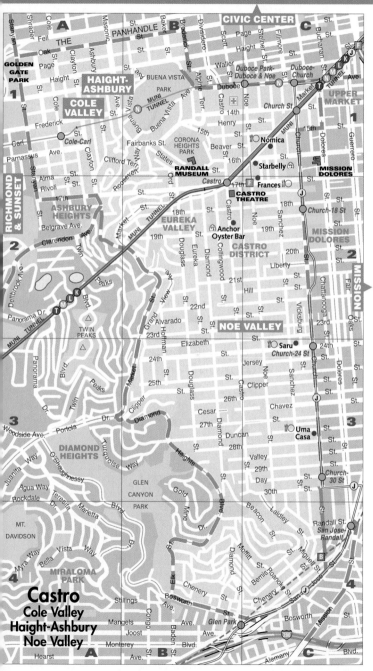

Castro
Cole Valley
Haight-Ashbury
Noe Valley

gourmands may prefer the likes of **La Mediterranee** for worthwhile cuisine, word on the street is that the best flavors here are served on the run. In fact, look no further than the kitschy kiosk **Hot Cookie** for that ideal bit of sweet.

COLE VALLEY

Neighboring Cole Valley may be small in size, but flaunts big personality. Cradling a mix of yuppies and families, this snoot-free quarter also embraces global flavors as seen in purveyors like **Say Cheese**, filled with top-quality international varieties. On Monday nights, dog-lovers treat the whole family to dinner at **Zazie**. Equally fun is a visit to **Val de Cole**, a wine shop offering value table wines to go with a delish dinner. The back garden patio at quaint **Cafe Reverie** is a stroller-friendly spot for a snack, whereas the 1930's throwback **Ice Cream Bar** with a soda fountain and lunch counter is mobbed by hipsters. Counter-culturalists have long sought haven in the hippiefied Haight-Ashbury where, despite the onslaught of retail chains, smoke shops and record

stores still dominate the landscape. But despite that, **Inovino** continues to thrive as a favored wine bar among locals and visitors for its tasty Italian small plates and an interesting selection of—you guessed it—*vino*. The Valley's aversion to fine dining and adoration for laid-back spots is further evident in lines that snake out the door of Puerto Rican favorite, **Parada 22** for authentic *pernil asado*; or **Cha Cha Cha**, a groovy tapas bar flowing with fresh-fruit sangria. Nurse that hangover with greasy hash browns and hotcakes at **Pork Store Cafe**, or head to **Haight Street Market** for a ready-made gourmet feast. On game night, kick back with a pint and plate of wings at old-school **Kezar Pub**.

NOE VALLEY

Noe Valley is known for its specialty shops, and Italian emporium **Pasta Gina** sells everything you might need for a night in with *nonna*. **Noe Valley Bakery** bakes the best bread around, after which a pour of coffee from **Castro Coffee Company** is a must. Imported chocolates are front and center at **Chocolate Covered**, while **Marcello's** is *the* hub for fast and fabulous pizza. Keeping pace with this sense of "spirit," **Swirl on Castro** is a sleek space that is big on boutique wines. But, if booze doesn't fit your mood, then opt for a soothing brew at **Spike's Coffees & Teas**, specializing in artisan loose-leaf teas.

ANCHOR OYSTER BAR 😊
Seafood

𝕏

MAP: B2

Landlubbers seeking a taste of the sea can be found pulling up a stool at this Castro institution, where waves of waiting diners spill out the doors. This tiny, minimally adorned space filled with old-fashioned charm is better for twosomes than groups.

While the menu may be petite, it's full of fresh fare like a light and flavorful Dungeness crab "burger" on a sesame bun; Caesar salad combining sweet prawns and tangy anchovy dressing; or a cup of creamy Boston clam chowder loaded with clams and potatoes. As the name portends, raw oysters are a specialty, so briny that the accompanying mignonette may not be necessary. And of course, the cioppino is unmissable as this signature item turns deadly when paired with delicious and buttery garlic bread.

- 579 Castro St. (bet. 18th & 19th Sts.)
- 𝒫 (415) 431-3990 — **WEB:** www.anchoroysterbar.com
- Lunch Mon – Sat   Dinner nightly   **PRICE:** $$

FRANCES 🍴○
Californian

𝕏𝕏 | ♿

MAP: C2

This tiny, intensely personal restaurant from Chef/owner Melissa Perello has been a local hit from the get-go. Chic and always packed, it's as perfect for a low-key date night as it is for dinner with the kids. And while reservations are a nigh-impossible score, the gracious staff saves ten counter seats for walk-ins—and serves every diner with equal aplomb.

Perello eschews trendy powders and foams for hearty, seasonal fare, like charred baby octopus with homemade yogurt and olive tapenade. Honey-brined pork chop rests over creamed escarole and fennel slaw; and McGinnis Ranch carrots are roasted with sunchokes for an interesting blend of sweet and savory. Desserts like a black sesame pavlova with chicory root ice cream offer a fresh, light conclusion.

- 3870 17th St. (at Pond St.)
- 𝒫 (415) 621-3870 — **WEB:** www.frances-sf.com
- Dinner Tue – Sun   **PRICE:** $$

NOMICA ⚍⚎

Fusion

XX | 🍸 🫗 ♿ 🖥   **MAP:** C1

Japanese and Western flavors collide at this hip Castro address, where "cassoulet" is actually a five-spice duck leg with soybeans and duck-fat rice; chicken wings come stuffed with gyoza filling; and chicken and waffles are done karaage-style with accents of shiso béarnaise and matcha salt. Even the cocktails incorporate unusual features like sea beans and shiitakes.

But despite the culinary culture clash, Nomica's food is playful and satisfying, and anxious foodies bend over backwards to score an advance order of its coveted whole chicken in brioche (which requires 24 hours' notice). With its vast selection of Japanese whiskey and awamori, it's a big draw for young professional types, who congregate at the bar for sips and quirky bites.

▦ 2223 Market St. (bet. 15th & 16th Sts.)
℘ (415) 655-3280 — WEB: www.nomicasf.com
▦ Dinner Mon – Sat   **PRICE: $$$**

SARU ⚍⚎

Japanese

X   **MAP:** C3

Hilly Noe Valley is the perfect setting for this jewel of a sushi restaurant, and lest you have an original idea, the line here will thwart you in your tracks. The menu is thoroughly Japanese, with a few California touches—think grilled shishito peppers tossed with crunchy daikon in a ponzu dressing.

Be sure to start with the signature tempura-fried seaweed cracker topped with spicy tuna and avocado. Then, perfectly sized tasting spoons of seared ankimo with scallions, as well as halibut tartare with yuzu make for delightful quick bites. Though rolls are available, regulars opt for the nigiri, which might include kampachi, baby snapper, and snow crab. If you'd like the chefs to choose, several omakase (including an all-salmon variation) are also on offer.

▦ 3856 24th St. (bet. Sanchez & Vicksburg Sts.)
℘ (415) 400-4510 — WEB: www.akaisarusf.com
▦ Lunch & dinner Tue – Sun   **PRICE: $$**

STARBELLY 🐶

Californian

✕✕ | 🍺 ⛓ 🏠 🛋

The simplest things are often the best, as a meal at Starbelly deliciously proves. Whether you're twirling a forkful of spaghetti with garlicky tomato sauce, jalapeños, and house-made bacon, or tucking into a juicy burger on a grilled sesame seed challah bun, you're sure to savor something beautifully made, seasonal, and unfussy. Desserts are just as satisfying, like a salted caramel pot de crème served with rosemary shortbread cookies.

A nexus of the Castro social scene, the cheerful, woodpaneled space is always full of locals hopping from table to table to greet their friends, and the back patio (heated and sheltered when it's foggy) is an appealing refuge.

Be sure to make reservations: this is a local favorite, and for good reason.

▨ 3583 16th St. (at Market St.)
📞 (415) 252-7500 — **WEB:** www.starbellysf.com
▨ Lunch & dinner daily   PRICE: $$

UMA CASA 🍴

Portuguese

✕✕ | ⛓

High ceilings and azulejo-adorned walls set the scene at this Noe Valley jewel, which succeeds longtime local spot Incanto. It's also one of the few high-end San Francisco restaurants spotlighting the cuisine of Portugal, and Chef Telmo Faria delivers a traditional seafood-centric menu. Read: grilled sardines, salt cod fritters, as well as garlic- and chili-inflected shrimp moçambique.

Most diners opt to share a flurry of small plates, commencing with potato chips and piri-piri sauce. The entrées are satisfying, too. Try the alcatra, red wine-braised short ribs, or pan-roasted sea bass with molho cru, the Portuguese take on chimichurri. Finally, sip on one of the bar's signature low alcohol cocktails, made with port, sherry, and other fortified wines.

▨ 1550 Church St. (at Duncan St.)
📞 (415) 829-2264 — **WEB:** www.umacasarestaurant.com
▨ Dinner Tue – Sun   PRICE: $$

CIVIC CENTER

HAYES VALLEY · LOWER HAIGHT · TENDERLOIN

Anchoring this old, new, and now fashionable district is the gilded beaux arts-style dome of City Hall, whose architectural splendor gleams along the main artery of the Civic Center. Following in these footsteps, refined details grace the neighborhood's prized cultural institutions like the War Memorial & Performing Arts Center, as well as the Asian Art Museum. On Wednesdays and Sundays, SF's oldest market, **Heart of the City**, erupts in full form on the vast promenade outside City Hall. This independent and farmer-operated arcade is a hit among locals thanks to an extensive offering of high-quality, locally sourced, and attractively priced produce—not to mention rare Asian ingredients like young ginger and Buddha's hand. Ground zero for California's marriage equality movement and countless political protests, City Hall's plaza is also home to galas like LovEvolution; the

SF Symphony's biennial Black & White Ball; as well as the annual St. Patrick's Day parade and festival.

Neighboring Tenderloin successfully alleviates this region's now-defunct repute as a "food desert." Similar, in some ways, to Manhattan's Meatpacking District and home to a vast Asian—particularly Vietnamese—population, this once tough but now trendy "underbelly" boasts an incredible array of authentic ethnic eateries. Gone are those gangs of organized crime, and in place Larkin Street (also known as "**Little Saigon**") is crowded with mom-and-pop shops like **Saigon Sandwich**—leading the way with spicy *báhn mì* made from fresh and crusty baguettes for only a song. Nearby, **Turtle Tower** has amassed quite a patronage (celebrity chefs included) for fragrant *pho ga*; while romantic little **Bodega Bistro** is best known for bold aromas, French flavors, and more *pho*. Score points among family and friends by treating them to an excellent selection of classic cocktails reinterpreted at **Bourbon & Branch**. Note that reservations are a must at this swanky, dimly

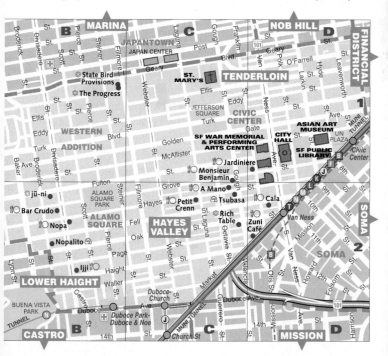

lit, and sultry hideaway-cum-former speakeasy, settled on Jones Street. But, for a more sober and substantial affair, local suits may head on over to **Elmira Rosticceria** for a range of Italian-inspired eats—take advantage of their flourishing take-out business during the lunch rush. Of course, come nightfall, the Tenderloin's muddle of strip clubs and bars becomes a hot hub for a decadent nightlife. And boasting an impressive selection of craft libations, **Tradition** is a hip venue housed on Jones Street that redefines the hand-crafted American cocktail experience by serving traditional drinks as well as updated versions in a vintage speakeasy setting.

West of the Civic Center, Hayes Valley is undeniably polished, with a coterie of designer boutiques set amid a medley of sleek retreats. Some residents find themselves smitten by **Chantal Guillon**, which spotlights exquisitely flavored macarons served in a French-style setting. Carnivores delight in **Fatted Calf Charcuterie** where fresh, smoked, and cured meats abound in loaded display cases. Here the cheese selection is solid too, so do all your stocking up, pre-picnic. Then, sate all these salty eats with a quenching sip from **True Sake**, a super-cool and all-sake business; just as caffeine junkies get their daily dose of **Blue Bottle** straight from the kiosk on Linden Street. Finish with a tour of Europe at **Miette**, an impossibly charming confiserie jammed with rare chocolates, salted licorice, taffy, and gelées; or **Christopher Elbow Artisanal Chocolate** for a smidge of bliss.

LOWER HAIGHT

Steps to the west, the Lower Haight attracts sporty troupes and hipster groups for sake-infused cocktails at **Noc Noc**, followed by fantastic live tunes at **The Independent**, a standing room-only music venue. Some dress to impress the über-cool crowd at **Maven**, where inventive cocktails, tasty bites, and groovy tunes guarantee a great night out. Speaking of beats, the Fillmore Jazz District continues to seduce (and save) music lovers today. Settled by African-American GI's at the end of World War II, the Lower Haight hummed with jazz greats like Billie Holiday and Miles Davis. With the attempted resurgence of the jazz district, the Fillmore today goes on to resound with music from rock icons like Jimi Hendrix and The Dead. Of course, the annual Fillmore Jazz Festival is a must-see celebration of musical magnificence.

A MANO ¶○

Italian

XX | ♿   **MAP:** C2

"A mano" is Italian for "by hand," and that's exactly how your pasta will be made at this delicious newcomer, where diners can frequently witness dough being rolled, cut, and folded just minutes before arriving at the table. Options include vivid green pea and pesto tagliatelle and delicately shaped agnolotti dal plin. For those who'd rather eschew carbs, there are hearty mains like braised short ribs.

The crowd is diverse, with young professionals and families alike sharing margherita pizzas and spicy chicken meatballs. Loud, funky music and floor-to-ceiling windows that open onto the bustle of Hayes Valley's main drag add to the lively vibe. Order up another cocktail or an affordable glass of Italian red to make the fun last a little longer.

■ 450 Hayes St. (bet. Octavia & Gough Sts.)
☎ (415) 506-7401 — **WEB:** www.amanosf.com
■ Dinner nightly   **PRICE:** $$

BAR CRUDO ¶○

Seafood

▣ | 🍺 ♿   **MAP:** B2

Visitors without reservations should be prepared to wait for a table at this Divisadero gem. In fact, they may even find people lined up on the sidewalk for a seat at the counter. As the name suggests, this seafood haven offers supreme crudos. Whether it's Arctic char with horseradish crème fraîche, wasabi tobiko, and dill; or scallop with sweet corn purée, tarragon oil, and popped sorghum, the combos are delicious. Shellfish platters are available, and there are a few hot dishes like seafood chowder chockfull of fish, shrimp, squid and bacon.

Inside, the space is often standing room-only, with just a few tables; most guests gather around the bar. Grab a glass of wine or beer, peek into the kitchen, and be sure to check out the futuristic art on the walls.

■ 655 Divisadero St. (bet. Grove & Hayes Sts.)
☎ (415) 409-0679 — **WEB:** www.barcrudo.com
■ Dinner Tue – Sun   **PRICE:** $$

CALA ¶○

Mexican

✗✗ | 🍸 ♿   **MAP:** D2

A Mexico City superstar with the seafood-centric Contramar, Gabriela Cámara has brought her magic touch to this Civic Center hottie, where she serves similar food. Nothing is lost in translation: filleted black cod with red chile adobo is silky and smoky after a wood grilling in collard leaves, while Cámara's famed tuna tostadas get a Bay Area sustainability update with ocean trout. And you won't want to miss the griddled blackbean sopes, which seem simple but sing with flavor.

Cala's minimalist aesthetic matches that of Contramar, with vaulted, skylight-dotted ceilings, a planter box full of climbing vines, and lots of light wood for a rustic-urban feel. Service can be spotty, but for a flavorful, unfussy meal, it's quickly become a hot ticket.

▓ 149 Fell St. (bet. Franklin St. & Van Ness Ave.)
℘ (415) 660-7701 — **WEB:** www.calarestaurant.com
▓ Dinner nightly   **PRICE:** $$$

IJJI ¶○

Japanese

✗ | ♿   **MAP:** B2

Seeking top-notch nigiri that doesn't break the bank? Head to this intimate Divisadero hangout, which boasts just 17 seats—10 at tables, where items are served à la carte, and seven more at an omakase-centric sushi bar. Needless to say, reservations are a must.

While Ijji's nigiri aren't quite as dazzling as some of the city's starred spots, the silky, soy-brushed kanpachi; delicate firefly squid with white miso; and decadent toro are each an outstanding value for the restaurant's mid-range price point. The limited menu also features a few cooked dishes, like slivers of meaty king trumpet mushrooms in a nutty sesame paste. Just don't expect to socialize with the chefs: laser-focused on making sure your fish is perfect, they tend to keep mum.

▓ 252 Divisadero St. (bet. Haight & Page Sts.)
℘ (415) 658-7388 — **WEB:** www.ijjisf.com
▓ Dinner nightly   **PRICE:** $$$

JARDINIÈRE ☊○
Californian

XxX | 🍇 🍸 ♿ 🍽 🧾

MAP: D1

For a memorable night on the town, don your best dress, find a hand to hold, and head to this longtime favorite—tinged with a sense of bygone romance. Stop off at the circular bar and join the well-heeled couples sipping cocktails pre- or post-opera. Prime seats on the upstairs balcony overlook the bustling lower level, and stunning arched windows show off views of the street. Approachable, seasonal dishes abound on Jardinière's menu, from tender tajarin pasta with morel mushrooms and butter to a Mediterranean-inspired duo of lamb belly and shoulder with fresh fava beans and smoked yogurt sauce.

Indecisive sweet tooths will thrill to the bonne bouche, an array of candies, cookies, small cakes, and profiteroles that makes a striking conclusion.

🔲 300 Grove St. (at Franklin St.)
☎ (415) 861-5555 — **WEB:** www.jardiniere.com
🔲 Dinner nightly

PRICE: $$$

MONSIEUR BENJAMIN ☊○
French

XX | ♿ 🧾

MAP: C1

Chef Corey Lee's take on timeless bistro cuisine is as sleek and striking as the space it's served in. Fit for the cover of a magazine, this black-and-white dining room's minimalist, yet intimate décor is trumped only by its pièce de résistance: an exhibition kitchen where you'll find the meticulous brigade of cooks hard at work, producing impressively authentic French food.

Begin with the pâté de campagne, enhanced with liver and shallots and presented with strong mustard, cornichons, and country bread. The Arctic char amandine is excellent, dressed with fragrant beurre noisette and served over a bed of crispy haricot verts and sunchokes. For a sweet and fruity finish, purists will delight in the dessert menu's crêpe façon gâteau.

🔲 451 Gough St. (at Ivy St.)
☎ (415) 403-2233 — **WEB:** www.monsieurbenjamin.com
🔲 Lunch Sat – Sun   Dinner nightly

PRICE: $$$

JŪ-NI ❀
Japanese

✗✗ | ⌣ ᵜ   **MAP:** B2

"Jū-ni" is Japanese for "twelve," which also happens to be the number of seats in this petite, omakase-only spot just off the busy Divisadero corridor. Its segmented, L-shaped sushi bar ensures personalized attention from the trio of chefs, often led by Chef/owner Geoffrey Lee. They're a young, lively crew, and they've designed this space with a crowd of similarly young, moneyed professionals in mind. Note the spotlights above the counter, placed for perfect Instagram snaps of dishes, and the thoroughly curated sake menu.

A meal may begin with a tasting of seasonal vegetables—think tomatoes over edamame hummus—before proceeding to an array of nigiri, painstakingly sourced straight from Tokyo's own Tsukiji fish market and delicately draped over well-seasoned pillows of rice. Standouts include sakura masu with a salt-cured cherry blossom leaf, buttery Hokkaido scallops, and the signature ikura—cured in soy, sake and honey and finished with a grating of velvety frozen monkfish liver.

Decadent supplements, like torched A5 Wagyu beef and luscious uni, can be added along the way. But the meal finishes with a surprisingly gentle sendoff: sweet, tender mochi dabbed with adzuki bean paste.

▮ 1335 Fulton St. (bet. Broderick & Divisadero Sts.)
☏ (415) 655-9924 — **WEB:** www.junisf.com
▮ Dinner nightly   PRICE: $$$$

NOPA ⊗

Californian

XX | 🍸 ♿ 🛋️

MAP: B2

Before you're able to enjoy a single forkful at this Bay Area sensation, you'll have to secure a table—and that takes some serious effort. Reservations are snapped up at lightning speed, and hopeful walk-ins must line up prior to the start of service to add their name to the list.

The good news? Your efforts will be well rewarded. Inside, an open kitchen, soaring ceilings, and hordes of ravenous sophisticates produce a cacophonous setting in which to relish Nopa's wonderful, organic, wood-fired cuisine. Dig into a bruschetta of grilled levain spread with smashed avocado, pickled jalapeños, lemon-dressed arugula, and shaved mezzo secco, or go for the roasted King salmon fillet over creamed corn, smoky maitakes, crisp green beans, and sweet tomato confit.

▓ 560 Divisadero St. (at Hayes St.)
✆ (415) 864-8643 — **WEB:** www.nopasf.com
▓ Lunch Sat – Sun Dinner nightly   **PRICE:** $$

NOPALITO ⊛

Mexican

X | ♿ 🚻

MAP: B2

Whether they're digging into a refreshing ensalada de nopales or sharing a platter of blue-corn tacos stuffed with spicy-smoky marinated fish, local couples and families adore this sustainable Mexican spot. Sister to Cal-cuisine icon Nopa, Nopalito is so beloved that an equally good and popular Inner Sunset location is also thriving.

The small, cheerful space with reclaimed wood and bright green accents doesn't take reservations; call ahead to get on the list, or try takeout. Once seated, friendly servers will guide the way with house-made horchata for the kids and an extensive tequila selection for grown-ups. Both groups will certainly agree on a sweet finish: the excellent vanilla bean flan topped with orange-caramel and orange supremes is unbeatable.

▓ 306 Broderick St. (bet. Fell & Oak Sts.)
✆ (415) 437-0303 — **WEB:** www.nopalitosf.com
▓ Lunch & dinner daily   **PRICE:** $$

PETIT CRENN ¶○

French

✕✕ | ♿ 🛏   **MAP:** C2

In a homey corner of booming Hayes Valley, Chef Dominique Crenn serves a menu more approachable (in both technique and price) than her acclaimed Atelier Crenn. With its open kitchen, chalkboard menus, and nautical feel inspired by Crenn's native Brittany, Petit Crenn is a hit among locals.

While the eats are rib-sticking—think wood-roasted trout with cider sabayon, or rustic bread slathered with espelette aïoli and sautéed mushrooms—the execution of this kitchen is precise, as evidenced in the exquisite gem lettuce salad—which is so much more than its name suggests—or even the rolled omelette tucked with fragrant herbs. Whether you opt for the early evening à la carte seating or multi-course prix-fixe, expect to leave sated and smitten.

▦ 609 Hayes St. (bet. Buchanan & Laguna Sts.)
℘ (415) 864-1744 — **WEB:** www.petitcrenn.com
▦ Lunch & dinner Tue – Sun   **PRICE:** $$$$

TSUBASA 😳

Japanese

✕   **MAP:** C2

Amidst the pricey boutiques and top-dollar restaurants of Hayes Valley, a good deal can be hard to come by. However, Tsubasa is a delightful exception, offering well-made nigiri, sashimi, and maki at a price point that belies the high quality of its fish.

The sleek dining room offers table seating, but the best seats in the house are at the sushi bar, where you'll be presented with generously portioned nigiri that range from cleanly flavored turbot to intense, vinegar-kissed saba (mackerel). There are also more elaborate maki, like a salmon and avocado roll topped with raw scallops and miso sauce. But the deepest pleasures are simple ones: excellent miso soup, a tuna roll with beautifully seasoned rice, and rich, custardy tamago.

▦ 429 Gough St (bet. Hayes & Ivy Sts.)
℘ (415) 551-9688 — **WEB:** www.tsubasasf.com
▦ Lunch Tue – Sat   Dinner Tue – Sun   **PRICE:** $$

THE PROGRESS ✿

Californian

✕✕ | 🍸 ♿

MAP: B1

This is the rare restaurant that guarantees its diners will never be bored, thanks to the sophisticated energy that flows directly from a notably ambitious kitchen.

Service is friendly and attentive. Sure, they may make an error in describing a dish, but they do it with panache. The gorgeous space has that Nordic look that California so loves, with plenty of bare wood, skylights, and an affluent crowd appearing informal in their Patagonias.

Be sure to try one of their clever cocktails, like the savory and refreshing house martini, finished with a droplet of rosemary oil.

The reasonably priced prix-fixe begins with snacks and moves on to family-style dining. Sunchokes are at the center of an exceptionally good combination of crisp roti, buttermilk-sunchoke-ranch dressing, thin slices of turnip, radish, artisanal cheese, and Burgundy truffle. Slow-cooked rabbit is enriched with dark jus and smoked prune romesco. When they hit their mark, food like this transcends its ingredients and technique to result in something genius. When they occasionally miss it, you feel like you've eaten a plate of weird vitamins. Desserts like "deluxe" vanilla ice cream are far more decadent than they sound.

■ 1525 Fillmore St. (bet. Geary Blvd. & O'Farrell St.)

𝒞 (415) 673-1294 — **WEB:** www.theprogress-sf.com

■ Dinner nightly

PRICE: $$$

RICH TABLE ✿

Contemporary

XX | 🍹

A rustic-chic décor, highlighting reclaimed and raw wood, gives Rich Table a farmhouse feel, and the crowds that pack it are equally stylish. The young professionals and pre-theater diners know that reserving in advance is a must. If you're not lucky enough to secure a table, get in line 30 minutes before opening to snag one of the dozen coveted bar seats.

Why all the fuss? Because Chefs/owners Evan and Sarah Rich execute casual California fare with fine-dining precision, interweaving a bevy of global influences along the way. An Indian-influenced foie gras torchon is set over a pool of tangy mango lassi and toasted meringue, all to be heaped upon buttery brioche. The seared pierogies, stuffed with ricotta, morels, and peas are pristine enough to win a Polish grandmother's approval, and a char siu-style pork chop is beautifully smoky and charred.

The super-hip staff is thoroughly polished and happy to recommend a cocktail or wine. They'll push the duo of famous "snacks" —crispy sardine-threaded chips and umami-packed porcini doughnuts with raclette dipping sauce. But skip them in favor of a seasonal dessert, like a tart cherry ice with almond ice cream and shiso.

▨ 199 Gough St. (at Oak St.)
℘ (415) 355-9085 — **WEB:** www.richtablesf.com
▨ Dinner nightly   **PRICE: $$$**

STATE BIRD PROVISIONS ✿

American

✕✕

MAP: B1

Welcome to the dining evolution, where streams of plates are passed between guests in dim sum-style, and the supremely seasonal California cooking is always very good, even vibrant and unexpected. You may not understand all of what you ordered, but prices are reasonable so pile on a few extra items and try everything that comes your way. No one leaves here hungry.

Servers circulate through the room with platters or push carts brimming with creative and utterly unique dishes. Highlights include a Vietnamese salad of deep-fried pork belly with plum, mint, basil, and cilantro in a lime-fish sauce vinaigrette. Heartier but wow-inducing bites of crisp pan-fried ravioli stuffed with guinea hen and bathed in rich broth will have you wishing for a larger portion. Other exquisite creations include shaved hearts of palm with yuba ribbons, Lacinato kale, Asian pear, sesame seeds, and more served in a generous pool of tahini and chili oil for a wonderful spicy, creamy contrast.

Be forewarned: getting a reservation here is the ultimate challenge and walk-in spots require lining up around 4:30 P.M. Best to avoid nights when large parties are booked—this may negatively impact your experience.

▨ 1529 Fillmore St. (bet. Geary Blvd. & O'Farrell St.)

℮ (415) 795-1272 — **WEB:** www.statebirdsf.com

▨ Dinner nightly

PRICE: $$

ZUNI CAFÉ ¶○

Mediterranean

✗✗ | ⚹ ⌂ ⟐ ⟐

D2

CIVIC CENTER

Almost forty years young and still thriving as if it were newborn, locals and visitors remain drawn to this SF institution. Famous for its laid-back California vibe and great, locally sourced eats, this iconic space embraces its unique shape, and is styled with bold artwork-covered walls, a copper bar counter, and wood-burning oven sending out delightful pizzas that fill the room with mouthwatering aromas.

Given its ace location, Zuni makes for a divine lunch destination—and proof is in the many business folk, trendy ladies-who-lunch, and tourists who fill its tables midday. Menu treasures include sliced persimmon scattered with shaved Jerusalem artichoke and baby arugula leaves, tailed by toothsome artisanal rigatoni clutching fragrant lamb sugo.

▧ 1658 Market St. (bet. Franklin & Gough Sts.)
✆ (415) 552-2522 — **WEB:** www.zunicafe.com
▧ Lunch & dinner Tue – Sun

PRICE: $$

Share the journey with us!
@MichelinGuideSF
@MichelinInspectors

FINANCIAL DISTRICT

EMBARCADERO · UNION SQUARE

Booming with high-rises and large-scale companies, the Financial District is world-renowned. While the city itself is reputed for its easygoing vibe and cool 'tude, the financial sector is ever-bustling with the prominence of Fortune 500 companies, multi-national corporations, major banks, and big law. Settled along the west of the waterfront, expect to see streetcars, pedestrians, and wildly tattooed bicycle messengers on weekdays clogging the routes of the triangle bounded by Kearny, Jackson, and Market streets. Come noon, lines snake out

the doors of better grab-and-go sandwich shops and salad spots. Of course, there is always a steady stream of expense-account clients who continuously patronize this neighborhood's host of fine-dining establishments; whereas along Market Street, casual cafés and chain restaurants keep the focus on families, tourists, and shoppers alike.

EMBARCARDERO

Despite all that this area has to offer, its greatest culinary treasures lies within the famed **Ferry Building**. This 1898 steel-reinforced sandstone structure is easily recognized by its 244-foot clock tower that rises up from Market Street and way above the waterfront promenade— **The Embarcadero**. It is among the few survivors of

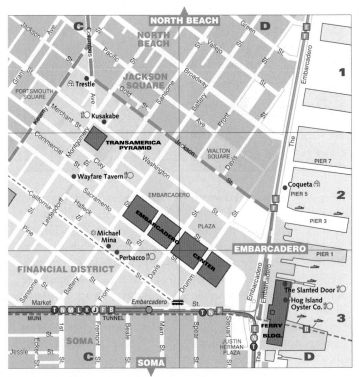

the 1906 earthquake and fire that destroyed most of this neighborhood. Thanks to a 2004 renovation, the soaring interior arcade makes a stunning showcase for regional products, artisanal foods, rare Chinese teas, and everything in between. Popularly referred to as the **Ferry Building Marketplace**, surrounding food community by highlighting small producers. Two of the most popular among them are **Cowgirl Creamery**'s farmstead cheeses, and Berkeley's **Acme Bread Company**, whose organic breads are a sight (and smell) to behold! Following this philosophy, find numerous

every diligent foodie is destined here for the likes of Chef Amaryll Schwertner's breakfast specialties at the beloved **Boulettes Larder**, where guests literally sit in the kitchen as their spread is prepared—multigrain griddle cakes with ricotta and seasonal fruit are a favorite for good reason. This emporium also pays homage to the organic and exotic mushrooms, medicinal herbs, and themed products at **Far West Fungi**. Here, patient enthusiasts can even purchase logs on which to grow their own harvest. Legendary **Frog Hollow Farm** is also stationed nearby, offering pristine seasonal fruit alongside homemade chutneys, marmalade, and fresh-baked pastries. Known for their Parisian-style chocolates and caramels, **Recchiuti Confections** has elevated their craft to an art form that can only be described as "sublime."

Completing this gourmet trend are gleaming bottles of **McEvoy Ranch Olive Oil** from their Petaluma ranch that also includes an impressive array of olive oil-based products. While such world-class food shopping may whet the appetite of many, more immediate cravings can be satisfied at the Building's more casual dining delights like **DELICA**, popular for beautifully prepared Japanese fusion food, from signature sushi rolls to savory croquettes. Join the corporate lunch rush seated at picnic tables in **Mijita** (run by Traci Des Jardins of **Jardinère** fame) to sample such treats as *queso fundido* or Baja-style fish tacos. Alternatively, claim a patio seat at **MarketBar** for market-inspired salads, flatbreads, and American brasserie fare. While this is a great spot to sit and take in the view, the most decadent takeout option is still **Boccalone Salumeria** for their

comprehensive charcuterie. Whether purchasing these salty eats by the platter, pound, or layered in a single-serving "cone," prepare for an unapologetically carnivorous treat. On Tuesday, Thursday, and Saturday mornings, high-minded chefs share laughs with the locals at **Ferry Plaza Farmer's Market**, which deals in everything from organic produce and baked goods to fresh pastas and tons more. On market days, open-air stands and tents line the picturesque sidewalk in front of the Ferry Building and rear plaza overlooking the bay.

Tourists and unwearied locals are sure to enjoy some visual stimulation at The Bay Lights—an undulating light installation by artist Leo Villareal—illuminating the west span of the Bay Bridge. **The Embarcadero** boasts the best view of this beautiful piece. Meanwhile, corporate types know to head on over to the **Embarcadero Center** (spanning five blocks and boasting reduced parking rates on weekends) to get their midday shopping fix in the sprawling three-story indoor mall, or to grab a quick lunch at one of their many eateries ranging from mini-chains to noodle shops. A speck of sweet from **See's Candies** or caffeine from **Peet's** makes for an ideal finale.

UNION SQUARE

Upscale department stores like Barneys, Neiman Marcus, and Saks Fifth Avenue preside over Union Square, where foodies gather for a gourmet experience and fashionistas flock to the parade of designer shops. And, just as noodle lovers form a queue outside **Katana-Ya** for their steaming bowls of slurp-worthy ramen, shopaholics and local bargain hunters alike pop into **Tout Sweet Patisserie** (housed inside Macy's) for a pick-me-up in the form of pastries, candies, and macarons. Take home a few extra goodies, if only to appreciate their beautiful packaging.

AKIKO'S 🍴

Japanese

✗ | ☯

MAP: B2

Though Akiko's may look like an average neighborhood sushi joint from the outside (especially since it's often confused with a nearby spot of the same name), a meal here is a reminder that appearances can be deceiving. Those planning on dining in will want to make a reservation, as the small, industrial space is mighty popular—especially those coveted counter spots.

Second-generation Chef/owner Ray Lee does wonders with nigiri from around the globe, from silky New Zealand King salmon to full-flavored Cyprian sea bream. Cooked dishes like gently battered agedashi tofu, in a flavorful broth accented with "pearls" of ikura, are just as appealing. And be sure to sample the excellent applewood-aged soy sauce, which brings out the flavors of each dish.

▦ 431 Bush St. (bet. Grant & Kearny Sts.)
☎ (415) 397-3218 — **WEB:** www.akikosrestaurant.com
▦ Lunch Mon – Fri   Dinner Mon – Sat   **PRICE: $$$**

COQUETA 😊

Spanish

✗✗ | ♿

MAP: D2

A tasty little morsel of a space serving up mouthwatering tapas, Michael Chiarello's Pier 5 destination offers shimmering views of the bay from its rustic dining room, equipped with rough-hewn wooden tables, cowhide rugs, and a big, theatrical open kitchen and bar. There's a bit more space on the tented outdoor patio, but if your heart is set on a table, book early.

Its name is Spanish for "flirt," and Coqueta's alluring menu has caused more than one enraptured diner to over-order. Some fine options: crunchy-creamy chicken and pea croquetas, mini sandwiches of smoked salmon with queso fresco and truffle honey, and wood-grilled octopus with tender fingerling potatoes. Complete the experience with the Asturian apple pie with Cabrales blue cheese ice cream.

▦ Pier 5 (at The Embarcadero)
☎ (415) 704-8866 — **WEB:** www.coquetasf.com
▦ Lunch Tue – Sun   Dinner nightly   **PRICE: $$**

CAMPTON PLACE ❁
Indian

XxX | 😳 � & ⊡ 🍴 🛋 ✋   **MAP:** B2

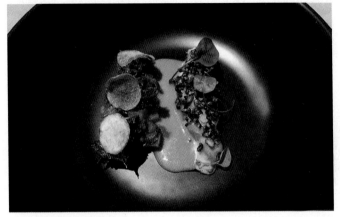

With its sleek booths, wall-to-wall windows, plush carpeting, and pristinely robed tables, this elegant oasis in the Taj Hotel is as formal and traditional as one would expect. A striking blown glass chandelier hanging from the coffered ceiling adds an element of the unexpected. An odd mix of gourmands and hotel guests keep the vibe at Campton Place desultory inside, but by greeting each diner as they enter, the staff maintains a sense of refinery that is true to this contemporary Cal-Indian menu.

The full talent of this kitchen is showcased in the seven-course vegetarian or Spice Route non-vegetarian tasting menus. Courses arrive on charcoal-glazed ceramics and allude to Indian spices. This is illustrated in puffed black rice-coated lobster dressed with a coastal-inspired coconut curry poured tableside. Other dishes like battered and fried cauliflower with creamy rice and turmeric foam, or black cod set atop vibrantly spiced green papaya cover all bases of flavor and texture.

Just as slow-cooked meat dishes have an elegant undertone of garam masala, a dessert like pumpkin cake served with refreshing Buddha's hand sorbet is sprinkled with colorful spices for an enticing presentation.

▨ 340 Stockton St. (bet. Post & Sutter Sts.)
📞 (415) 955-5555 — **WEB:** www.camptonplacesf.com
▨ Lunch & dinner daily   **PRICE:** $$$$

DEL POPOLO ☺

Pizza

✗ | &

If you've got eyes for killer pies, you'll want to make a beeline to this chic and simple Italian hot spot. The open space is centered around a big, blazing oven, and crowds arrive early to score every last no-reservations seat. (The host is happy to text when yours is ready.)

Del Popolo may have gotten its start as a food truck, but one bite of the wood-fired pizza and its clear how it earned its address. Chewy, blistered, and caramelized, the crusts arrive laden with toppings both traditional (mozzarella, tomato sauce, house-made sausage) and California cool (roasted winter squash, mascarpone, spring onions). Don't sleep on the antipasti, either—a smoked, cumin-infused sweet potato with pecan salsa verde and a poached egg is dizzyingly delicious.

◼ 855 Bush St. (bet. Mason & Taylor Sts.)
℘ (415) 589-7940 — **WEB:** www.delpopolosf.com
◼ Dinner Tue – Sun   PRICE: $$

HOG ISLAND OYSTER CO. ⵏⵔ

Seafood

✗ | 🍸 & ⛱

Can't make the trip to Marin to shuck oysters on Hog Island's docks? They'll bring Tomales Bay's finest to you at this buzzing cityside outpost in the Ferry Building, which draws long lines of both tourists and locals for platters of some of the sweetest, freshest bivalves on the West Coast. You'll receive all the accompaniments—lemon, Tabasco, mignonette—but they're good enough to slurp solo.

Once you've had your fill, be sure to sample the other aquatic offerings: Peruvian-style crudo with silky sea bass; a hefty bowl of cioppino loaded with prawns, clams, mussels, and squid; and the exceptional Manila clam chowder, a bestseller for good reason. Throw in the expansive Bay views from the patio and dining room, and those lines come as no surprise.

◼ 1 Ferry Building (at The Embarcadero)
℘ (415) 391-7117 — **WEB:** www.hogislandoysters.com
◼ Lunch & dinner daily   PRICE: $$$

KIN KHAO ✿
Thai

✗ | 🍸 ⚬ 🍽

Tucked into an alcove of the unprepossessing Parc 55 hotel, this restaurant won't win any awards in the décor department—it's spare and casual, with tables set with chopstick canisters and bowls of chili oil. But when it comes to delivering authentically layered, fiery Thai flavor with a produce-driven northern California flair, it has no equal.

Kin Khao's menu conjures up dishes from across Thailand and is a virtual homage to local purveyors. Imagine a meaty and rich five spice duck noodle soup infused with duck bones and stocked with bok choy, noodles, and delightfully tender duck leg confit; or a deliciously fresh take on som tum, with julienned green papaya tossed with golden tomatoes, long beans, dried shrimp, and crushed red chili. More traditional options may include classic pad kee mao showcasing wide, flat noodles stir-fried with a potent mixture of ground pork bits, bell pepper, onion, and holy basil.

Needless to say, those avoiding spicy food or craving plain old pad Thai should look elsewhere. But, if you're craving a vibrant and zesty meal, then strap in for a wild and enticing ride. Come dessert, try the black rice pudding served warm and with myriad toppings.

▨ 55 Cyril Magnin St. (entrance at Ellis & Mason Sts.)
☎ (415) 362-7456 — **WEB:** www.kinkhao.com
▨ Lunch & dinner daily   **PRICE:** $$

KUSAKABE 🍴

Japanese

XX | ○⌄ ⅐   MAP: C1

Serene with warm lighting and clean lines, distinctive creativity is the motto of this sushi-focused operation. Inside, a stunning counter crafted from a piece of live-edge elm, oyster-hued leather chairs and a ceiling of wood slats complete the Japan-chic look.

While the preparation of their nightly omakase might seem like a production line, by employing myriad cooking techniques, the kitchen ensures that every bite is memorable. Begin with warm kelp tea, before embarking on a sashimi parade of bluefin slices served with a yuzu-onion-sesame sauce. A soup course may feature a soy foam-miso broth with rice dumplings and duck meatballs. And finally, a top rendition of sushi yields shima aji with daikon and ayu that is torched just enough to blister the skin.

▪ 584 Washington St. (bet. Montgomery & Sansome Sts.)
✆ (415) 757-0155 — **WEB:** www.kusakabe-sf.com
▪ Dinner Mon – Sat   **PRICE: $$$$**

PERBACCO 🍴

Italian

XX | 🕸 ⅐ 🧼   MAP: C3

Slick financial types flex their expense accounts at this longtime Northern Italian retreat. Its polished décor belies a comforting menu of house-made pastas and items like roast chicken and meatballs at lunch, with slightly more refined takes at dinner. Dishes are executed with care—from slow-roasted vitello tonnato and semolina-dusted petrale sole to handmade pastas.

The space is larger inside than it looks, with plenty of booths and seats at the gleaming marble bar up front, and buzzy tables in the back with a view of the open-plan kitchen. Well-versed servers will encourage saving room for the end of the meal—as the cheese display, an impressive selection of grappas, and the inventive, delicious desserts are all highlights.

▪ 230 California St. (bet. Battery & Front Sts.)
✆ (415) 955-0663 — **WEB:** www.perbaccosf.com
▪ Lunch Mon – Fri   Dinner Mon – Sat   **PRICE: $$**

MICHAEL MINA ⸙

Contemporary

XxX | 🕸 ♿ 🍽 🖐

Long a favorite address for power players, super-chef Michael Mina's San Francisco flagship has softened its hard-charging edge a bit, altering the décor and removing a few tables to create a more intimate ambience. Nonetheless, you're still likely to see plenty of expense-account types, along with a handful of occasion-celebrating couples receiving attentive service from the suited waitstaff.

Change has also come to the kitchen, where a new chef de cuisine has made waves without shifting too much (Mina's famed "trio" presentations are still alive and well). The focus remains on luxurious ingredients coaxed into harmonious balance, from black-truffle rice "snowballs" crowned with sliced raw tuna to potato-leek soup accented with uni and trout roe. Even the banana tarte Tatin boasts a double dose of truffle—a drizzle of black truffle caramel atop, with white truffle ice cream alongside.

A five-course menu allows you to select your own options (including Mina's signature lobster pot pie), or you can put yourself in the kitchen's hands for a larger, ten-course affair. Be sure to spend time with the wine list as well: it offers an impressive roster of both familiar labels and unusual varietals.

▦ 252 California St. (bet. Battery & Front Sts.)
℘ (415) 397-9222 — **WEB:** www.michaelmina.net
▦ Lunch Mon – Fri   Dinner nightly   **PRICE: $$$$**

THE SLANTED DOOR 🍴

Vietnamese

XX | 🍸 ⚕ 🍽 🖼 🤙   **MAP:** D3

Reservations are a challenge at this modern stunner with a killer view of the Bay Bridge, which has managed to stay atop tourists' hit lists even as its Northern Californian spin on Vietnamese food has steadily become less inspired. It's an efficient and professional place, but with little warmth; the hospitality is hit-or-miss at best.

Instead of the cellophane noodles with crab or overpriced shaking beef, diners should stick to more solid offerings like gau choy gow, featuring pan-fried dumplings with Gulf shrimp and vibrant garlic chives accompanied by a zippy soy and fish-sauce dip. Half-orders are encouraged, so take advantage by sampling more than one of the delectable vegetable sides, like crisp and spicy broccoli with pressed tofu.

▪ 1 Ferry Building (at The Embarcadero)
☎ (415) 861-8032 — **WEB:** www.slanteddoor.com
▪ Lunch & dinner daily   **PRICE:** $$

TRESTLE 😊

American

XX | ⚕   **MAP:** C1

In SF's dizzyingly expensive dining landscape, this little hot spot, which offers a three-course menu for $35, is an incredible steal—provided you're willing to sacrifice freedom of choice. The two options for each course change daily based on what's freshest: our repast featured creamy wild mushroom risotto, fork-tender short ribs with charred onions and romesco, as well as a milk chocolate devil's food pudding cake with Mission figs. But yours might be different.

As with any killer deal, there are caveats: reservations are necessary (and hard to score), and the noise level is through the roof. But the historic brick space is lots of fun, with cool, contemporary art and a namesake central trestle table. The fact that the price is right only adds to the allure.

▪ 531 Jackson St. (at Columbus Ave.)
☎ (415) 772-0922 — **WEB:** www.trestlesf.com
▪ Dinner nightly   **PRICE:** $$

WAYFARE TAVERN 🍴

Gastropub

XX | ♿ 🖨 👜

(MAP icon)

Though it feels like it's been around for decades, celebrity chef Tyler Florence's FiDi favorite is actually a toddler—at least in tavern years. Nonetheless, it's become a standby for business types doing deals or enjoying post-work cocktails. Complete with dark wood and leather furnishings, a private billiards room, and bustling bar, Wayfare Tavern has the air of a gastropub-turned-private club.

Hearty Americana with seasonal accents defines the menu. Meals here usually begin with piping-hot popovers, and then proceed on to buttermilk-brined fried chicken—both of which are the chef's signature dishes. Even fish specials, like pan-roasted salmon with wilted leeks, are pure comfort, as is a strawberry cheesecake finished with a graham cracker tuile.

▨ 558 Sacramento St. (bet. Montgomery & Sansome Sts.)
℘ (415) 772-9060 — **WEB:** www.wayfaretavern.com
▨ Lunch & dinner daily   **PRICE:** $$$

Look for the symbol 🍳
for a brilliant breakfast to
start your day off right.

MARINA

JAPANTOWN · PACIFIC HEIGHTS · PRESIDIO

Following the havoc wreaked by the 1906 earthquake, San Francisco began reconstructing this sandy marshland by selling it to private developers. They, in turn, transformed the Marina into one of the most charming residential bubbles in town. Picture young families, tech wealth, and an affluent vibe straight out of a 21st century edition of The Yuppie Handbook, and you're in the Marina! Pacific Heights is considered the area's upper echelon—known for older family money and members who couldn't care less about being edgy. Here, bronzed

residents can be found jogging with their dogs at Crissy Field, or sipping hot chocolate from the **Warming Hut**. Parents can be seen pushing Bugaboos in haute couture boutiques or vying for parking in luxe German-engineered SUVs.

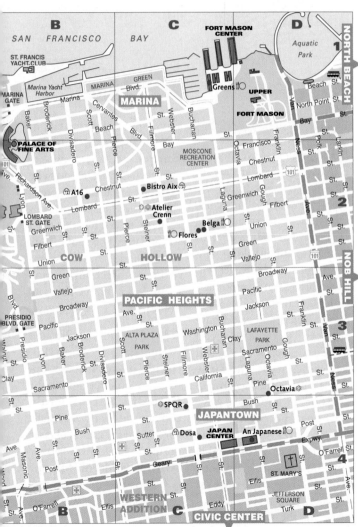

CASUAL EATS

Marina girls as well as Pac Heights socialites are always on the go, and quick-bite cafés are their calling card. Find these denizens gathering at **Jane** for pastries and paninis to nibble along with sips from a range of excellent teas, coffees, and smoothies. **Cafe GoLo** brings to life a classic American coffeehouse replete with expected breakfast specials, salads, and sandwiches; while **The Tipsy Pig** is a welcoming gastropub boasting an impressive bevy of bites and brews. True burger buffs in the Marina seem to have an insatiable appetite for locally founded **Roam Artisan Burgers**. Equally popular and sought-after are the contemporary,

flavor-packed offerings at SoCal favorite, **Umami Burger**. In truth, quality cuisine has little to do with a Marina restaurant's success: the locals are unapologetically content to follow the buzz to the latest hot spot, where the clientele's beauty seems to be in direct proportion to its level of acclaim and popularity.

However, in the Presidio (home to Lucasfilm HQ) squads of tech geeks opt for convenience at nearby **Presidio Social Club**, cooking up tasty, regionally focused fare in a classic northern Californian setting. **"Off the Grid-Fort Mason"** is California's most coveted street food fair that gathers every spring through fall and features a fantastic collection of vendors and food trucks—from **Curry Up Now** and the **Lobsta Truck**, to **Johnny Doughnuts** and everything in between. Then again, food is mere sustenance to some, and simply a sponge for the champagne and chardonnay flowing at the district's numerous watering holes. The bar scene here is not only fun but also varied, with a playground for everyone. Oenophiles plan far in advance for the annual **ZAP Zinfandel Festival** in the winter; while preppy college kids swap European semester stories at sleek wine spots like **Ottimista Restaurant & Bar** or **Nectar Wine Lounge**. Couples on the other hand can find more romance by the fireplace at posh **MatrixFillmore**.

JAPANTOWN

Evident in the plethora of restaurants, shopping malls, banks, and others businesses, the Asian community in the Marina is burgeoning. Thanks to the prominent Japanese population and abundant cultural events, **Japantown** is an exceptional and unique destination for tourists and locals alike. The **Northern California Cherry Blossom Festival** and **Nihonmachi Street Fair** bring to life every aspect of Asian-American heritage and living. Date-night is always memorable at the **AMC Dine-In Kabuki 8** theater, which happens to be equipped with two full bars. For a post-work snack, prepared meals, or even authentic imported ingredients, **Super Mira** is a market that offers a host of traditional eats. But for lunch on the run, grab excellent sushi, sashimi, or bento boxes at nearby **Nijiya Market**. Visitors and laid-back locals sojourn to **Daikoku by Shiki** (in the Kintetsu Mall) if only to admire their assortment of beautiful Japanese ceramics, cast-iron teapots, sake sets, and glazed bowls. Just a couple blocks from Japantown is perhaps the best spice shop in the country. Featuring walls lined with stacks of jars, **Spice Ace** boasts of extensively curated spices, extracts, and salts, that can all be sampled before purchase.

AN JAPANESE 🍴

Japanese

✗

MAP: D4

This tucked-away space in Japantown promises a great evening complete with specialized Japanese cuisine. At the helm of the kitchen is the talented chef, Kiyoshi Hayakawa, who along with his wife, the head server, and a second sushi chef, provides a concise menu with a $30 à la carte minimum. Serious sushi lovers however can always go for the two nigiri-only menus or an all-out omakase with some hot appetizers.

The nigiri are excellent—their gently seasoned rice draped with exceptionally pristine fish. And for the finale, a buttery slice of seared Wagyu beef. Cooked dishes might include a vivid matsutake mushroom soup featuring an intense kelp broth.

Though the dress code is casual, the room is still small and very hushed, making for an intimate meal.

■ 22 Peace Plaza, Ste. 510 (bet. Buchanan & Laguna Sts.)
✆ (415) 292-4886 — **WEB:** www.sushiansf.com
■ Dinner Tue – Sat

PRICE: $$

A16 😊

Italian

✗✗ | 🐝 ♿

MAP: B2

An undying favorite of yuppies, families, and tourists alike, A16 is known for rustic Italian cooking and a vast selection of delicious, unusual wines from all over the boot. Dinner reservations are indispensable, especially if you want one of the prime counter seats facing the open kitchen and wood-burning pizza oven.

The menu's pies, pastas, and antipasti change with the season, so you could sample anything from a highly enjoyable zuppa di ceci verde flecked with green garbanzo beans and parsley, to perfectly al dente cavatelli tossed in a slow-cooking lamb sugo made extra hearty with the addition of plump barlotti beans. For dessert, look no further than the fig crostata with vanilla gelato, which tastes like the work of a particularly talented nonna.

■ 2355 Chestnut St. (bet. Divisadero & Scott Sts.)
✆ (415) 771-2216 — **WEB:** www.a16sf.com
■ Lunch Wed – Sun   Dinner nightly

PRICE: $$

ATELIER CRENN ✿✿

Contemporary

✕✕✕ | ✿ ♿ ▣

Located along an attractive strip in the affluent Marina, Chef Dominique Crenn's gorgeous and contemporary restaurant hums with creative energy. Past the entrance and charming foyer, is a newly designed dining room that feels roomier yet cozy, peppered with homey charm, an earthy palette, sleek tables, and soft lighting.

A cadre of servers dressed in dark suits is poised, polished, and unfailingly professional. The menu is structured like a poem written by the chef herself and is cleverly adapted to welcome diners, with each course providing an elegant turn of prose. Highlighting an array of luxurious ingredients to suit the whims of the season are dishes like an orb of grilled Koshihikari rice topped with steamed Hokkaido uni and treated with a savory white wine and fennel broth. Inspired by the chef's childhood memories of foraging with her father are grilled porcinis crowned by translucent sheets of lardo and coupled with parmesan custard.

Albeit cerebral, the kitchen flaunts a welcoming, celebratory air. This is also expressed through a playful dessert tasting of Mayan-inspired corn crisps topped with frozen corn mousse, or sapote ice cream in a bee pollen-sprinkled wafer cone.

■ 3127 Fillmore St. (bet. Filbert & Pixley Sts.)
☎ (415) 440-0460 — **WEB:** www.ateliercrenn.com
■ Dinner Tue – Sat   **PRICE: $$$$**

BELGA 🍴

Belgian

✗✗ | 🍹 🍺 ♿ 🏮 🎦 🛋 🧺   **MAP:** C2

Belgian brews and bites are the cornerstones of this fresh recruit in the former Café des Amis, which has kept its brasserie look but pivoted from Paris to Brussels. All the classics are accounted for: well-salted frites with garlic aïoli; bowls of mussels; and of course, house-made sausages—try the combo board, which comes with andouille, boudin noir, boudin blanc, and currywurst, not to mention a generous bowl of spaetzle. Flatbreads and salads round things out.

The Euro-café vibe is fun with red banquettes, classic bistro chairs, and marble floors to complement the big beer selection (both European and domestic) and cocktails. Young Marinaites have, understandably, caught on quickly: the bar and dog-friendly patio are constantly abuzz.

▪ 2000 Union St. (at Buchanan St.)
✆ (415) 872-7350 — **WEB:** www.belgasf.com
▪ Lunch & dinner daily   **PRICE:** $$

BISTRO AIX 🐶

Mediterranean

✗✗ | 🍸 ♿   **MAP:** C2

In the competitive Marina market, lovely Bistro Aix remains a charming and relatively affordable neighborhood option for thoughtfully made Southern French fare with a California touch. The dining room offers two distinct culinary experiences, beginning with seats in front at the convivial marble bar and small bistro tables. Beyond this, find the sunny bubble of the intimate back atrium, verdant with olive trees and flooded with natural light. A well-heeled crowd enlivens the space.

Dishes are simple and well executed, like roasted eggplant with toasted sesame seeds, gypsy peppers, and a topping of creamy burrata; or the excellently grilled sea scallops with earthy chanterelles and silky beurre blanc. Thoughtfully chosen French wines complement each dish.

▪ 3340 Steiner St. (bet. Chestnut & Lombard Sts.)
✆ (415) 202-0100 — **WEB:** www.bistroaix.com
▪ Dinner Mon - Sat   **PRICE:** $$

DOSA ☺

Indian

✕✕ | 🍹 ⚐ 🍽   **MAP:** C4

Grandeur and glamour infuse every inch of this stylish restaurant, whose soaring ceilings, colorful walls, and swanky demeanor complement the bold and fragrantly spiced food. As the name suggests, dosas are a highlight here, with crisp exteriors, spicy fillings, and excellent accompanying sambar and chutney. Warm servers will help translate street faves like bhel puri (a sweet-sour blend of puffed rice, crispy noodles, green mango, and chutney); or shake things up with idli fries, tailed by a Bengali gimlet with gin, curried nectar, and lime. Desserts are every bit as exotic as the rest of the menu, and may reveal rasmalai—patties of fresh cheese in sweet cream flavored with cardamom and rosewater.

Fans revel in the second, smaller location on Valencia Street.

▦ 1700 Fillmore St. (at Post St.)
🕾 (415) 441-3672 — **WEB:** www.dosasf.com
▦ Lunch Wed – Sun   Dinner nightly   **PRICE:** $$

FLORES 🍴

Mexican

✕✕ | 🍹 ⚐ 🎪 ⬚ 🍽   **MAP:** C2

It's always a fiesta at this lively Latin spot on Cow Hollow's main drag, where you're as likely to find young families sharing a bowl of guac as you are Marina girls getting tipsy on mezcal margaritas. Patterned tiles, bright murals and chill beats create a modern vibe, and though you may have to wait (only limited reservations are available), the friendly staff will make it worth your while.

Flores is among the city's best upscale Mexican spots—with the bonuses of heftier portions and a lower price tag. You'll be able to taste the difference in the handmade corn tortillas that encase an oozy huitlacoche quesadilla, and the tender, citrusy carnitas. Save room for churros: the spicy "Mexican hot chocolate" dipping sauce is well worth the calories.

▦ 2030 Union St. (bet. Buchanan & Webster Sts.)
🕾 (415) 796-2926 — **WEB:** www.floressf.com
▦ Lunch Sat – Sun   Dinner nightly   **PRICE:** $$

GREENS 🍴

Vegetarian

✗ | ♿ | 🛥

MAP: C1

Annie Somerville's pioneering vegetarian restaurant has been around since 1979, but neither the menu nor the surroundings show Greens' age. Instead, fresh, energetic cuisine abounds, with a light touch and slight global inspiration. Brunch draws a big crowd, so be prepared to wait for those perfectly fried eggs over griddled potato cakes. Vegetarians and carnivores will rejoice after sampling the honest, colorful, down-to-earth seasonal entrées at dinner, followed by delightful desserts like a huckleberry upside down cake with a subtle kick from Meyer lemon.

Housed in historic Fort Mason, the warehouse-style space is rustic but refined, with sweeping views of the Golden Gate Bridge and sailboats on the Bay.

For a quick lunch, there's also a to-go counter.

◾ Building A, Fort Mason Center
℘ (415) 771-6222 — **WEB:** www.greensrestaurant.com
◾ Lunch Tue – Sun   Dinner nightly   **PRICE:** $$

HONG KONG LOUNGE II 😊

Chinese

✗✗ | 🥢

MAP: A4

If the bland peach exterior of this restaurant doesn't entice you, trust that a juicy treasure lies beneath: some of the Bay's best dim sum offered at lunch. Skipping the carts for a made-to-order approach, the sizable menu groans with winners, including flaky, buttery baked pork buns, sautéed pea shoots delectably flavored with garlic, and one of the best egg custard tarts you're ever likely to taste—even if you've visited Hong Kong.

Throw in above-average tea options and a sizable vegetarian menu, and it's no wonder that this tiny gem draws legendary waits on weekend mornings. Just don't turn tail and head for the other Hong Kong Lounge further down Geary—despite their names, the two aren't affiliated, and the food isn't quite the same.

◾ 3300 Geary Blvd. (at Parker Ave.)
℘ (415) 668-8802 — **WEB:** www.hongkonglounge2.com
◾ Lunch & dinner Wed – Mon   **PRICE:** $$

OCTAVIA ✿
Californian

XX | 🍇 ⬚   **MAP:** D3

Chef/owner Melissa Perello may already be a local culinary personality at Frances, but her sequel, Octavia, shines even brighter from its home in the tony lower Pacific Heights. Packed with a dynamic and diverse group of diners, the airy, open space feels minimalist and bistro-chic, from the white-tiled kitchen to those raw-wood benches lined with woolen pillows. Service is polite and efficient.

Chef Perello has a gift for elevating straightforward dishes through the use of superb ingredients and beautifully executed technique, beginning with a smoked trout fillet on a bed of cream cheese with green mustard seeds and steamed potatoes. Kale salad is deliciously crunchy and nicely matched with diced fennel, creamy avocado, salty aged parmesan, and breadcrumbs in a light vinaigrette. A petite filet of beef arrives tender and perfectly cooked to order, atop potatoes mashed with olive oil, grilled broccolini, and cabbage dressed in rapini pesto. Desserts are imaginative and masterful, so save room for their completely new take on profiteroles, soft and fresh, filled with poppy seed ice cream accented with tart rhubarb and kumquat.

Tables fill early, so be sure to reserve well in advance.

■ 1701 Octavia St. (at Bush St.)
☏ (415) 408-7507 — **WEB:** www.octavia-sf.com
■ Dinner nightly   **PRICE:** $$$

SOCIALE 😋

Italian

XX | 🛖 ⌷   **MAP:** A4

Italian in name but Californian in spirit, Sociale is a go-to for comfort fare that blends the best of both worlds. Creamy burrata is served over pumpkin purée and garnished with pepitas and pecans, while braised pork belly in a heady, robust sauce melts in the mouth. Dessert is a must; you'll be hard-pressed to find a table that can resist ordering the signature chocolate oblivion cake, a sinfully rich ganache enhanced with olive oil, sea salt, and amaretti cookie crumble.

Located at the end of an alley with a heated patio, the vibe here is bistro-chic, with a hint of European flair accented by the warm, accommodating staff and the Italian and French chanteuses on the playlist. It's the kind of neighborhood gem that everyone wishes they had on their block.

▨ 3665 Sacramento St. (bet. Locust & Spruce Sts.)
✆ (415) 921-3200 — **WEB:** www.sfsociale.com
▨ Dinner Mon – Sat   **PRICE:** $$

Look for our symbol 🍺
spotlighting restaurants
with a notable beer list.

SPQR ✿
Italian

✕✕ | 🎗 ♿︎

Pleasant and homey with excellent modern Italian cooking, there is little wonder why this destination is always bustling. Book in advance and assume that the dining counter reserved for walk-ins is already overflowing for the night. The space itself is narrow with tightly packed wood tables and furnishings; it would seem cramped were it not for the soaring ceiling, skylights, and open kitchen to brighten the mood. No matter where you look, the passion and enthusiasm for Italian specialties are palpable here—even contagious.

From antipasti to dolce, celebrated Chef Matthew Accarrino's extensive menu evolves with the seasons, yet remains as satisfying as it is impressive. Memorable and very creative pastas include supremely rich linguine in Alfredo sauce with abalone liver, grated bottarga, and the faintest hint of Meyer lemon. A degustazione of suckling pig arrives as six unique preparations, including medallions of succulent loin, slices of crisp-edged porchetta, and a cool pork terrine with pops of mustard seed.

Desserts feature the wonderfully sweet-tart flavors of thick and creamy maple panna cotta topped with wine-poached apple, a cloud of whipped cream, and cookie crumble.

■ 1911 Fillmore St. (bet. Bush & Pine Sts.)
✆ (415) 771-7779 — **WEB:** www.spqrsf.com
■ Lunch Sat – Sun   Dinner nightly   **PRICE:** $$$

SPRUCE ⁕

Californian

✕✕ | 👫 🍸 ♿ 🍽 🔥 🖐

MAP: A4

Set in one of San Francisco's snazziest neighborhoods, Spruce draws a regular crowd of wealthy retirees and corporate types by day. Evenings bring couples out for date night. The dining room, with its cathedral-style ceilings and skylight, is masculine yet modern—think studded leather chairs and splashes of charcoal and chocolate. A small front café serves coffee and pastries, while the marble bar lures happy-hour crowds for a cocktail or glass of wine from the extensive list.

Micro-seasonal and thoroughly Californian, Spruce spotlights cooking that's both simple and undeniably elegant. Rustic and homey starters may include hand-shaped ravioli filled with fresh ricotta and bathed in a broth of its tart whey with fava leaf purée. A roulade of guinea hen stuffed with pork and duck sausage is exquisitely moist, juicy, and accompanied by thick fingers of nutty-sweet brown ale toast perfect for sopping up every last drop.

For dessert, a dense and decadent crème fraîche cheesecake is thick and creamy, with plenty of sweet vanilla flavor and a classic graham-cracker crust; juicy citrus segments and a quenelle of brilliantly tart Makrut lime ice cream add zing.

▨ 3640 Sacramento St. (bet. Locust & Spruce Sts.)
✆ (415) 931-5100 — **WEB:** www.sprucesf.com
▨ Lunch Mon – Fri   Dinner nightly   **PRICE: $$$**

MISSION

BERNAL HEIGHTS · POTRERO HILL

It's like the sun never goes down in the Mission—a bohemian paradise dotted with palm trees and doted on by scores of artists and activists, as well as a thriving Hispanic community. Here, urban life is illustrated through graffiti murals decorating the walls of funky galleries, thrift shops, and independent bookstores. Sidewalk stands burst with fresh plantains, nopales, and the juiciest limes this side of the border. Mission markets are known to be among the best in town and include **La Palma** **Mexicatessen** teeming with homemade *papusas*, chips, and fresh cheeses. **Lucca Ravioli** is loved for its legion of imported Italian goods; and the petite grocer, **Bi-Rite**, is big on prepared foods and flowers. Across the street, **Bi-Rite** **Creamery** is a cult favorite for ice cream. Moving on from markets to hip coffee haunts, **Ritual Coffee Roasters** is the leader of the pack. Join their fan base in single file outside the door, order a special roast from the barista, and find yourself in awe of this pleasing, very potent berry. Coffee connoisseurs also pay their respects at the original **Philz Coffee** for brews that cannot be beat.

CLASSIC MEETS CUTTING-EDGE

The Mission is home to many contemporary hangouts, although those bargain *mercados* and dollar stores might suggest otherwise. **Dynamo Donut + Coffee** over on 24th Street is a dreamy retreat for these fried and sugary parcels of dough, complete with delectable flavors such as lemon-buttermilk and chocolate-star anise. **Walzwerk** charms with East German kitsch and is the go-to spot for traditional delights; while carb fiends know to stop by **The Sandwich Place** for freshly baked bread loaded with flavorful fillings. Here in the Mission, pizza reigns supreme and thin-crust lovers are happy to wait in line at **Pizzeria Delfina** for a wickedly good slice with crisped edges. A destination in its own right, **Tartine Bakery's** exceptional breads, pastries, and pressed sandwiches are arguably

unmissable. However, to best experience this region's range of culinary talents, forgo the table and chairs and pull up at a curb on Linda Street, where a vigilant street food scene is brimming with a wealth of international eats.

DAYTIME DELIGHTS

The city's hottest 'hood also offers a cool range of sweets. For instance, a banana split is downright retro-licious when served at the Formica counter of 90-year-old **St. Francis Fountain**. If that's not enough, the sundaes here are made with Mitchell's Ice Cream, famous since 1953. Modish flavors like grasshopper pie and Kahlua mocha cream are in regular rotation at the newer **Humphry Slocombe**; while **Mission Pie** is another local gem that tempts with a spectrum of flavors—both sweet and savory. For more bold plates, **Plow** in Potrero Hill is a top breakfast and brunch hit. The space is small but massively popular, so expect to wait a while before your first bite of lemon-ricotta pancake—there's even a menu for the little "plowers"

who arrive by stroller. At lunch head to Peru by way of abuela-approved **Cholo Soy** for authentic, homemade, and always-affordable fare. **La Taqueria**'s carne asada burrito is possibly the most decadent around, but when it comes to tacos, it's a tossup on whether **El Gallo Giro** or **El Tonayense** takes the title for best truck in town.

NIGHT BITES

The **Monk's Kettle** brags a beer list beyond par, with around 200 rotating craft brews on their carte. But, if heady cocktails are what you crave, then dash over to **Trick Dog** for tantalizing concoctions and creative small plates that go a long way in sating that late-night appetite. Then dance the night away (as well as these indulgences) at **El Rio** on Salsa Sunday—the dive bar with a bustling back patio. Growling stomachs also seem game to brave the harsh lighting at the many taquerias around, including **Taqueria Cancún** for a veggie burrito or **El Farolito** for mind-blowing meats.

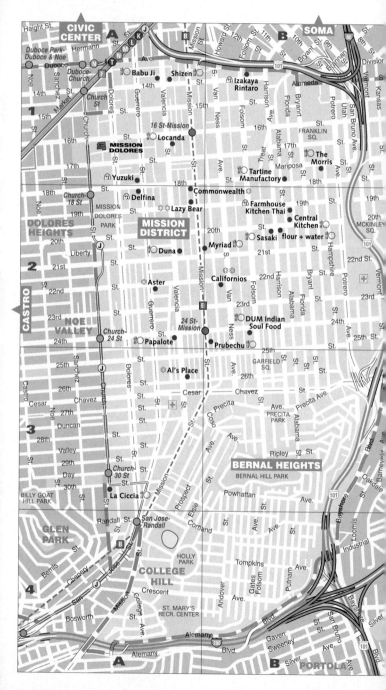

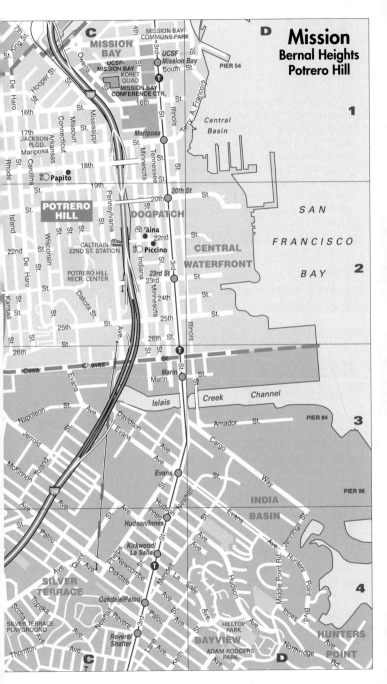

Mission
Bernal Heights
Potrero Hill

MISSION BAY

MISSION BAY COMMONS PARK

UCSF Mission Bay South

UCSF-MISSION BAY KORET QUAD

MISSION BAY CONFERENCE CTR.

PIER 54

Central Basin

17th JACKSON PLGD.

Papito

POTRERO HILL

DOGPATCH

'āina

CALTRAIN 22ND ST. STATION

Piccino

POTRERO HILL RECR. CENTER

CENTRAL WATERFRONT

S A N

F R A N C I S C O

B A Y

Islais Creek Channel

Cesar Chavez

Marin

Napoleon

Amador

PIER 94

Davidson

Evans

Cargo

Way

Evans

PIER 96

INDIA

BASIN

Hudson/Innes

Kirkwood/La Salle

SILVER TERRACE

Oakdale/Palou

SILVER TERRACE PLAYGROUND

Revere/Shafter

HILLTOP PARK

BAYVIEW

ADAM RODGERS PARK

HUNTERS POINT

'ĀINA 🙂

Hawaiian

✗ | ♿ 🏠 ⛱

MAP: C2

Catch some aloha vibes at this Hawaiian pop-up gone permanent in the Dogpatch, which imports many of its ingredients directly from the islands. The brunch menu riffs on all the classics, from house-made "spam" musubi in lettuce-leaf wraps to warm, fluffy malasada doughnuts stuffed with guava custard and rolled in palm sugar. Binchotan-charred octopus over kalo coconut cream is a must order, while ti leaf-steamed trout with smoked mushrooms and crispy trout skin chips is perfect for sharing. The space isn't glamorous, but it's relaxed and comfortable, with beautiful wood tables, greenery, and floods of light.

Don't miss the excellent low-ABV cocktails, either. The coconut milk punch with sweet vermouth and hibiscus-rose sugar is a knockout.

▨ 900 22nd St. (at Minnesota St.)
℘ (415) 814-3815 — **WEB:** www.ainasf.com
▨ Lunch Wed – Sun   Dinner Tue – Sat   **PRICE: $$**

BABU JI 🍴

Indian

✗ | 🖬

MAP: A1

This vibrant Indian canteen, from husband-and-wife team Jessi and Jennifer Singh, hopped the globe from Australia to New York before planting its roots in San Francisco. Its latest home in the trendy Mission pairs nicely with the fun, flavorful, and creative food that emerges from Chef Jessi's kitchen, where the curries are as vivid as the multi-hued décor itself.

Most diners choose the six-course tasting menu, which covers a range of bright, flavorful dishes like chili-flecked, yogurt-marinated kebabs with ginger-beet purée, succulent shrimp curry, sweet-and-sour "General Tso's" cauliflower, and tandoori chicken. Grab a beer from the communal fridge, catch a Bollywood flick projected on the wall, and enjoy the pulsating energy of this lively room.

▨ 280 Valencia St. (bet. 14th & Brosnan Sts.)
℘ (415) 525-4857 — **WEB:** www.babujisf.com
▨ Dinner Mon – Sat   **PRICE: $$**

AL'S PLACE ✿

Californian

✗✗ | ♿ ⛩

Vegetables are the star of the menu at this bright-blue oasis on busy Valencia Street, which adheres to a mostly pescatarian philosophy, with carnivorous options available on the side. If that sounds like a dealbreaker, it shouldn't be—Chef/owner Aaron London (a.k.a. AL) is wildly adept with the seasons' bounty, making a dish of blistered squash with pickled kohlrabi, hummus, and creamy burrata feel as lush and luxurious as the offerings at a steakhouse.

London's menu is chockablock with such creativity, from the brine-pickled French fries and flavorful ras el hanout olives that kick off each meal, to the silky grits topped with tangy goat's milk curds, Brussels sprouts, chanterelle, and yuzu. At times, the combinations can read like a five-car pile-up—cured trout, mashed turnips, and bagna cauda?—But the crew always manages to smoothly navigate the layers of flavor, blazing new roads in diners' imaginations.

Like the menu, Al's space is bright, open, and cheerful, with plenty of natural light, bold colors, and a casual but engaging staff. Embrace the energy, perhaps with a glass of French wine or a craft beer, and let the boisterous, creative spirit of the restaurant win you over.

■ 1499 Valencia St. (at 26th St.)
℘ (415) 416-6136 — **WEB:** www.alsplacesf.com
■ Dinner Wed – Sun

PRICE: $$

ASTER ✿
Californian

✗✗ | ♿

The idea of a fine-dining space that features mainstream music, spare décor, and young clientele in jeans may seem overdone, but Aster makes everything appear new and inventive, never forced. Set in a quiet residential neighborhood, its tawny banquettes, wood tables, and strands of lights fashion a studied yet casual vibe that never feels like it is trying too hard. The staff is attentive yet friendly, and eager to please.

The kitchen heightens every element of healthy, light Californian cuisine made from only the best organic ingredients around.

Like the space, the food has no sense of excessive complication; everything is cooked, seasoned, and paired perfectly. Here, a simple garden salad is a graceful blend of tangerine, turnips, and flowers tossed with pumpkin seeds over a bed of mashed avocado. This might be followed by a thick, generous trout fillet, seared to crisp-skin perfection and set atop snap pea purée. Lighter main courses leave room for enjoying their excellent desserts, such as a sweet poached pear stuffed with vanilla ice cream beneath a crunchy pistachio scone and pear coulis. The fixed-price menu is reasonable for the trendsetting combination of cuisine and space.

■ 1001 Guerrero St. (at 22nd St.)
℘ (415) 875-9810 — **WEB:** www.astersf.com
■ Dinner nightly

PRICE: $$$

CALIFORNIOS ✿✿

Mexican

✕✕

Set in a bohemian area known for its street tacos and bare bones eateries, Californios aims to elevate the Mission district's south-of-the-border fare to contemporary Mexican cuisine and it more than succeeds. A complex, layered mole here isn't just likely to please—it's bound to turn your entire understanding of this nation's cuisine on its head.

The luxurious space only ups the appeal. Caramel-hued banquettes pop against dark-lacquered walls, while chandeliers and shelves of cookbooks further punctuate the upscale mien of the intimate room. You'll feel as though you're dining in Chef Val M. Cantu's very own atelier, made extra personal by the deeply knowledgeable staff, who seems to pride themselves on knowing every detail about the dishes coming out of the open kitchen.

One lengthy tasting menu is served nightly. It changes often, but expect inventive items like squid-ink tostadas heaped with guacamole, Monterey squid, and truffles. A wonderfully spicy flauta is filled with duck barbacoa; while butter-poached lobster is tucked into blue corn tortillas and topped with fennel and aji amarillo. Sorbet made from local guavas, nestled in a spread of pistachio butter is an astounding send-off.

▨ 3115 22nd St. (bet. Capp St. & Van Ness Ave.)

☏ (415) 757-0994 — **WEB:** www.californiossf.com

▨ Dinner Tue – Sat   PRICE: $$$$

CENTRAL KITCHEN 🍴
Californian

XX | ♿ ⬚　　　　　　　　　　　　　　**MAP:** B2

A chic and sleek crowd of Mission foodies gathers at this trendy restaurant, nestled in a complex beside sister shop/deli Salumeria, cocktail bar Trick Dog, and coffee shop Sightglass. Wend your way to the central courtyard, with a trickling fountain and large glass doors leading into the main space, where a vast open kitchen faces the simple wood tables.

Kitchen renovations resulted in a wood-burning hearth and expanded pasta program. Along the way, you might taste a mound of burrata surrounded by melon cubes, cucumber slices, and purslane tossed in a chili-herb vinaigrette. Gamey pork trotter agnolotti is balanced by lemon verbena; while hearth-roasted hen served in a black chili sauce and paired with chicken cracklings is nothing less than compelling.

■ 3000 20th St. (at Florida St.)
✆ (415) 826-7004 — **WEB:** www.centralkitchensf.com
■ Dinner Mon – Sat　　　　　　　　　　**PRICE:** $$$

DELFINA 😊
Italian

XX | ♿　　　　　　　　　　　　　　**MAP:** A2

One of the city's greats for rustic Italian meals, Delfina is nestled on a block of gems for food lovers including Bi-Rite (and its creamery), Tartine Bakery, and sister spot Pizzeria Delfina. But even with this rarefied competition, Delfina books well in advance and draws lines for its few walk-in seats.

The simple, yet lively dining room is attended to by a warm staff, and the bill of fare shifts with the seasons. Soul-satisfying dishes might include house-made francobolli with prosciutto and mascarpone, as well as perfectly roasted chicken with silky olive oil-mashed potatoes. Seasonal desserts, like warm pear Charlotte with salted caramel and brandy anglaise are delightful.

■ 3621 18th St. (bet. Dolores & Guerrero Sts.)
✆ (415) 552-4055 — **WEB:** www.delfinasf.com
■ Dinner nightly　　　　　　　　　　**PRICE:** $$

COMMONWEALTH ✿

Contemporary

XX | ♿

The cool kids of the Mission flock to this upscale spot, all sleek vibe and warm welcome. Set on one of the neighborhood's grittiest stretches, the one-story brick building wears its history in the form of an old painted doughnut ad—and though frosted windows keep the environs at bay, Commonwealth cares for its own by donating a portion of profits from each night's six-course tasting menu to charity.

Everything here is offered à la carte, but most opt for the aforementioned tasting menu, for which the cheerful servers are happy to mix and match dishes. The results are as creative and ambitious as the techie-hipster clientele, with breathtakingly beautiful, Asian-influenced bites: think sea urchin under a canopy of seaweed brioche topped with tomato and watermelon pearls, or seared diver scallop in a corn-and-white miso emulsion with tarragon and fennel.

Along the way, expect surprises utilizing the best seasonal produce, like tangy sudachi sorbet in a pool of sake soda, or pressed cantaloupe infused with honey and togarashi. It all pairs nicely with an intriguing, terroir-driven wine list—or if you're feeling adventurous, a nightly frozen cocktail chilled with liquid nitrogen.

▨ 2224 Mission St. (bet. 18th & 19th Sts.)
☏ (415) 355-1500 — **WEB:** www.commonwealthsf.com
▨ Dinner nightly   **PRICE:** $$

DUM INDIAN SOUL FOOD ⅈ○

Indian

✗✗ | ♿   **MAP:** B2

Smart diners know to order the biryani at this food-truck-gone-permanent: it's steamed in a covered pot, according to the traditional dum method. But while rice is nice, you'll also want to sample fusion-forward dishes showcasing the chef's CIA training and exacting technique, like garam masala-spiced fried chicken with charred green beans and creamy makhani sauce, or tender, tangy pork vindaloo, wrapped burrito-style in a whole-wheat paratha with cilantro chutney.

Though it's set in a casual corner of the Mission, DUM's space is sleek and stylish, with aqua walls and glam off-white furnishings. Nonetheless, prices are reasonable—especially given the huge portion sizes—and local foodies have quickly absorbed it into their regular rotation.

■ 3111 24th St. (bet. Folsom & Shotwell Sts.)
𝒞 (415) 874-9045 — **WEB:** www.dumsf.com
■ Lunch & dinner Wed – Sun   **PRICE:** $$

DUNA ⅈ○

Eastern European

✗ | ♿   **MAP:** A2

The chefs behind the much-loved, now-shuttered Bar Tartine have moved down Valencia, operating a spot that once again displays their prodigious skills with Eastern European flavors and extensive in-house fermentation. Duna's space is far simpler than Bar Tartine's, with counter service and a rather brief menu. However, the results remain explosive.

The menu is heavy on "spoonable" soup-salad hybrids like the "Dad's favorite," a tangle of cucumber, dill, and sliced onion in a tangy buttermilk dressing. Hand-rolled spätzle are bathed in a rustic stewed tomato and onion sauce, while crisp potato pancakes get a punch from creamy, chili-flecked pumpkin seed dip. Pair them with a salad and one of the house-fermented kefir sodas, in unusual flavors like sumac.

■ 983 Valencia St. (bet. 20th & 21st Sts.)
𝒞 (415) 484-1206 — **WEB:** www.duna.kitchen
■ Dinner Wed – Sun   **PRICE:** ⊜

FARMHOUSE KITCHEN THAI 😳

Thai

✗ | ♿   **MAP:** B2

For authentic Thai flavors in a lively space, this cutie is hard to beat—and has a dedicated following among the young techies and families who reside in the neighboring industrial lofts. The space is eclectic with interesting art installations, flower arrangements, and accents that spin to the seasons. It's the kind of affordable weeknight spot designed for repeat business.

The menu is extensive but the kitchen manages to prepare dishes with careful attention to detail, bold flavors and top quality ingredients—from marinated flank steak rolled around cucumber and cilantro, to coconut- and turmeric-marinated barbecue chicken with black sticky rice. The herbal rice salad featuring green mango, dried shrimp, and chili is a signature and deservedly so.

▪ 710 Florida St. (bet. 19th & 20th Sts.)
☏ (415) 814-2920 — **WEB:** www.farmhousesf.com
▪ Lunch & dinner daily   **PRICE:** $$

FLOUR + WATER 🍴

Italian

✗ | ♿ ▢   **MAP:** B2

As the name implies, two ingredients create a world of possibilities at this always-packed Mission hot spot. Neapolitan pizzas and handmade pastas (like al dente garganelli with whole-grain mustard and braised pork) will have you sighing after each bite, and a selection of more traditional mains (such as seared duck breast with chanterelles and pecorino-dusted charred Brussels sprouts) score every bit as big as the noodles and pies.

Laid-back service, up-to-the-moment music, and a buzzy, effervescent vibe make flour + water the epitome of California cool.

Throw in a glass of their refined Italian wine, along with an alluring dessert like the salted caramel apple tart, and you can see why getting a table here is well worth the challenge.

▪ 2401 Harrison St. (at 20th St.)
☏ (415) 826-7000 — **WEB:** www.flourandwater.com
▪ Dinner nightly   **PRICE:** $$

IZAKAYA RINTARO 🐶

Japanese

🍴 | ♿ 🖥

MAP: B1

Delicate izakaya cuisine with a produce-centric NorCal sensibility awaits at this Japanese sanctum, which transforms even the most humble dishes into art. Freshly made soft tofu is infused with fragrant bergamot peel, while meaty king trumpet mushrooms join classic chicken thighs and tender tsukune on the menu of smoky, caramelized charcoal-grilled skewers. The blancmange, infused with white sesame and topped with sweet black soybeans, is particularly unmissable.

Housed in the former Chez Spencer, which was destroyed in a fire, Rintaro has kept its predecessor's gorgeous (and charred) arched ceiling beams, but added a delicate, wood-framed bar and booths. The result is a serene environment perfect for sharing and sampling the exquisite food.

▉ 82 14th St. (bet. Folsom & Trainor Sts.)
☏ (415) 589-7022 — **WEB:** www.izakayarintaro.com
▉ Lunch Thu – Sat   Dinner nightly   **PRICE:** $$

LA CICCIA 🍴○

Italian

🍴🍴

MAP: A3

Sardinian cuisine takes the spotlight at this family-run charmer, which draws a loyal crowd of Noe Valley regulars—particularly parents on a well-earned date night. The intimate, dark green dining room is always full, and nestled right up against the kitchen, from which the chef regularly pops out to greet guests in a blend of Italianenglish.

Start with the house-made bread and the home-cured salumi of the day (think citron-studded mortadella). The pasta longa with cured tuna heart slivers twirls fresh, delicious linguini with sea urchin and tomato, and an entrée of stewed goat is gamey but tender, served alongside braised cabbage, black olives, and fried capers. For a pleasant conclusion, cap it all off with the fluffy and airy ricotta-saffron cake.

▉ 291 30th St. (at Church St.)
☏ (415) 550-8114 — **WEB:** www.laciccia.com
▉ Dinner Tue – Sat   **PRICE:** $$

LAZY BEAR ✿✿

Contemporary

✕✕ | 🍸 &

Communal eating is at the heart of this fine-dining dinner party. Lazy Bear may have its origins as an underground phenom, but today anyone can try to score a seat. That is, after jumping through a few virtual hoops: buy a ticket in advance and wait for an e-mail listing house rules to be followed in earnest. Rest assured this is all worth the effort.

The nightly tasting menu is dished out in a cool, bi-level warehouse and starts upstairs in the loft with aperitifs and snacks like Kumamoto oysters with apple-fennel mignonette. Then move downstairs to a dining room boasting two giant tree slabs as communal tables, each lined with 20 chairs. Diners are given a pencil and pamphlet informing them of the menu (with space for note-taking underneath) and are invited to enter the kitchen to chat with the talented cooks themselves. This leaves the young crowd dreamy-eyed with chef worship. The entire experience is more about the kitchen than the dining room, which isn't to everyone's taste.

Highlights include an elegant matsutake mushroom consommé with hints of redwood oil; and a decadent slice of deeply marbled Miyazaki ribeye, lightly seared and served with Asian pear and bone marrow-pumpkin pureé.

▦ 3416 19th St. (bet. Mission & San Carlos Sts.)
𝒞 (415) 874-9921 — **WEB:** www.lazybearsf.com
▦ Dinner Tue – Sat   **PRICE:** $$$$

LOCANDA ⅋○

Italian

XX | 🍷 ⅋ 🛋 🖐

This chic Roman-style osteria packs in the hipsters with a lively scene, killer cocktails, and inspired pastas, like radiatore tossed in tomato-lamb ragù with pecorino and hints of fresh mint. Hearty main courses might include smoky and tender pancetta-wrapped chicken served over nutty farro verde. None of this is surprising, considering Locanda is from the team behind Mission favorite, Delfina.

Reservations here are a tough ticket, but the attire and vibe are casual and welcoming (if noisy). Can't get a table? Seats at the bar, where the full menu is served, are a solid backup.

Locanda's ultra-central address makes parking a challenge, so plan on using the valet or allotting extra time.

◼ 557 Valencia St. (bet. 16th & 17th Sts.)
☎ (415) 863-6800 — **WEB:** www.locandasf.com
◼ Lunch Sat – Sun Dinner nightly

PRICE: $$

THE MORRIS ⅋○

Contemporary

XX | 🍸 ⅋

After working at a number of SF's top restaurants, veteran sommelier Paul Einbund has settled down at this neighborhood charmer in the Mission, named for his father. Unsurprisingly, The Morris boasts a killer selection of wine (displayed in a handsome glass cellar), along with top-notch cocktails and a sophisticated yet highly craveable comfort-food menu.

Quell your hunger with slices of Tartine country loaf—baked just down the street—as you peruse the menu, which offers appealing bites both small (pork cracklins with honey and Aleppo pepper?) and large (charred broccolini with succulent grilled squid in chili-lime dressing). Be sure to also try their signature smoked duck. Brined for two days, aged for four, it is a smoky, tender, meaty marvel.

◼ 2501 Mariposa St. (at Hampshire St.)
☎ (415) 612-8480 — **WEB:** www.themorris-sf.com
◼ Dinner Mon – Sat

PRICE: $$$

MYRIAD ❚❘○
International

❌ | ♿ ⬛

Not sure what to eat tonight? Bring your indecision and your appetite to this globe-trotting gastropub, which turns out skillfully prepared dishes from across cultures. Whether you're feeling like a dose of Moroccan (roasted lamb sandwich with tomato jam and feta), Mexican (cochinita pibil), French (farm toast with fromage blanc and roasted plums), Italian (ricotta zeppole with caramel sauce), or any combination of the above, there's a dish that's sure to satisfy. There's also a selection of beer and wine to match every delightful bite.

Myriad sprawls over two long and narrow rooms, where hipster couples and families with kids trade bites of the shareable dishes. If you're paralyzed by choice, friendly servers are happy to lend a hand.

⬛ 2491 Mission St. (bet. 20th & 21st Sts.)
✆ (415) 525-4335 — **WEB:** www.myriadsf.com
⬛ Lunch & dinner daily   **PRICE:** $$

PAPALOTE ❚❘○
Mexican

❌

MAP: A2

Head to this little standout for a lighter take on the gut-busting taqueria treats that define the Mission. Papalote manages to deliver the goods without the guilt, and the difference is clear in the outstanding fish tacos: corn tortillas piled with fresh, flaky white fish (sautéed in butter and garlic) along with sliced romaine and chopped tomato.

Unlike the competition, Papalote doesn't have a salsa bar, but it doesn't need one: its defining feature is its gobsmackingly good, house-made roasted tomato salsa, which you'll want to slather on dishes like the pitch-perfect breakfast burrito, stuffed with scrambled eggs, chorizo, cheese, and guacamole. The space and service are bare-bones, but with food this good, you won't care.

⬛ 3409 24th St. (bet. Poplar & Valencia Sts.)
✆ (415) 970-8815 — **WEB:** www.papalote-sf.com
⬛ Lunch & dinner daily   **PRICE:** ☜

PAPITO 🍴

Mexican

✗ | 🛖 🛋️   **MAP:** C1

It might be French-owned (neighboring bistro Chez Maman is a sibling), but Papito is 100% Mexican, as your first bite of the outstanding shrimp tacos, piled with spicy adobo and sweet mango salsa, will attest. An ear of caramelized, grilled corn slathered in spicy mayo, lime juice, and cotija cheese will transport you to the streets of D.F., while the smoky coloradito sauce that bathes tender chicken enchiladas will have you scraping your plate for more. Papito's flavors are big, but its space is no more than a shoebox, so be prepared to wait or take your order to-go. If you dine in, the vibrant look matches the energetic food, with bright walls and a bustling side bar.

Note: Hayes Valley's Papito, once a satellite, now has different owners.

◾ 317 Connecticut St. (at 18th St.)
𝒫 (415) 695-0147 — **WEB:** www.papitosf.com
◾ Lunch & dinner daily   **PRICE:** ⚭

PICCINO 🍴

Italian

✗✗ | ♿ 🛖 🛋️   **MAP:** C2

A progenitor of the increasingly hot Dogpatch restaurant scene, Piccino embodies the neighborhood's many flavors, drawing families with kids in tow, young tech types, gregarious retirees, and more. Its memorable yellow exterior houses a relaxed, artsy-urban interior with lots of wood and natural light, a perfect venue for unwinding with friends.

Everyone comes here for deliciously blistered pizzas like the funghi, with roasted mushroom duxelles, sautéed wild mushrooms, stracchino, and slivers of garlic. Though pizza is a focus, Piccino excels in appetizers like tender, skillfully prepared polpette in tomato sauce, and must-order desserts such as a delectable hazelnut-cocoa nib cake. Their adjacent coffee bar is an area favorite.

◾ 1001 Minnesota St. (at 22nd St.)
𝒫 (415) 824-4224 — **WEB:** www.piccino.com
◾ Lunch & dinner daily   **PRICE:** $$

PRUBECHU 🍴○

Chamorro

✗ | ♿   **MAP:** B2

Owned by two natives of Guam, Prubechu is the only Bay Area restaurant that serves the island's Chamorro cuisine. It's a shoebox-sized space without a full kitchen, but the intrepid staff manages to turn out utterly unique, utterly delicious meals like none you've ever had.

Diners can choose between a tasting menu offering intricate Chamorro interpretations, or a small selection of homey à la carte dishes. Either way, the results are thrilling, from a flavorful chicken sausage steamed with luscious coconut milk in a banana leaf, to umami-rich dried pork shoulder with nettle purée. The nutty, creamy toasted rice porridge with caramel soy and a tempura-battered soft-cooked egg is a standout, as is a gently sweet and caramelized banana doughnut.

▓ 2847 Mission St. (bet. 24th & 25th Sts.)
☍ N/A — **WEB:** www.prubechu.com
▓ Dinner Tue – Sat   **PRICE:** $$

SASAKI 🍴○

Japanese

✗✗ | ♿   **MAP:** B2

Masaki Sasaki is well known among Bay Area sushi enthusiasts, having worked at a number of the area's top spots. Now, he's finally launched his own restaurant, housed on the ground floor of a quaint Mission Victorian. With only 12 seats at the sushi counter, reservations are a must, but each guest is rewarded with personal attention from Masa-san.

As with many high-end temples of sushi, only one omakase-style menu is offered. But Sasaki throws out the rulebook on proceeding from light to heavy fish. Commence with silky maguro, rich mackerel, and creamy monkfish liver, before veering back to a lighter crab and pickled cucumber dish. A parade of nigiri is equally deft, with specially seasoned rice individually chosen for each type of fish.

▓ 2400 Harrison St. (at 20th St.)
☍ (415) 829-8997 — **WEB:** www.sasakisf.com
▓ Dinner Tue – Sat   **PRICE:** $$$$

SHIZEN ⅚○

Vegan

XX | &

MAP: A1

At first glance, this stylish izakaya and sushi bar could be another in a line of similar places that dot the San Francisco landscape, were it not for a major twist: everything on the menu is vegan. Purists and die-hard carnivores may scoff, but the food is exceptional, skillfully manipulating vegetables and starches to recreate seafood-centric Japanese favorites.

Spicy tuna gets a run for its money from the impressive tofuna rolls, with chili-inflected minced tofu and cucumber, crowned with creamy avocado and dusted in chili "tobiko." A yuba salad with miso dressing and tempura-battered shiitake mushrooms stuffed with faux-crab are equally compelling. Throw in a sleek, contemporary setting, and Shizen is a winner for eaters of all stripes.

■ 370 14th St. (at Stevenson St.)
𝒞 (415) 678-5767 — **WEB:** N/A
■ Dinner nightly   **PRICE: $$**

TARTINE MANUFACTORY ⅚○

Californian

X | & 🍽

MAP: B1

Like its much-loved loaves, Tartine Bakery's spinoff turns rusticity into an art form. Sharing a massive industrial space with the Heath Ceramics factory, it boasts big windows, lots of light, and a crowd of millennial worker bees seeking morning ham-and-cheese Danishes and afternoon pick-me-ups of house-roasted coffee and cherry-almond bostocks. Also on the menu: beer, wine, soft-serve ice cream, and perfectly tangy house-made shrub sodas.

In the evening, the bread ovens shut down to create a more intimate space for dinner, with entrées like roast chicken and little gem salad. Still, the best time to visit is while the sun is up and the scent of bread is wafting through the air, despite the notably casual self-service.

■ 595 Alabama St. (at 18th St.)
𝒞 (415) 757-0007 — **WEB:** www.tartinemanufactory.com
■ Lunch & dinner daily   **PRICE: $$**

YUZUKI

Japanese

✕ | 👃 ♿

MAP: A1

Formerly an izakaya, this elegant Japanese restaurant has changed chefs and focus, offering delicate Washoku-style fare (read: no sushi). A meal might begin with thin slices of lightly torched mackerel, artfully arranged on shiso leaves. Then transition to tender Wagyu beef tataki, airy shredded vegetable and shrimp tempura, and a delicate sundae of azuki beans, mocha, and kelp gelée over vanilla ice cream.

With Tartine Bakery and other great gourmet spots sharing its block, there's no denying the fact that Yuzuki has a lot of competition. But with such an exquisite array of plates, not to mention outstanding organic sake and nutty buckwheat tea for sipping, it will transport you to Japan—provided you can snag a tough-to-get reservation.

▢ 598 Guerrero St. (at 18th St.)
☏ (415) 556-9898 — **WEB:** www.yuzukisf.com
▢ Dinner Wed – Sun

PRICE: $$

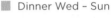

Sunday brunch plans?
Look for the 🍳!

NOB HILL

Thanks in large part to its connection to the Gold Rush industry magnates, Nob Hill is San Francisco's most privileged neighborhood. Its many plush mansions, strategic location complete with breathtaking views of the Bay, and accessible cable car lines that chug up to the top, ensure that it remains home to the upper crust. Speaking of which, note the familiar tinkle from wind chimes and postcard-perfect brass rails checking tourists who dare to lean out and take in the sights. Despite the large scale devastation following the 1906 earthquake, this iconic part of town bordering the gorgeous Golden Gate Bridge and Alamo Square's "Painted Ladies" was able to retain its wealthy reputation thanks to an upswell of swanky hotels, door-manned buildings, and opulent dining rooms. Unsurprisingly, "Snob Hill" today continues to echo of mighty egos and wealthy families who can be

seen making the rounds at **Big 4**, cradled within The Huntington Hotel. Named after the 1800s railroad titans, this stately hermitage is known for its antique memorabilia and nostalgic chicken potpie. A stop at **Swan Oyster Depot** for some of the finest seafood in town is a sure way to impress your out-of-town, tourist-trapped friends, but be prepared to wait up to several hours on busy days for one of their coveted few seats. Cocktails and small

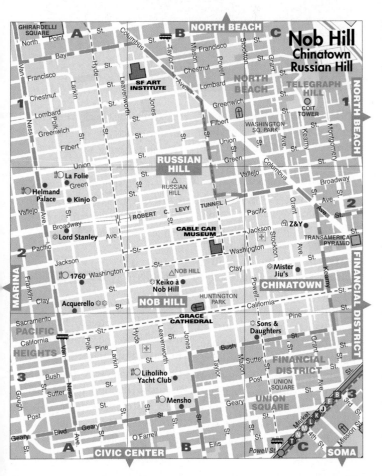

plates ensure epic levels of enjoyment at the extravagant **Top of the Mark** restaurant, boasting a sleek, lounge-like vibe and panoramic vistas of the sun setting over the cityscape. Moving from day to night, a handful of food-centric saloons fortuitously sate the tastes of young professionals with pennies to spare. At the top is **Cheese Plus**, showcasing over 300 international varieties, artisan charcuterie, and of course, chocolate for added decadence. Just steps away, **The Jug Shop** is an old-time, reliable, and very personable destination among locals who can be seen lapping up micro-brew beers and global wines. For a total departure, kick back with a *mai tai* (purportedly invented at Oakland's Trader Vic's in 1944) at **Tonga Room & Hurricane Bar**—a tiki spot in the *très* chic Fairmont Hotel, decked out with an indoor swimming pool that also functions as a floating stage.

RUSSIAN HILL

Slightly downhill and north toward Polk Street, the vibe mellows on the approach to Russian Hill, named after a Russian cemetery that was unearthed up top. Chockablock with cute boutiques, dive bars, and casual eateries, this neighborhood's staircase-like streets are scattered with

predominantly un-Russian groups and singles that seem more than willing to mingle. Good, affordable fare abounds here, at such popular haunts as **Caffé Sapore** serving breakfast specials, sandwiches, soups, and salads; as well as **Street** for fine, seasonal American cuisine. Tacky taqueria-turned-nighttime disco, **Nick's Crispy Tacos**, is a perennial favorite. The downright sinful and delicious chocolate earthquake from **Swensen's Ice Cream**'s flagship parlor (in business since 1948) is undoubtedly the town's most treasured dessert. From flashy finds to tastefully decorated destinations, **Bacchus Wine Bar** is an elegant and ever-alluring Italian-style spot lauded for both its beautiful interiors and exceptional wine, beer, and sake selections.

CHINATOWN

Scattered with large parks—Huntington Park is perhaps the city's most coveted stretch of greenery—Nob Hill's scene begins to change as you venture east to the country's oldest **Chinatown**. Here, authentic markets, dim sum palaces, souvenir emporiums, banks, and other businesses, which employ scores of the immigrant community, spill down the eastern slope of the Hill in a wash of color and vibrant Chinese characters.

Amid these steep streets find some of the city's most addictive and crave-worthy barbecue pork buns at old and almost antique dim sum houses where jam-packed dining is the name of the game. Even gastronomes flock here to scour the shelves at family-owned and operated **Wok Shop**, bursting with unique cookware, linens, tools, and all things Asian. Others may prefer to avoid the elbow-to-elbow experience and take home a slice of Chinatown by way of juicy dumplings, buns, and sweets from **Good Mong Kok Bakery**. Soldier on from this excellent and inexpensive take-out spot only to spin out a sugar-rush over creamy, oven-fresh custard tarts at **Golden Gate Bakery**; or prophetic little samples in the making at **Golden Gate Fortune Cookie Factory**. The amazing and very affordable **House of Nanking** is another rare (read: necessary) pleasure. Don't bother ordering from the menu—the owner will usually grab them from your hands and take over the ordering. But really, nobody is complaining. Finally, the **Mid-Autumn Moon Festival** brings friends and families together over mooncakes—a traditional pastry stuffed with egg yolk and lotus seed paste—and to reflect upon summer's bounty.

ACQUERELLO ✿✿
Italian

XxX | 🕸 | 🗖

MAP: A2

With its air of old-world sophistication, Acquerello is the kind of establishment where one dresses for dinner, which is always an occasion. The room feels embellished yet comfortable, with vaulted wood-beamed ceilings, warm terra-cotta walls, and contemporary paintings. It seems to draw celebrants of a certain age who are happy to splurge on a white truffle-tasting menu.

Each prix-fixe promises expertise and finesse, with a carefully curated wine list to match. Count yourself lucky if your meal begins with their famed parmesan budino surrounded by black truffle "caviar." Pasta must not be missed, such as the very fine and vibrant tajarin with a tableside shaving of impossibly earthy white truffle. Venison medallions wrapped in crisped pancetta are served with beautiful simplicity alongside pear slices, onion jam, chanterelles, and butternut squash purée. Refreshing desserts include delicate almond milk-panna cotta covered with vin santo jelly and crowned by buttery crushed almonds, quince, and tufts of dehydrated Balsamic vinegar.

Save room for one of the best mignardises carts you will ever encounter, stocked with superlative house-made chocolates, macarons, pâtes de fruits, and caramels.

■ 1722 Sacramento St. (bet. Polk St. & Van Ness Ave.)
℘ (415) 567-5432 — **WEB:** www.acquerello.com
■ Dinner Tue – Sat

PRICE: $$$$

HELMAND PALACE ¶○

Afghan

XX | ᒼ ⌛

MAP: A2

A drab exterior and an awkward Van Ness address haven't always worked in Helmand Palace's favor, but the food-savvy know it's one of the Bay Area's best for Afghan cuisine. The well-appointed interior is worlds away from the busy thoroughfare's steady stream of traffic, with linen-draped tables, big blue-cushioned armchairs, and warm, inviting service.

Every meal here kicks off with a basket of fluffy flatbread, served with three irresistible dipping sauces. The kaddo, caramelized baby pumpkin and ground beef in a garlic-yogurt sauce, is a perennial favorite, as is the chapendaz, marinated beef tenderloin over a tomato-pepper purée, rice, and lentils. Vegetarians will find numerous dishes to enjoy, all of them just as flavorful as the carnivorous feast.

▨ 2424 Van Ness Ave. (bet. Green & Union Sts.)
✆ (415) 345-0072 — **WEB:** www.helmandpalacesf.com
▨ Dinner nightly   **PRICE:** $$

LA FOLIE ¶○

French

XXX | 🕸 ᒼ ⌷ ⌛

MAP: A2

Few grandes dames of high-end French cuisine remain in the city, but this long-running spot from Chef/owner Roland Passot has held strong. With two formal dining rooms featuring starched tablecloths, polished servers, and a tall art deco wine case, it's a favorite among occasion-celebrating couples and the luxury-loving tourist crowd.

Diners can build their own three-to-five course prix-fixe, with classic dishes like a double bone-in lamb chop or a tower of crispy goat cheese, eggplant, and portobello mushroom. Thicker wallets can splurge on the chef's-choice tasting menu or the array of sumptuous supplements, like foie gras and butter-poached lobster. For dessert, chocolate lovers should be sure not to miss out on the velvety Valrhona mousse.

▨ 2316 Polk St. (bet. Green & Union Sts.)
✆ (415) 776-5577 — **WEB:** www.lafolie.com
▨ Dinner Tue – Sat   **PRICE:** $$$$

KEIKO À NOB HILL ❀

Fusion

XxX | 🕸 ▭

Elegant, discreet, and romantic, Keiko à Nob Hill blends unique culinary style with traditional appeal. Cushioned banquettes wrap the square dining room, outfitted with subdued lighting, fabric-covered walls, and heavy brown trim, resulting in a space that is lovely (if of a certain age).

It is always best to be prompt: the formal service team is gracious but handles each night's single seating with precision, serving all guests at once. Arriving on time is crucial as this kitchen takes its work and its mission rather earnestly.

Chef Keiko Takahashi's nightly tasting menu is a twelve-course progression of French culinary technique with subtle hints of Japanese flavors. Her success is undeniable from the first taste of Japanese spiny lobster presented in a martini glass with lobster-tomato water foam and a chilled layer of fruity bell pepper mousse. Moist, fragrant, and remarkably delicious Cornish hen arrives tucked with razor-thin shavings of black truffle beneath its skin, complemented with parmesan foam, Ibérico ham-cream sauce, and asparagus. A simple parfait is an extraordinary finale that includes coffee pâte de fruit, marron glacé, and bits of crunchy meringue atop whipped cream with grilled pears.

▪ 1250 Jones St. (at Clay St.)
☏ (415) 829-7141 — **WEB:** www.keikoanobhill.com
▪ Dinner Tue – Sun   PRICE: $$$$

KINJO ❀

Japanese

XX | &

MAP: A2

A partnership between the owners of Saru and Ijji and a former chef of Sushi Ran, sushi-focused Kinjo has made a splash in Russian Hill. Though its gray-and-glass exterior is discreet in appearance, the Zen-like inner sanctum decorated in light wood is palatial for a sushi restaurant. Tables expand the capacity to around 30 diners, but the best seats are—as always—at the venerable counter, where guests receive personalized service from the speedy and courteous chefs.

Diners are offered a choice of two set menus, each of which wends its way through cooked dishes like cherry leaf-cured trout and seafood in a flavorful broth with pea shoots, before arriving at a procession of nigiri. Sourced from around the globe, the selection might include red wine-cured Australian chutoro, luscious Hokkaido uni, and a trio of fish smoked tableside under a glass cloche. Other treats along the way: caviar-topped oysters, spoons of corn and lobster, and appetizing homemade tofu.

Each menu also includes a delicate dessert, like amazake panna cotta with candied sesame and strawberry sorbet. But before it arrives, you may be tempted to order even more nigiri from the à la carte menu—they're simply that good.

◾ 2206 Polk St. (at Vallejo St.)
☏ (415) 921-2222 — **WEB:** www.kinjosf.com
◾ Dinner Tue – Sun

PRICE: $$$$

LIHOLIHO YACHT CLUB ⵑ〇
Hawaiian

XX | 🍸 ♿   **MAP:** B3

There are no yachts to be found on the urban Tenderloin/Nob Hill border, but hordes of enthusiasts remain quite eager to book passage on Liholiho's love boat. Fusing Californian technique with the flavors of Chef/owner Ravi Kapur's native Hawaii, this sleek and sunny Instagrammer's paradise is known for strong cocktails, shareable plates, and near-impossible reservations. Two bars are available for walk-ins, but those tend to fill up quickly.

Watched over by a big '70s-era snapshot of Kapur's mom, the dining room hums with groups savoring beef tongue bao, luscious coconut-clam curry, and nori crackers heaped with tuna poke. If you turn your nose up at Spam, a Hawaiian staple, try the house-made (and off-menu) version. It just might convert you.

◼ 871 Sutter St. (bet. Jones & Leavenworth Sts.)
☎ (415) 440-5446 — **WEB:** www.liholihoyachtclub.com
◼ Dinner Mon – Sat   **PRICE:** $$$

MENSHO ⵑ〇
Japanese

X   **MAP:** B3

This little ramen shop is the first in the U.S. from the chef behind the highly popular Tokyo outposts, and its wait times are nothing short of epic—even in line-crazed San Francisco. No matter how early you arrive, snagging one of the 28 communal seats is at least a 30-minute affair that can easily run up to two hours. And the dicey Tendernob address means the line is often beset by aggressive panhandlers.

Only true aficionados can say if the ramen is worth it, but the tori paitan variety is one undeniably spectacular bowl, packed with springy, chewy noodles and outstanding duck chashu in a luxuriously creamy, umami-rich broth. Just know you'll be asked to slurp it down quickly: the hungry, huddled masses outside are anxious to take your seat.

◼ 672 Geary St. (bet. Jones & Leavenworth Sts.)
☎ (415) 800-8345 — **WEB:** www.mensho.tokyo
◼ Dinner Tue – Sun   **PRICE:** ⚆

LORD STANLEY ✿

Californian

XX | ♿

Like the husband-and-wife team who own it, Lord Stanley is half European and half Californian. Superlative ingredients and a sun-filled space lend it an undeniable West Coast vibe, while house-made breads, confections, and an intriguing wine list of European vintages make it clear that these chefs were trained across the pond.

Yet this is a charming little establishment right at home in its central Polk Street location, filled with a casual crowd of locals streaming in—imagine windows which offer a stellar, sweeping view of the neighborhood. Inside, the dining room is furnished with small bistro tables, while a larger communal table on the balcony welcomes groups. Bare wood tabletops set with handcrafted cutlery and warmed by candlelight set a simple and cozy atmosphere for enjoying meals that highlight artisanal and organic ingredients. Not unlike the space, the cooking here is approachable yet refined. A Berkshire pork chop is meltingly tender, balanced with just the right blend of sweet and sour flavors. Come dessert, a deconstructed dark chocolate pudding with sesame crisp is unmissable.

Be sure to quiz the attentive staff on the dishes—they'll happily explain each intricate layer.

◼ 2065 Polk St. (at Broadway)
✆ (415) 872-5512 — **WEB:** www.lordstanleysf.com
◼ Dinner Tue – Sat   PRICE: $$$

MISTER JIU'S ✿

Chinese

XX | 🍸 ♿

Chef/owner Brandon Jew has brought some of the sparkle back to Chinatown with this contemporary treasure, which puts a modern Californian spin on the Cantonese classics that once made the neighborhood a national dining destination. Impressively, the chef also makes all his Chinese pantry staples in-house, like the oyster sauce that coats a stir-fry of smoked tofu with long beans, tripe, and tendon; or lap cheong (Chinese sausage), which comes stuffed into roasted quail with sticky rice and jujube.

The menu is full of these clever touches, from the tomalley that adds depth to a rich Dungeness crab egg custard to the "tentacles" of fried fennel that echo the texture of salt-and-pepper squid.

Set in a longtime Chinese banquet hall, Mister Jiu's is bright and airy, with dramatic brass lotus chandeliers overhead. Food is served family-style, making it ideal for groups. But solo diners will also enjoy the sophisticated front bar, which serves up thoughtful, complex cocktails with Asian inflections like lemongrass milk and green tea.

Desserts are excellent, equally skillful and may incorporate black sesame, red bean, and osmanthus cream into preparations that will satisfy any sweet tooth.

▪ 28 Waverly Pl. (bet. Clay & Sacramento Sts.)
☎ (415) 857-9688 — **WEB:** www.misterjius.com
▪ Dinner Tue – Sat   **PRICE: $$$**

1760 🍽

Contemporary

✕✕ | 🍸 ♿   **MAP:** A2

Fine dining with a bold Asian twist is the lure at this sleek spot, where the chef is fusing old-school bistro favorites (focaccia, lobster bisque) with island-inspired flavors. A quick scan of the menu will reveal palate-pleasers such as calamansi, ginger, coconut, and tamarind, resulting in tantalizing creations like succulent baby back ribs with hoisin barbecue sauce or ravioli stuffed with sweet corn purée and bathed in a lemongrass-infused red curry.

Owned by the team behind Acquerello, 1760 (named for its address) draws an older, upscale crowd to its gallery-like space. Generally speaking, the more refined your appetite, the greater the reward, as portions while tasty are petite and the recommended 2-3 plates per person may still not fill you up.

🔲 1760 Polk St. (at Washington St.)
📞 (415) 359-1212 — **WEB:** www.1760sf.com
🔲 Dinner Mon – Sat   **PRICE:** $$$

Z & Y 😊

Chinese

✕   **MAP:** C2

Some like it hot, and here they are in heaven. Be forewarned: timid palates should steer clear of the super-spicy Sichuan dishes that have made Z & Y a Chinatown smash hit. Nearly every dish is crowned with chilies, from the huge mound of dried peppers that rests atop tender, garlicky bites of fried chicken to the flaming chili oil anointing tender, flaky fish fillets in a star anise-tinged broth with Sichuan peppercorns aplenty.

The well-worn dining room may seem unremarkable and the service perfunctory, but the crowds are undeterred. Plan to wait among eager fans for a seat, then settle in for delicate pork-and-ginger wontons swimming in spicy peanut sauce and more chili oil. Allot time to navigate the challenging parking situation.

🔲 655 Jackson St. (bet. Grant Ave. & Kearny St.)
📞 (415) 981-8988 — **WEB:** www.zandyrestaurant.com
🔲 Lunch & dinner daily   **PRICE:** $$

SONS & DAUGHTERS ✤

Contemporary

✕✕

MAP: C3

Everyone at this inviting space is warmly professional, including the eager, well-paced staff. Add in the mature, stylish crowd, architecturally detailed dining room—a hybrid between your grandmother's home and an art gallery with its black-and-cream palette, leather banquettes, and vintage chandeliers—and you'll be counting down the days until your next visit.

Small but mighty, this kitchen under the guidance of Chef Teague Moriarty turns out a seasonal, nine-course fixed menu that consistently pleases. A meal here might begin with an unctuous butternut squash soup garnished with fried salsify; or crunchy asparagus accompanied by gently pickled mushrooms and topped with shaved cured egg yolk. Then a block of exquisitely smooth foie gras is crowned with strawberry purée and fried almonds for a delicious and nutty bite, while crisp bits of lamb are incorporated with minted peas to form a clever counterpoint of sweet and savory flavors.

Deep red and juicy cherry ice cream is a sublime dessert. But it is the combination with intensely moist pistachio cake, tart verjus granite, juniper foam, and fresh cherries that showcase the technical prowess of this gifted kitchen.

▣ 708 Bush St. (bet. Mason & Powell Sts.)
✆ (415) 391-8311 — **WEB:** www.sonsanddaughterssf.com
▣ Dinner Wed – Sun

PRICE: $$$$

NORTH BEACH

FISHERMAN'S WHARF · TELEGRAPH HILL

Relatively compact yet filled with cool restaurants, casual cafeterias, and a hopping nightlife, North Beach has that authentic Californian vibe that makes it just as much a local scene as a tourist mecca. Steps from the docks and nestled between bustling **Fisherman's Wharf** as well as the steep slopes of Russian and Telegraph Hills, this neighborhood owes its vibrant nature to the Italian immigrants who passed through these shores in the late 1800s. Many were fishermen from the Ligurian coast, and the seafood stew (cioppino) that was prepared and perfected on their boats evolved into a quintessential San Francisco trademark. Though Italian-

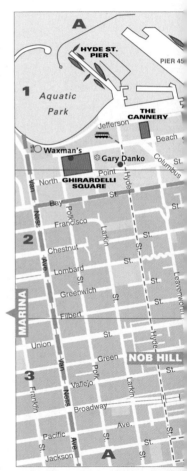

Americans may no longer be in the majority here, classic ristorantes, pizzerias, and coffee shops attest to their idea of the good life. At the annual **North Beach Festival** held in mid-June, a celebrity pizza toss, Assisi Animal Blessings, and Arte di Gesso also pay homage to this region's Italian roots. Foodies however can rest assured that dining here isn't all about lasagna-loving, red-sauce joints. Brave the

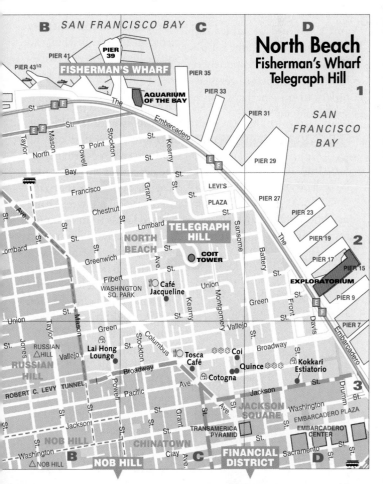

crowd of locals and visitors for some of the most fantastic fish and chips this side of the pond and fish tacos this side of the border, at **The Codmother Fish and Chips**. This veritable local favorite is essentially a small kiosk with a window to place your order and a handful of tables on the front patio. Clearly, it isn't about the dining experience here, and most people get their orders to go—perhaps for a stroll along the wharf?

TELEGRAPH HILL

Cutting its angle through North Beach, Columbus Avenue is home to the neighborhood's most notable restaurants, bars, and lounges.

Thanks to **Molinari's**, whose homemade salami has garnered a commendable following since 1896, whimsical, old-world Italian delicatessens are a regular fixture along these blocks. Pair their impressive range of imported meats and cheeses with some *vino* for a perfect picnic in nearby Washington Square Park. Preparing wood-fired pizzas featuring classic combinations since 1935, **Tommaso's Ristorante Italiano** is another citywide institution, situated on the southern end of North Beach. The décor and ambience may be a vestige from the past, but that hasn't prevented devoted locals from cramping its quarters. Fine-dining can also come with a throwback feel and **Bix** is a grand example. This bi-level arena with a balconied dining room, classic cocktails, and jazz club-ambience makes for a divine date-night. Getting acquainted with North Beach is a never-ending but very telling experience. After all, these neighborhood venues were also home to a ragtag array of beret-wearing poets in the 1950s and remain a popular excursion for the Beat Generation. Those so-called beatniks—Allen Ginsberg and Jack Kerouac to name a few—were eventually driven out by busloads of tourists. Nonetheless, bohemian spirits still linger here, at such landmarks as the City Lights bookstore and next door at **Vesuvio**, the quintessential boho bar.

FEASTING IN FISHERMAN'S WHARF

Fisherman's Wharf, that mile-long stretch of waterfront at the foot of Columbus Avenue, ranks as one of the city's most popular sites. There aren't many locals here and it teems with souvenir shops, street performers, and noisy rides. But you should stop by if only to feast on a sourdough bread bowl crammed with clam chowder, or fresh crabs cooked in huge steamers right on the street. Then, sample a bite of culinary history at **Boudin Bakery**. While this shop has bloomed into a full-scale operation complete with a museum and bakery tour, it stays true to its roots by crafting crusty sourdough every day, using the same mother (dough)

first cultivated here in 1849 from local wild yeast. Not far behind, **Ghirardelli Square** preserves yet another taste of old San Francisco. This venerable chocolate company, founded by Domenico "Domingo" Ghirardelli in 1852, flaunts a host of delectable wares at the equally famous **Original Ghirardelli Ice Cream & Chocolate Shop at Ghirardelli Square**. When roaming around here, don't forget to glimpse their impressive manufacturing equipment, while enjoying a hot fudge sundae. On your way out, be sure to take away some sweet memories in the form of those chocolate squares.

CAFÉ JACQUELINE 🍴

French

✗

MAP: C2

You'll float away on a cloud at the first taste of Jacqueline Margulis' signature soufflés, light and fluffy masterworks that have kept her tables full for over 35 years. Since the chef makes each of her creations by hand, expect to spend three or so hours at the table—it's the perfect romantic escape for couples lingering over a bottle of wine.

To sate your appetite while you wait, a bowl of light carrot soup or a delicate cucumber salad in champagne vinaigrette will do the trick. But the soufflés are the real draw, and keen diners plan on both a savory and a sweet course. For the former, a combination of flaky salmon, tender asparagus, and caramelized Gruyère is a delight. And the utterly perfect lemon soufflé will haunt any dessert lover's dreams.

▧ 1454 Grant Ave. (bet. Green & Union Sts.)
✆ (415) 981-5565 — **WEB:** N/A
▧ Dinner Wed – Sun   **PRICE: $$$$**

COTOGNA 😊

Italian

✗✗ | ♿ 🏠 🛋 🍽

MAP: C3

Though rustic compared to high-end sibling Quince, Michael and Lindsay Tusk's casual Italian offshoot would be elegant by any other standard. Stylish, bright, and a hot-ticket reservation, the space centers around an exhibition kitchen, from which crisp pizzas and hearty roasted meats emerge. The absolutely delicious menu highlights Chef Tusk's pristine pastas, like butternut squash cappellacci in caramelized brown butter drizzled with bitter cocoa reduction. Seasonal starters are equally pleasing, like kale and radicchio salad in tangy vinaigrette with hard-boiled farm egg and pecorino. A pretty wedge of the lime meringue tart with huckleberry compote is zippy, refreshing, and none-too-sweet.

The three-course prix-fixe offers an exceptional value.

▧ 490 Pacific Ave. (at Montgomery St.)
✆ (415) 775-8508 — **WEB:** www.cotognasf.com
▧ Lunch Mon – Sat   Dinner nightly   **PRICE: $$**

COI ✿✿✿
Seafood

XxX | 🕸 ⚤ 🛋 🍽

Chef Matthew Kirkley displays a distinct sense of artistry in his cooking, as if each plate were a portrait. Yet his precision and meticulous technique ensure that there is much more substance—and flavor—to Coi's seafood-centric cuisine.

Batons of bay leaf bavarois are topped with a thin layer of champagne gelée, meaty crab with pickled parsley leaves and pink grapefruit to garnish. A spritz of saltwater at the end lends a sense of brininess to the entire dish. Variations on Maine lobster include morsels of roasted tail meat and butter-poached claw, joined by foie gras terrine, wrapped in nori, and crowned with lobster roe and pickled red cabbage leaf. The tasting menu nicely transitions into inspired desserts, like the virtual solar system of chocolate orbs, filled with mandarin praline, crémeux, mousse, and more, beneath a whimsical "shooting star" of caramel crunch.

Despite its location just blocks from the Broadway clubs, the vibe inside this dining room is hushed and Zen-like, thanks to low ceilings, soft lighting, and well-paced service. While thoughtful wine pairings are available, diners should also consider their innovative tea coupling, highlighting rare and aged blends.

🔲 373 Broadway (bet. Montgomery & Sansome Sts.)
📞 (415) 393-9000 — **WEB:** www.coirestaurant.com
🔲 Dinner Thu – Mon   **PRICE: $$$$**

GARY DANKO ✿

Contemporary

XxX | 器 ᕼ ♢ ☝   **MAP:** A1

The elite meet to eat at this throwback favorite, which has been hosting the crème de la crème of the city (and its visitors) since the '90s. Set near Ghirardelli Square in Fisherman's Wharf, it features two lovely wood-paneled dining rooms and a small, bustling bar, all of them regularly full of hobnobbing business types and couples celebrating big occasions. With bursting flower arrangements, attentive servers, and well-dressed diners everywhere you look, it's hard not to be captivated.

The menu focuses on classic cuisine with some global twists; diners can create their own three- four- or five-course prix-fixe, or hand over the reins to the chef's tasting menu. Luxurious dishes include a luscious rock shrimp and Dungeness crab risotto, accented with butternut squash; branzino with fennel purée, olives, and a saffron-orange emulsion; as well as a perfectly cooked herb-crusted lamb loin, draped over date-studded farro and rainbow carrots.

While Danko may not be on the cutting-edge of fine dining, its top-notch wine list and outstanding service epitomize old-school luxury. Like the chocolate soufflé with vanilla bean crème anglaise that caps the meal, this is a classic for a reason.

▦ 800 North Point St. (at Hyde St.)
✆ (415) 749-2060 — **WEB:** www.garydanko.com
▦ Dinner nightly   **PRICE:** $$$$

KOKKARI ESTIATORIO 🍴

Greek

✕✕ | ♿ ⬚   **MAP:** D3

Zeus himself would be satisfied after a soul-warming meal at this Greek favorite, which serves up San Francisco chic with a side of old-world taverna hospitality. Translation? Once you're seated at the bar or settled near one of the roaring fireplaces, the thoughtful staff will cater to your every need. Kokkari's sophisticated menu leans heavily on the wood grill and rotisserie, which produce smoky souvlaki with warm pita and tangy chickpea salad, as well as roasted head-on prawns in garlic butter. Braised lamb shank with orzo is a feast, but resist the urge to conquer the Olympus-sized portions: you'll want to sample the galaktoboureko, crispy phyllo rolls filled with creamy custard and topped with honey, figs, and crème fraîche ice cream.

🔲 200 Jackson St. (at Front St.)
☎ (415) 981-0983 — **WEB:** www.kokkari.com
🔲 Lunch Mon – Fri   Dinner nightly   **PRICE:** $$

LAI HONG LOUNGE 🍴

Chinese

✕ | ♿ 🍴   **MAP:** B3

This windowless dim sum lounge looks small from the outside, but there's room for over 100 diners inside its cherry-red dining room—with dozens more hopefuls lined up on the street outside. The largely Chinese crowd attests to the authenticity of the food, which ranges from steamed pork buns and taro dumplings to chicken feet with peanuts. (If you're hoping to skip out on the wait, go at dinner instead of lunch, or call for takeout.)

Smiling servers roll carts featuring no end of tasty options, so you'll have to make some hard choices. Favorites include gingery wonton soup, full of soft and savory little dumplings; enormous rice noodle rolls stuffed with ground beef and aromatic herbs; and crispy, golden pan-fried tofu with a silky interior.

🔲 1416 Powell St. (bet. Broadway & Vallejo St.)
☎ (415) 397-2290 — **WEB:** www.lhklounge.com
🔲 Lunch & dinner daily   **PRICE:** $$

QUINCE ✿✿✿

Italian

✗✗✗✗ | 🦀 🍸 ♿ 💺 🤚 **MAP: C3**

An air of refinement touches this dining room—note the massive Murano chandelier, the stylish guests, and everything in between. No wonder this is where affluent tourists and locals alike come to celebrate their special occasions. From the moment the champagne cart arrives at your table to the last bite of the guéridon's mignardises, service is perfectly timed and attentive. The room is as lovely as ever, but has recently been tweaked to allow more space for private parties.

There was a time when Quince was home to traditional Italian cooking, but Chef Tusk's menu is increasingly contemporary. So while tortellini may sound familiar, this delicate pasta is a refined balance of the umami, earthy, and sweet flavors of red kuri squash, colatura di alici, and lapsang souchong black tea. Lasagnette is a masterpiece with dozens of layers of Swiss chard, guinea hen, and wild mushrooms. Crisp-skinned duck breast is beautifully roasted and impossibly tender, served in a pool of duck jus with turnips and black trumpets, alongside a pleasingly bitter tardivo radicchio salad, topped with a skewer of duck offal. Desserts offer a smart and harmonious finale to your meal.

The wine list is wonderful, but pricey.

🟦 470 Pacific Ave. (bet. Montgomery & Sansome Sts.)
📞 (415) 775-8500 — **WEB:** www.quincerestaurant.com
🟦 Dinner Mon – Sat   **PRICE: $$$$**

TOSCA CAFÉ ¶○

Italian

✗✗ | 🍸   **MAP:** C3

This historic bar has been expertly revived under NYC stars, April Bloomfield and Ken Friedman, who spent millions to add a kitchen and make its old-school charm seem untouched. White-coated bartenders shake and stir behind the glorious carved wood bar, while diners feast in the cushy red leather booths. Tables are few, so expect a wait if you don't have a reservation.

The food is Italian-American with Bloomfield's signature meaty influences, like flavorful, gamey grilled lamb ribs that nearly fall off the bone. Pastas are strong, from creamy gemelli cacio e pepe to rich, spicy bucatini all'Amatriciana, but don't neglect their vegetables: a dish of tender cauliflower and potatoes in a rich taleggio sauce with crunchy breadcrumbs is a showstopper.

▓ 242 Columbus Ave. (bet. Broadway & Pacific Ave.)
✆ (415) 986-9651 — **WEB:** www.toscacafesf.com
▓ Dinner nightly   **PRICE:** $$$

WAXMAN'S ¶○

American

✗✗ | ♿ 🪑 🖨   **MAP:** A1

With this bright, airy restaurant set just steps from the waterfront in Ghirardelli Square, acclaimed NYC chef, Jonathan Waxman, has returned to his Bay Area roots, bringing his rustic American food with him. This hot spot's hearty cooking will appeal to the array of visitors who stream into the square each day, but this is no tourist trap—in fact, it's the perfect place to unwind from a hectic day of sightseeing, perhaps with a glass of pinot gris on the lovely patio.

On the menu, you'll find Waxman's famed roast chicken, with its crisply caramelized skin and zippy salsa verde as well as his signature golden-brown smashed potatoes. But don't miss the rotating offerings, either—from seared calamari salad to buttery strawberry crostata, everything's made with the season's best.

▓ 900 North Point St. (bet. Larkin & Polk Sts.)
✆ (415) 636-9700 — **WEB:** www.waxmanssfo.com
▓ Dinner Tue – Sat   **PRICE:** $$$

RICHMOND & SUNSET

Named after an Australian art dealer and his home (The Richmond House), quiet yet urban Richmond is hailed for the surf that washes right up to its historic Cliff House and Sutro Baths. Springtime adds to the area's beauty with Golden Gate Park's blushing cherry blossoms and whimsical topiaries— nevermind those bordering pastel row-houses in desperate need of a lick of paint. More than anywhere else in the city, this sequestered northwest enclave is ruled by a sense of Zen, and residents seem deeply impacted by it—from that incredibly stealthy sushi chef to über-cool Sunset surfer dudes. Given its multi-cultural immigrant community, Richmond's authentic cuisine options are both delicious and varied. Begin with an array of European specialty items at **Seakor Polish Delicatessen and Sausage Factory**, proffering an outstanding selection of smoked, cured meats, sausages, pickles, sauerkraut and more.

NEW CHINATOWN

While Richmond does cradle some western spots, it is mostly renowned for steaming bowls of piping-hot *pho*, as thick as the marine layer itself. This area has earned the

make you feel like a kid in a candy store, Hong Kong–style delights (on offer even late at night) at **Kowloon Tong Dessert Café** will do a bang-up job. Clement Street, also an inviting exposition for the adventurous home cook and curious chef, features poky sidewalk markets where clusters of bananas sway from awnings and the spices and produce on display are as vibrant as the nearby **Japanese Tea Garden** in bloom. While the Bay Area mantra "eat local" may not be entirely pertinent here, a medley of global goodies abound and everything from tamarind and eel, to live fish and pork buns is available for less than a buck. There is a mom-and-pop joint for every corner and culture. In fact, this is *the* 'hood to source that 100-year-old egg or homemade kimchi by the pound. The décor in these divey shops is far from remarkable and at times downright seedy, but really, you're here for the food, which is undeniably authentic. Buses of Korean tourists routinely pull up to **Han Il Kwan** for a taste

nickname "New Chinatown" for good reason; and plates of deliciously moist and juicy *siu mai* are meant to be devoured at **Shanghai Dumpling King** or **Good Luck Dim Sum**. Speaking to this neighborhood's relatively new nickname, **Wing Lee Bakery** is famed for its comprehensive selection of dim sum—both sweet and savory. And while you're at it, don't miss out on Frisco's finest roast duck, on display at **Wing Lee BBQ** next door. Those looking to replicate this Asian extravaganza at home should start with a perfect wok, stockpot, noodle bowl, and rice cooker among other stellar housewares and kitchen supplies available at **Kamei**. If that doesn't

Richmond & Sunset

South Bay

CHINA BEACH

LAND'S END

COASTAL TRAIL

PACIFIC OCEAN

LINCOLN

THE LEGION OF HONOR

SEA CLIFF

THE PRESI

Washingto

Lincoln

Blvd

PARK

Lake St.

California St.

Clement

SUTRO BATHS RUINS

CLIFF HOUSE

Seal Rock Dr.

Point Lobos Ave.

Geary

SUTRO HEIGHTS PARK

48th

45th

43rd

41st

39th

37th

33rd

31st

29th

27th

25th

23rd

21st

19th

17th

Lake St.

Pizzetta 211

Kappou Gomi

Fiorella

Clemer

Sichua Home

RICHMOND

Anza St.

Balboa

RICHMOND

Balboa

Great

La Playa

Cabrillo

47th Av

OCEAN BEACH

Fulton

St.

Ave.

Ave.

Ave.

Ave.

St.

St.

St.

Cabrillo

Ave.

Spreckels Lake

GOLDEN

John F. Kennedy

West

Park Presidio

Stov Lake

Chain of Lakes

John F. Kennedy Dr.

GATE

Dr.

PARK

Highway

Dr.

Middle

Martin

Luther

King Jr.

Lincoln

Martin Luther King Jr. Dr.

Way

Lincoln

45th

43rd

41st

37th

35th

31st

29th

27th

25th

23rd

19th

Irving

Irving

Ocean Beach

Judah

Judah-Sunset

Judah

Judah-19 Av

La Playa

Outerlands

Kirkham

Ave.

Ave.

Ave.

Lawton

Moraga

22nd

Kirkha

St.

St.

St.

OCEAN BEACH

Lawton

Ave.

St.

Moraga

Noriega

36th

Noriega

SUNSET

43rd

St.

37th

Ortega

Pacheco

Sunset Reservoir

24th

Ortega

Great

48th

Pacheco

Quintara

Quintara

45th

St.

41st

39th

35th

33rd

31st

29th

25th

21st

Quintara

Rivera

Rivera

PACIFIC OCEAN

Santiago

Ave.

Santiago

Taraval-22 Av

47th

Taraval-Sunset

Taraval

St.

PARKSIDE

Tar

19th

Taraval

Ulloa

23rd

Ulloa

GOLDEN GATE NATIONAL RECREATION AREA

Ave.

Vicente

Sunset

St.

Ave.

Vicente

Ave.

Wawona

SF Zoo

Wawona

Sloat

Yorba

PINE LAKE PARK

Crestlake Dr.

Sloat Blvd.

A

B

C

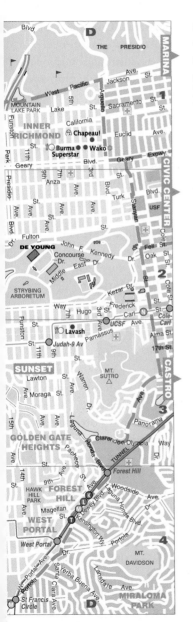

of home. The space may be congested and service can be a disaster, but the kitchen's nostalgic cooking keeps the homesick hordes coming back for more. Native-born aficionados can be found combing the wares at **First Korean Market**, poised on Geary Boulevard and packed with every prepared food and snack under the sun. Meanwhile, culture vultures gather for an intense Burmese feast at **B Star Bar**, after which a refreshing sip at **Aroma Tea Shop** is nothing if not obligatory. Their owners even encourage free tastings of exclusive custom blends of individually sourced teas from around the world.

SUNSET

A dash more updated than bordering Richmond, Sunset—once a heap of sand dunes—retains a small-town vibe that's refined but still rough around the edges. Here, locals start their day with fresh-baked pastries at **Arizmendi Bakery** and then stroll around the corner for some much-needed caffeine at the **Beanery**. Asian appetites routinely frequent **Ebisu**—a Japanese restaurant—for their sashimi and creative sushi rolls. Tourists taking in the sights at the de Young Museum or Academy of Sciences love to linger over lunch at **Wooly Pig Cafe**. Their namesake "Wooly Pig" sandwich, crafted from toasted challah and overflowing with pork belly, mizuna greens, and pickled shallots, is guaranteed to knock your socks off. Yes, the space is tiny with only a smattering of tables, but with gorgeous Golden Gate Park just a block away, their offerings make for perfect picnic treats. Over on Noriega Street, the line lengthens out the door and down the sidewalk at **Cheung Hing**. If that isn't a sign that something special is going on here, sample the kitchen's Chinese barbecue including whole roast duck, or take slices of tender-charred pork to-go. In fact, those leaving with bags of roasted meat can be assured of envious glares from the crowds waiting around. As the sun sets in the Sunset, savor dinner at **Pisces** **California Cuisine**, which flaunts dishes composed of local, seasonal, and nutritional ingredients. Reflecting the same philosophy, **Thanh Long** on Judah Street has gained a substantial local fan-base who seem unperturbed at the thought of waiting endlessly for their famous garlic noodles and whole-roasted Dungeness crab. Outer Sunset residents who are at the mercy of time may rest assured as **Noriega Produce Market** resides just around the corner, and is as immaculate as any farmer's market for sustainable, organic produce. Finally, no repast can be termed "regal" without a bit of sweet at **Holy Gelato!**—a quirky shop serving coffees, teas, and creamy gelatos in a wide range of flavors—including crème brûlée, goat cheese, and honey-lavender. Top off this sugar high at age-old, Asian kitsch fave, **Polly Ann Ice Cream**, with such inventive flavors as durian, jasmine tea, or taro—and know that nothing but happy dreams can follow.

BURMA SUPERSTAR ⏃○

Burmese

✗ | ♿   **MAP:** D1

Like any celebrity, it's easy to recognize this unusual dark wood superstar from the eager crowds swarming like paparazzi. Everyone endures their no-reservations policy to Instagram their favorite Burmese dishes. See the iPhones poised over the famed rainbow and tea-leaf salads or samusa soup (also available as a lunchtime combo). Regulars stick to traditional items, marked by asterisks on the menu. Palate-tingling options include rice noodles with pickled daikon and tofu in a spicy tomato-garlic sauce, or pork and kabocha squash stewed in a gingery broth with coconut sticky rice. A creamy Thai iced tea is the perfect counterbalance to the spicy, boldly flavored fare.

Hipper digs, a cooler crowd, and updated favorites can be found at sib—Burma Love.

■ 309 Clement St. (bet. 4th & 5th Aves.)
✆ (415) 387-2147 — **WEB:** www.burmasuperstar.com
■ Lunch & dinner daily   **PRICE:** $$

CHAPEAU! 😊

French

✗ | ♿   **MAP:** D1

For an oh-so-French experience on Asian food-centric Clement, denizens head to Philippe Gardelle's authentic bistro, where tightly spaced tables and paintings of the titular hats create a convivial atmosphere. Packed with regulars receiving bisous from the chef, Chapeau! is warm and generous, a vibe that's aided by its strong Gallic wine list.

Dishes are traditional with a bit of Californian flair, like fingerling potato chips in a frisée and duck confit salad or salted-caramel ice cream that tops the pain perdu. The cassoulet, wholesome with braised lamb, rich with smoky sausage, and earthy with white beans, is perfect for a foggy night in the Avenues. Come before 6:00 P.M. on certain nights for a $40 early bird prix fixe, or create your own from their many set menus.

■ 126 Clement St. (bet. 2nd & 3rd Aves.)
✆ (415) 750-9787 — **WEB:** www.chapeausf.com
■ Dinner nightly   **PRICE:** $$

FIORELLA 🍴

Italian

🏃 | ♿ 🛋

MAP: C1

In the foggy Outer Richmond, this casual neighborhood pizzeria has quickly become as hot as its wood-fired oven. Local families come in droves to share a pie or a plate of pasta in the vintage-chic dining room, where laid-back servers chat with patrons beneath funky wallpaper depicting a bevy of Bay Area landmarks and legendary locals.

The chewy, blistered crusts churned out of the kitchen are loaded with flavor, whether in a classic Margherita or salami pie with provolone and red chili. Throw in a seasonal salad, a pile of chicken wings tossed in a Calabrian chili-honey glaze, and a glass of Italian wine from the compact list. And be sure to save room for the delectable warm almond- and Meyer lemon-ricotta cake, which gets toasted to perfection alongside the pies in the oven.

▦ 2339 Clement St. (bet. 24th & 25th Sts.)
☎ (415) 340-3049 — **WEB:** www.fiorella-sf.com
▦ Lunch Sat – Sun   Dinner nightly

PRICE: $$

KAPPOU GOMI 😊

Japanese

🏃

MAP: C1

Sushi-seekers should take a pass, but those yearning for elegant, traditional Japanese food will find kindred spirits at this precious gem. The serene, ultra-minimalist dining room isn't fancy, with only a few shelves of ceramics as décor. But the older Japanese women in traditional garb who run the show are endlessly polite and attentive, so long as you're not raising a din—or requesting a spicy tuna roll.

The eight-page menu offers a head-spinning number of options arranged by ingredient, like umami-rich wilted mizuna salad with fava beans and bonito sauce, or pale green edamame tofu with fresh cherries, cherry blossom noodles, and a sour-salty cherry paste. The exquisitely moist and flaky black cod, grilled with a slightly sweet sake marinade, is revelatory.

▦ 5524 Geary Blvd. (bet. 19th & 20th Aves.)
☎ (415) 221-5353 — **WEB:** N/A
▦ Dinner Tue – Sun

PRICE: $$

LAVASH 🍴

Persian

✗✗ | ♿   **MAP:** D3

You'll feel like you've dined in a Persian home after leaving family-run Lavash, which has become a neighborhood fixture thanks to warm service and sizable portions. Painted in hues of orange, gold, and rose, the casual and flower-filled space is inviting, and throughout a meal here, you'll see locals dropping in for takeout or just to chat.

Begin your feast with sabzi panir, a plate of fresh herbs, feta, cucumber, tomato, walnuts, and grapes that's perfect for ad hoc toppings on the cracker-like namesake bread. Then order up a skewer or two of tender and smoky ground beef and lamb koobideh, served over fluffy basmati rice. Finally, don't miss the crispy, sticky-sweet baghlava—it's available in traditional pistachio or as a chocolate "choclava."

◾ 511 Irving St. (bet. 6th & 7th Aves.)
✆ (415) 664-5555 — **WEB:** www.lavashsf.com
◾ Lunch & dinner Tue – Sun   **PRICE:** $$

OUTERLANDS 🍴

American

✗ | 🛖 🛋 🍳   **MAP:** A3

For the residents of this Outer Sunset foggy beachside community, this sweet spot is an ideal hangout. The salvaged wood-dominated décor is perfectly cozy, and all-day hours ensure crowds flock here for breakfast and Bloody Marys to start their day. A friendly staff, good, locally roasted coffee, and a nicely stocked bar with a fine listing of beers on tap encourages further lingering.

Stop in for fresh-baked pastries like coffee cake, scones, and glazed doughnuts; or dig into heartier fare like an open-faced sandwich topped with black eye pea purée, green tomato, and griddled ham slices. Once the sun sets over Ocean Beach, expect more ambitious cooking from the dinner menu, like smoked chicken with tomato panzanella and charred gem lettuce.

◾ 4001 Judah St. (at 45th Ave.)
✆ (415) 661-6140 — **WEB:** www.outerlandssf.com
◾ Lunch & dinner daily   **PRICE:** $$

PIZZETTA 211 ⅈ○

Pizza

✗

MAP: C1

This shoebox-sized pizzeria may reside in the far reaches of the Outer Richmond, but it's easily identifiable by the crowds hovering on the sidewalk to score a table. Once inside, you'll be greeted by pizzaiolos throwing pies in the tiny exhibition kitchen—ask for a counter seat to get a better view.

The thin, chewy, blistered pizzettas each serve one, making it easy to share several varieties. Weekly specials utilize ingredients like seasonal produce, house-made sausage, and fresh farm eggs, while standbys include a pie topped with wild arugula, creamy mascarpone, and San Marzano tomato sauce. Whatever you do, arrive early: once the kitchen's out of dough, they close for the day, and the omnipresent lines mean the goods never last too long.

▨ 211 23rd Ave. (at California St.)
℘ (415) 379-9880 — **WEB:** www.pizzetta211.com
▨ Lunch & dinner Wed - Mon   PRICE: $$

SICHUAN HOME 😃

Chinese

✗

MAP: C2

One of the brightest offerings on Geary Boulevard, Sichuan Home lures diners far and wide. Its spotless dining room is a vision of varnished wood panels and mirrors, with plexiglass-topped tables for easy chili oil clean-up and menus that feature tempting photos of each item.

A sampling of the wide-ranging Sichuan cuisine should include tender, bone-in rabbit with scallions, peanuts, and a perfect dab of scorching hot peppercorns. Fish with pickled cabbage gets a delightfully restorative hit of bold flavors from mustard greens and fresh green chilies, and red chilies star in aromatic dry-fried string beans with minced pork. For dessert, rich and velvety mango pudding, topped with grapefruit sorbet and fresh pineapple, is a tropical treat.

▨ 5037 Geary Blvd. (bet. 14th & 15th Aves.)
℘ (415) 221-3288 — **WEB:** N/A
▨ Lunch & dinner daily   PRICE: $$

WAKO ⌘

Japanese

✗ | ♿

Wako blends right in with the sea of Asian restaurants on Clement Street, but don't let its nondescript exterior fool you. Once inside, you will find a serene and spare dining room that is composed with beautiful, multi-hued wood surfaces and attended to by an exceedingly polite service staff. Fresh flowers add a bit of flourish and fun.

It's the kind of pristine culinary experience that connoisseurs and foodies crave. And since this kitchen boasts some of the best sushi in town, be sure to make reservations. The omakase (with a choice of two menus of varying length) may be the only option on offer, but rest assured as it's available throughout the restaurant. Nevertheless, a seat at the ubiquitous counter is likely to deliver a happier outcome.

From the non-sushi items, diners may be presented with poached monkfish liver, a creamy potato croquette dolloped with salmon roe, or a salad of shaved apple and mizuna. The real knockouts though arrive on rice: squid with a touch of shiso and Meyer lemon zest; silky salmon with house-made yuzu kosho; custardy uni imported from Japan, wrapped in roasted seaweed; and to finish, a melt-in-your-mouth slice of gently seared A5 Wagyu beef.

◾ 211 Clement St. (bet. 3rd & 4th Aves.)

✆ (415) 682-4875 — **WEB:** www.sushiwakosf.com

◾ Dinner Tue – Sat

PRICE: $$$

SOMA

Once the city's locus of industry, sprawling SoMa (short for South of Market) has entered a post-industrial era that's as diverse and energetic as San Francisco itself. From its sleek office towers and museums near Market, to the spare converted warehouses that house the city's hottest startups, SoMa teems with vitality, offering memorable experiences around every turn. Tourists may skip it for its lack of Victorians, but SoMa's culinary riches and cultural cachet are of a different, authentically urban kind—this is the neighborhood equivalent of a treasured flea-market.

FINE ARTS & EATS

Most visitors to this neighborhood tend to cluster in the artsy northeast corridor (bordering downtown) for trips to the Museum of Modern Art, Yerba Buena Center for the Arts, Contemporary Jewish Museum, as well as a profusion of other galleries and studios. For a pit stop,

join the tech workers snagging a caffeinated "Gibraltar" from local coffee phenomenon, **Blue Bottle**, nestled in the back of Mint Plaza (there is also a rotating schedule of food trucks that visit Mint Plaza). For a more serene setting, gaze into Yerba Buena Gardens with a cup of rare green tea and some spa cuisine at **Samovar Tea Lounge**.

In a city where everyone loves to eat, even the **Westfield San Francisco Centre** mall is a surprisingly strong dining destination, offering cream puffs, a chocolatier, tea shop, or even *bi bim bap* in its downstairs food court.

And local chain **Buckhorn Grill**, in the Metreon Mall, is a sparkling delight for deliciously marinated, wood-fired tri-tip. A hard day's shopping done, hit happy hour on Yerba Buena Lane with the yupsters fresh from their offices, indulging in a strong margarita at festive Mexican cantina, **Tropisueño**. But for a more sedate sip, make way to chic **Press Club**, which focuses on Californian wine and beer. In the midst of it all, the Moscone Center may draw conventioneers to overpriced hotel restaurants and clumsy chains, however, the savvier ones beeline to **ThirstyBear Organic Brewery**, where classic Spanish tapas and organic brews come without the crowds or crazy prices. Then stroll over to the Rincon Center for a unique meal at **Amawele's South African Kitchen**—an establishment that has won the hearts of local office workers with such classic eats as "bunny chow" (a curry-filled bread bowl).

PLAY BALL

SoMa's southeast quarter has undergone a revival in the last decade, with baseball fans flooding AT&T Park to watch the Giants—perennial World Series contenders. The park's food options are equally luring and include craft beer, sushi, and

Ghirardelli sundaes. Crabcake sandwiches at **Crazy Crab'z** have a fan club nearly as sizable as the team itself. Off the field, this corridor is dominated by the tech scene, which has transformed the area's former factories and warehouses into humming open-plan offices. An oasis of green amid these corporate environs, South Park is a lovely retreat, particularly with a burrito in hand from the vibrant taqueria, **Mexico au Parc**. Just outside the park, legions of young engineers in their matching company hoodies form long lines every lunchtime outside **HRD Coffee Shop**. It may look like a greasy spoon but serves inventive Korean-influenced dishes like spicy pork and kimchi burritos. Hip graphic designers can be seen speeding their fixed-gear bikes towards Market to pick up desktop fuel from **The Sentinel**, where former Canteen chef, Dennis Leary, offers house-roasted coffee in the mornings and excellent corned-beef sandwiches for lunch.

For a casual lunch, **21st Amendment** (a brewpub with hearty food and popular beers like Back in Black) is beloved; whereas Farmerbrown's **Little Skillet** might just have some of *the* best fried chicken and waffles in town. Silicon Valley commuters begin pouring out of the Caltrain station at 5:00 P.M., giving the area's nightlife an extra shot in the arm. For those in need of a more understated retreat, the 700-label selection at ripped-out-of-France wine bar, **Terroir**, will enchant natural-wine junkies.

SAN FRANCISCO ▶ SOMA

BEST OF THE WEST

SoMa's western half may appear grittier, but it is still a must for those in search of good food. After a brief closure and remodel, Vietnamese standby **Tú Lan** is once again drawing lines of customers for its killer imperial rolls, despite the drug-addled environs of its Sixth Street digs. Crowds also cluster regularly at neighboring **Popsons**, where an impressive selection of juicy burgers and thick ice cream shakes are definitely worth the wait—and extra calories! Indeed, very little is same old-same old on this side of the city—whether it's the tattooed skateboarders practicing their moves, the omnipresent cranes constructing condo towers, or the drag performers who can be found entertaining and regaling bachelorette parties over Asian-fusion food at hopping nightspot, **AsiaSF**. Amidst these edgy bars, kitschy boutiques, and design start-ups of Folsom delicious Ethiopean stews served alongside piles of spongy *injera* fuel a booming takeout business at **Moya**. From there, travel east to feast on flavorful Thai curries, noodles, and larb at **Basil Canteen**—located in the original Jackson Brewery building. Finally, hit those 11th Street bars for some serious drinking and dancing, before sealing the deal over a rich and heart-warming Nutella-banana triangle from late-night perma-cart, **Crêpes a Go Go**.

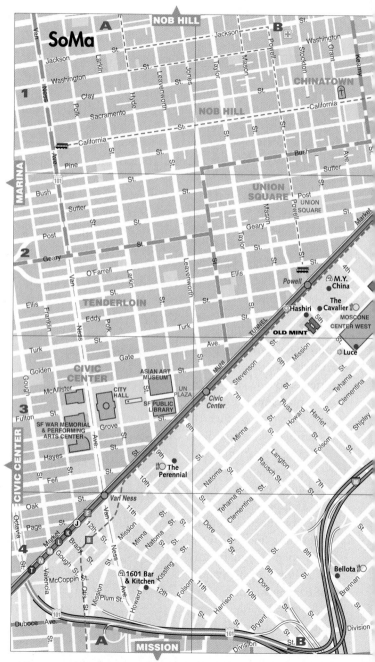

SoMa

NOB HILL

A

B

CHINATOWN

NOB HILL

MARINA

UNION SQUARE

UNION SQUARE

TENDERLOIN

Powell
M.Y. China
Hashiri
The Cavalier
MOSCONE CENTER WEST
OLD MINT
Luce

CIVIC CENTER

ASIAN ART MUSEUM
CITY HALL
UN PLAZA
SF PUBLIC LIBRARY
Civic Center

SF WAR MEMORIAL & PERFORMING ARTS CENTER

The Perennial

Van Ness

Bellota

1601 Bar & Kitchen

MISSION

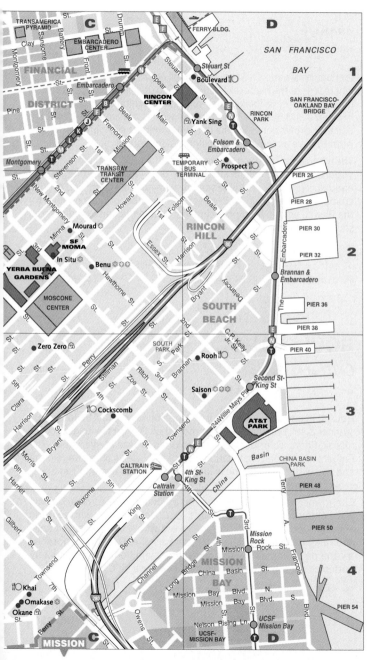

BELLOTA ¶O
Spanish

XX | 器 🍸 🕭 ⇄　　　　　　　　**MAP:** B4

Iberian flavors and Cali-cool join forces at this SoMa Spanish stunner, where legs of the namesake jamón ibérico de bellota hang in a central glass case. They're flanked by a sumptuous exhibition kitchen framed in bronze and hand-painted tiles, as well as a glamorous U-shaped bar. Chic professionals (some of them from the neighboring offices of Airbnb) have already staked their claim for date night.

The menu adds seasonal touches to traditional Spanish tapas: picture yogurt-braised chicken albóndigas drizzled with pomegranate agridulce; or a fluffy tortilla Española with rainbow chard and chorizo crumbles. Paellas sized for 2-4 people are another popular option—try the Pluma, with Ibérico pork shoulder, summer squash, and slivered squash blossoms.

▓ 888 Brannan St. (bet. 7th & 8th Sts.)
℘ (415) 430-6580 — **WEB:** www.bellotasf.com
▓ Lunch Mon – Fri　Dinner Mon – Sat　　　　**PRICE:** $$$

BOULEVARD ¶O
Californian

XX | 器 🕭 ⇄ 🍳　　　　　　　　**MAP:** D1

Housed in one of the city's most historic buildings, this Belle Époque stunner is still breathtaking after more than 20 years, with glamorous mosaic floors, colorful glass, and polished bronze at every turn. The Embarcadero-adjacent location offers lovely views of the Bay Bridge and the water, and business lunchers as well as evening romance-seekers adore its transporting vibe.

Chef/owner Nancy Oakes is known as a pioneer of Californian cooking, with comforting takes on standards like Dungeness crab with avocado and ruby-red grapefruit, burrata served with a side of shaved kale, and flaky halibut over a mashed potato cake. Sweets are notable: try the pear- and apple-studded winter symphony crisp or creamy butterscotch pudding with pecan granola for a bit of bliss.

▓ 1 Mission St. (at Steuart St.)
℘ (415) 543-6084 — **WEB:** www.boulevardrestaurant.com
▓ Lunch Mon – Fri　Dinner nightly　　　　**PRICE:** $$$

BENU ✿✿✿

Asian

XxX | 器 ᵹ 🖵 🍽

Don't miss the street views directly into Benu's kitchen as you enter—the chefs here are preparing a series of masterpieces. The interior is awash in earthy colors and sleek banquettes, and the slate-gray dining room is serene, with clean lines drawing the eye across the meticulous design. Given the restaurant's high caliber, the staff is impressively warm and relaxed.

Chef Corey Lee's nightly tasting is a unique marriage of contemporary Asian influences, while Master Sommelier Yoon Ha oversees an exceptional beverage program. Each meal begins with a thrilling parade of bites like silky egg custard with faux "shark fin," slivers of Jinhua ham, and umami-rich black truffle. The main courses might include a delectable "thousand-year-old" quail egg atop bright ginger cream, followed by delicate xiao long bao filled with rich lobster and lobster coral. Then fork-tender beef braised in pear juice reaches a new height of excellence when paired with charred scallion purée and black trumpet mushrooms. The memory of the osmanthus gelée with almond cake and apricots will remain long after the last plate has been cleared.

Finally, sojourn to their pretty courtyard to linger after this regal repast.

◼ 22 Hawthorne St. (bet. Folsom & Howard Sts.)
☎ (415) 685-4860 — **WEB:** www.benusf.com
◼ Dinner Tue – Sat   **PRICE: $$$$**

THE CAVALIER ⅝◯

Gastropub

XX | 🍸 ⅍ 🛋 🗄 🗄 🖐   **MAP:** B2

One of the city's high-profile hangouts, this is the third effort from the team behind Marlowe and Park Tavern. Everything here has a British bent, echoed in the hunting-lodge-gone-sophisticated décor with red-and-blue walls accented by taxidermied trophies and tufted banquettes. Across-the-pond classics have Californian twists like a deep-fried Scotch duck egg wrapped in truffled duck rillettes. The restaurant has quickly become a see-and-be-seen haunt of the tech oligarchy (complete with a private club). However, the food is spot-on and homey as seen in a corned beef-and-potato hash topped with a gently poached egg.

Though reservations are a must, its location in the Hotel Zetta means service runs from morning to night, giving diners plenty of options.

▪ 360 Jessie St. (at 5th St.)
📞 (415) 321-6000 — **WEB:** www.thecavaliersf.com
▪ Lunch & dinner daily   **PRICE:** $$

COCKSCOMB ⅝◯

American

XX | 🍸 ⅍ 🛋   **MAP:** C3

Carnivores will thrill to the offerings at this favored spot from offal-loving *Top Chef Masters* champ Chris Cosentino. It doesn't shy away from aggressively rich fare like wood-grilled bruschetta topped with uni butter, sweet Dungeness crab, and buttery lardo, or smoky butterflied roast quail in a rich, salty tetrazzini gravy. Even veggie-centric celery Victor gets a meaty spin, its tangy vinaigrette accented by crisp chicken-skin chicharrónes.

Thanks to the hearty menu and location in a tech-centric corridor, Cockscomb draws a mostly male crowd that packs in for shellfish platters and intense, boozy cocktails named for SF landmarks. Laid-back, yet attentive service and a soaring, industrial space make it the very picture of a hot spot.

▪ 564 4th St. (at Freelon St.)
📞 (415) 974-0700 — **WEB:** www.cockscombsf.com
▪ Lunch Mon – Fri   Dinner Mon – Sat   **PRICE:** $$$

HASHIRI ✿

Japanese

XxX | 🍷 ♿ 🍴

MAP: B2

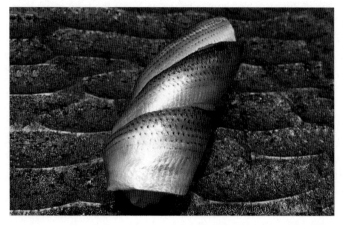

This omakase-only Japanese gem in Mint Plaza may be one of the city's most expensive restaurants, but those who can afford the bill will be rewarded with a truly luxurious experience. Every detail of Hashiri has been finely crafted, from the hand-painted dishes and crystal sake glasses to the parting seasonal treat presented to diners at the end of their meal. This dining room is home to a host of Asian diners and suits, but don't be surprised if you see a hoodie-clad millionaire or two seated next to you.

Chef Takashi Saito and team offer their own creative hybrid of two classic cuisines—the artistry of sushi fused with the ceremony of a kaiseki meal. Exceptional dishes showcase the best of the season and have included tender pen shell clam with citrus-splashed fava beans and bamboo shoots; or lightly grilled A5 Wagyu beef over celeriac purée and charred ramps. Then move on to some outstanding nigiri like buttery Spanish mackerel brushed with citrus, pungent aji with minced chives and ginger, chutoro, otoro, as well as Hokkaido uni.

Sake connoisseurs will enjoy the exclusive selection, while novices can rest assured as the helpful staff is happy to steer their way to the right choice.

▨ 4 Mint Plaza (at 5th St.)
✆ (415) 908-1919 — **WEB:** www.hashirisf.com
▨ Dinner Tue – Sat   **PRICE: $$$$**

IN SITU ✿
International

XX | ♿ ⬚

Like the SF Museum of Modern Art in which it's housed, Corey Lee's "culinary museum" bends notions of time and place to offer this unique array of iconic dishes from top chefs around the world, honoring more than two decades of innovative cooking. Guided by the dishes' creators, Lee has trained his cooks to faithfully replicate more than 100 menu items from a starry lineup that includes Chefs Thomas Keller, Albert Adrià, and David Chang.

The concise menu rotates seasonally, ensuring that diners will always have new "exhibits" to sample. They might include David Thompson's intensely spicy Chiang Mai-style guinea fowl larb salad, Mehmet Gürs' luscious lamb shank manti with yogurt mousse and tomato, and Hiroshi Sasaki's succulent glazed chicken thigh with a creamy onsen egg. If Adrià's decadent and masterfully prepared Jasper Hill Farm cheesecake with a hazelnut crust and white chocolate cookies is in the lineup, don't hesitate.

In addition to the culinary concept, In Situ's design is in keeping with its museum home, featuring a spare dining room and a few gems from SFMOMA's collection adding pops of color. Be forewarned that a sophisticated but casual crowd fills up this room quickly.

◾ 151 Third St. (bet. Howard & Minna Sts.)
☏ (415) 941-6050 — **WEB:** insitu.sfmoma.org
◾ Lunch Thu – Tue   Dinner Thu – Sun   **PRICE:** $$$$

KHAI 🍴◯
Vietnamese

χ | ⅊   **MAP:** C4

A celebrity in his native Vietnam, Chef/owner Khai Duong has chosen to settle down in a strip mall near the Design District, where he offers a ten-course tasting menu with two nightly seatings. The petite dining room is a bit eccentric, with its daytime takeaway counter mostly obscured by curtains. Still, you'll get a lot of face time with the chef, who's an active presence and a great character.

Trained in France, Duong offers beautifully crafted updates on classic Vietnamese dishes, from vermicelli with shredded omelet and pork belly to Hanoi's famous cha ca thang long, turmeric-marinated fish with dill and scallions. Other highlights include rich matsutake mushroom pâté, and for dessert, slippery coconut noodles with durian paste and coconut cream.

▦ 655 Townsend St. (bet. 7th & 8th Sts.)
℘ (415) 724-2325 — **WEB:** www.chefkhai.com
▦ Dinner Tue – Sat   **PRICE:** $$$$

M.Y. CHINA 🙂
Chinese

χχ | ⅊ 🔪   **MAP:** B2

Need proof that Yan Can Cook? Just snag a table at the famed PBS chef's elegant restaurant. Housed under the dome of the Westfield San Francisco Centre shopping mall, M.Y. China is a dark, sultry space full of posh Chinese furniture, antiques, and dramatic lighting. Shopping-weary patrons fill the dining room, whereas chowhounds hit the exhibition counter to watch the staff masterfully hand-pull noodles and toss woks.

The menu reads like an ode to regional Chinese cuisine, spanning chewy scissor-cut noodles with wild boar, fluffy bao stuffed with sweet and smoky barbecue pork, and, when it's in season, delectable pepper-dusted whole crab. Be sure to order strategically, as you'll want room for the flaky, buttery, creamy, and outright superb Macanese egg tarts.

▦ 845 Market St. (bet. 4th & 5th Sts.)
℘ (415) 580-3001 — **WEB:** www.tastemychina.com
▦ Lunch & dinner daily   **PRICE:** $$

LUCE ❀
Contemporary

XxX | ⚐ ⟟ ▤ ⛱ ▨

MAP: B3

Know that the ambience is pleasant, the space is elegant, the service team is quick and polite, and the food is consistently excellent. Also, know that you probably won't have a hard time getting a reservation at this InterContinental Hotel restaurant—Luce is often inexplicably empty. Let its lack of popularity be your reminder to come here when looking for a little privacy—think date night.

Soaring ceilings, dark and dramatic spherical lights, a transparent wall of wine bordering the kitchen, and shiny cushioned banquettes give the dining room a sumptuous, airy feel that promises the high level of luxury echoed in the cuisine. This may be one of the city's more venerable mainstays, but a contemporary sensibility is clear throughout the décor and menu.

Luce serves breakfast, lunch, and brunch, but dinner is when the serious diner arrives for an altogether stellar experience. Highlights include a generous portion of perfectly white halibut poached in California olive oil and placed on a colorful bed of fresh shelling beans with artichokes and clams. Desserts may combine the wonderfully light flavors of sweet corn panna cotta with kernels of honey-caramel popped corn and huckleberry compote.

▪ 888 Howard St. (at 5th St.)
✆ (415) 616-6566 — **WEB:** www.lucewinerestaurant.com
▪ Lunch & dinner daily

PRICE: $$$

MOURAD 🏵

Moroccan

XxX | 🎴 🍸 ♿ ⬜ 🤝   **MAP: C2**

This glamorous outpost at the base of the PacBell building introduces the unique soul of Chef/owner Mourad Lahlou's eponymous restaurant. This neighborhood's food-obsessed techies flock to the boldly designed space, replete with soaring ceilings, glowing central columns, and a superb (suspended) wine cellar. The servers may not know the menu inside out, but a good sommelier and live music keep the crowds contented and lively.

Chef Lahlou is at his best when reinterpreting modern Moroccan cuisine with ingredients such as za'atar, harissa, and dates. Begin with the subtle and original combination of nicely charred octopus accented with an herbaceous oil, chili powder, and diced merguez sausage, alongside an unctuous purée mixing chickpeas, citrus, and olives. Be sure to order the main courses in true Moroccan style—as shareable platters with plenty of sauces and sides. A remarkable take on lamb loin is cooked to perfection and intensely flavored with spiced black olives, surrounded by deliciously crunchy flatbreads.

Desserts embrace deconstruction and fusion, perhaps built on the powerful flavors of dark chocolate, jasmine cream, and ginger crumble.

◼ 140 New Montgomery St. (bet. Minna & Natoma Sts.)
✆ (415) 660-2500 — **WEB:** www.mouradsf.com
◼ Lunch Mon-Fri Dinner nightly   **PRICE: $$$**

OKANE 🐶

Japanese

𝄪 | ♿   **MAP:** C4

Can't afford to indulge in the exquisite sushi at Omakase? Consider heading to its next-door little sib, where the fish is still top-notch (it's all sourced from Japan) but the atmosphere is more laid-back. Okane draws lots of nearby Adobe and Zynga employees at lunch and big groups at dinner, all sharing bottles of sake and making the most of the small-plates menu.

Sushi is, of course, a must: the nigiri is pristine and delicious, as are more Americanized rolls like the Harajuku (filled with shrimp tempura, avocado, and salmon and topped with tuna, eel sauce, and lotus root chips). But don't sleep on the non-sushi dishes—the cod marinated in sake lees is grilled to perfection, and broiled salmon aburi with avocado and ikura is delicious, too.

▦ 669 Townsend St. (bet. 7th & 8th Sts.)
☏ (415) 865-9788 — **WEB:** www.okanesf.com
▦ Lunch Mon – Fri   Dinner nightly   **PRICE:** $$

THE PERENNIAL 🍴

Contemporary

𝄪𝄪 | 🍸 ♿ 🖐   **MAP:** A3

Quite possibly the world's most enviro-friendly restaurant, this popular spot is out to prove that sustainability can be delicious. Every ingredient is meticulously sourced, with much of the produce coming from the restaurant's own aquaponic farm in Oakland. From the modern dining room to the energy bill, the lowest possible carbon footprint is the goal.

Sure, but is it tasty? In a word, yes. From sustainable Kernza wheatgrass toasts topped with cauliflower to cheesy grain porridge thick with black trumpet mushrooms and artichoke hearts, there's a lot to savor (including hyper-homemade sodas and cocktails). And while the staff is happy to answer questions, they're not a drag—you won't get a seminar with your meal, unless you want one.

▦ 59 9th St. (bet. Market & Mission Sts.)
☏ (415) 500-7788 — **WEB:** www.theperennialsf.com
▦ Dinner Mon - Sat   **PRICE:** $$$

OMAKASE ✿

Japanese

⚙ | ♿

True, the vibe is friendly and the location is convenient for tech entrepreneurs, but superb Edomae sushi is the real reason why Omakase is always full. Ergo, reservations are required and punctuality is a must. The kimono-clad servers strain to place dishes in front of diners, who usually sit elbow-to-elbow at the tight L-shaped counter, but the chummy young professionals and gourmands don't seem to notice anything but the chefs.

Choose from two omakase menus; the more extensive (and expensive) one offers additional sashimi and nigiri. Begin with buttery ocean trout steamed in sake and presented with a wedge of heirloom black tomato and herb salad in rice wine vinaigrette. Beautifully arranged sashimi features bluefin tuna with red-fleshed sea perch, garnished with cured kombu, shiso leaf, wasabi, and a bit of chrysanthemum petal salad. Still, no dish can compare with the exquisite level of nigiri, which may showcase marinated chutoro, cedar-torched sea bream, Hokkaido uni with house-brined ikura, and a fluffy piece of lobster-infused tamago.

Extreme attention to detail is the hallmark of dining here, with customized portions of rice and wasabi adjustments for each guest's palate.

▨ 665 Townsend St. (bet. 7th & 8th Sts.)
℘ (415) 865-0633 — **WEB:** www.omakasesf.com
▨ Dinner nightly   PRICE: $$$$

PROSPECT 🍴

American

✗✗✗ | 🎴 🍸 ♿ 🖥 🤚   **MAP:** D1

For a polished and contemporary experience that doesn't sacrifice approachability, FiDi denizens turn to Prospect, a crowd-pleaser for the full-pocketbook crowd. Set on the ground floor of a soaring high-rise, its airy space offers attractive, roomy tables, adept service, and a popular, well-stocked cocktail bar.

Simple, well-constructed American fare abounds, with menu mainstays like an heirloom tomato salad with creamy dollops of burrata and crisp, garlicky breadcrumbs; or a perfectly flaky Coho salmon fillet set over earthy black rice, sweet yellow corn, and caramelized summer squash. Dessert should not be missed: the butter brickle icebox cake with honey-glazed plums and toasted pecan butter crunch is a truly memorable treat.

▪ 300 Spear St. (at Folsom St.)
📞 (415) 247-7770 — **WEB:** www.prospectsf.com
▪ Lunch Mon – Fri Dinner Mon – Sat   **PRICE:** $$$

ROOH 🍴

Indian

✗✗ | ♿ 🛶   **MAP:** D3

Amidst a slew of upscale Indian restaurants descending upon San Francisco, Rooh rises to the top, thanks to an innovative menu that fuses the subcontinent's myriad flavors with modern restaurant staples (oysters, pork belly, burrata). The bold India-goes-industrial décor is a bit paint-by-numbers, with vivid jewel tones and an oversized mural depicting a traditionally dressed woman. But the vibe is engaging and the cocktails quite unique.

Rooh's approach is casual, but tabs can grow stratospheric in this pricey tech corridor. For the best value, opt for a meal of delicious small plates like the piquant paneer chili, coated in crispy shreds of kataifi noodles. Wrap up with the exquisite carrot halwa cake, accented by cardamom kulfi and yogurt mousse.

▪ 333 Brannan St. (at Stanford St.)
📞 (415) 525-4174 — **WEB:** www.roohsf.com
▪ Lunch Sun – Fri Dinner Mon – Sat   **PRICE:** $$$

SAISON ✿✿✿
Californian

XxX | 🐝 🍸 🚷 🚰

The kitchen's footprint is as large as the dining room's in this grandiose brick warehouse, where the cooks themselves often attend to diners. As you savor each course, you'll have a full view of Chef Joshua Skenes and his team tending the live-fire hearth that's the soul of Saison's culinary philosophy.

Smoke, embers, and flame add a captivating depth to two of the restaurant's signature dishes: briny house-smoked caviar served "breakfast sandwich" style with egg custard and flaky biscuits, as well as butter-drenched bread topped with a lobe of perfect sea urchin. The richness of this cuisine is offset by delicate items, all of which portray strong Japanese influences—imagine a gentle tea of house-grown herbs. Then a visually arresting plate of radishes in a vinegar poaching liquid is juxtaposed with rustic barbecue quail for a perfect example of Skenes' storytelling.

As can be expected from such a culinary temple, the audience is wealthy, refined, and each detail, from the cashmere blankets to the Zalto stemware, is carefully considered. Yet the kitchen's passions remain pure at heart: a concluding sundae with smoked caramel and grilled peanuts will transport you to childhood pleasures.

▧ 178 Townsend St. (bet. 2nd & 3rd Sts.)
☏ (415) 828-7990 — **WEB:** www.saisonsf.com
▧ Dinner Tue - Sat

PRICE: $$$$

1601 BAR & KITCHEN 😊
Sri Lankan

XX | ♿
MAP: A4

Sri Lankan flavors infuse the dishes at this quiet winner, which also employs Western ingredients to arrive at its very own delicious concoctions. For a more extensive exploration of this island nation's cuisine, go for the degustation menu. Or stick to such decidedly untraditional items as lamprais, which might stuff a classically French bacon-wrapped rabbit loin and eggplant curry into a banana leaf. Halibut "ceviche" is more like a flavored sashimi, with hints of coconut milk and serrano chilies.

This contemporary space with its wraparound windows and slate walls is a perfect showcase for the food. Dine solo at the bar with a bittersweet Dubonnet sangria, or come with friends to share food and wine—the polished staff makes either experience enjoyable.

■ 1601 Howard St. (at 12th St.)
✆ (415) 552-1601 — **WEB:** www.1601sf.com
■ Dinner Tue – Sat   **PRICE: $$**

YANK SING 😊
Chinese

XX | ♿ 🖵 🔪
MAP: D1

With a higher price tag than the average Chinatown joint, Yank Sing is arguably the place in town for dim sum. The upscale setting boasts reasonable prices, but the zigzagging carts can get hectic. While peak hours entail a wait, one can be assured of quality and abundant variety from these carts rolling out the kitchen.

The signature Peking duck with its crispy lacquered skin and fluffy buns makes for a memorable treat, not unlike the deliciously sweet and salty char siu bao. Of course, dumplings here are the true highlight, and range from fragrant pork xiao long bao, to paper-thin har gao concealing chunks of shrimp. Don't see favorites like the flaky egg custard tarts? Just ask the cheerful staff, who'll radio the kitchen for help via headsets.

■ 101 Spear St. (bet. Howard & Mission Sts.)
✆ (415) 781-1111 — **WEB:** www.yanksing.com
■ Lunch daily   **PRICE: $$**

ZERO ZERO 🏠

Pizza

✗✗ | ♿ 🛋 🖐   **MAP:** C3

Zero Zero may be named for the superlative flour used in its blistered pies, but it is so much more than a pizzeria. While the Castro topped with oozing mozzarella and spicy soppressata is delicious, this casual spot offers far more than just a good slice. Absolute knockouts include a beautifully composed panzanella accompanied by basil pesto; while gnocchi tossed in a hearty pork belly ragù and decked with dollops of ricotta is light and bright, despite the indulgent ingredients.

A mix of families, hipsters, and business folk from the Moscone Center fill the warm, bi-level space. Group dining is ideal for sampling more of the menu, and the sizable bar will ensure that everyone's furnished with a terrific cocktail or pint of local draft root beer.

🔲 826 Folsom St. (bet. 4th & 5th Sts.)
📞 (415) 348-8800 — **WEB:** www.zerozerosf.com
🔲 Lunch & dinner daily   **PRICE:** $$

Look for our symbol 🍇
spotlighting restaurants
with a notable wine list.

EAST BAY

EAST BAY

A signature mash-up of wealthy families, senior bohemians, and college kids, Berkeley is extolled for its liberal politics and lush university campus. Snooty gourmands and reverential foodies consider it to be the Garden of Eden that sprouted American gastronomy's leading purist, Alice Waters. Her **Chez Panisse Foundation** continues to nurture the **Edible Schoolyard**, an organic garden-cum-kitchen classroom for students. Waters also founded **Slow Food Nation**, the country's largest celebration of sustainable foods; and her influence can be tasted in numerous establishments serving Californian cuisine.

GOURMET GHETTO

Budget-conscious Berkeleyites needn't look to restaurants alone for pristine, local, and organic food. Their very own **North Shattuck** corridor (also known as the "gourmet ghetto") gratifies with garden-fresh produce as well as takeout from **Grégoire**. This area is also home to aficionados who frequent co-ops like the **Cheese Board Collective**, **Cheese Board Pizza Collective**, and **Acme Bread Company** for first-rate produce and variety. The **Juice Bar Collective** keeps diet-conscious droves coming back for more; whereas meat addicts can't get enough of Chef Paul Bertolli's **Fra' Mani Handcrafted Foods**, where traditional Italian

flavors mingle with creative techniques. Every Thursday, the **North Shattuck Organic Farmer's Market** draws cooking enthusiasts from near and far who are looking to expand their culinary repertoire with a vast range of regionally sourced produce.

Meanwhile, hungover scholars can't imagine beginning a day without brunch at **La Note**, where the cinnamon-brioche pain perdu packs a walloping punch. Too rich? Test the spread at **Tomate Cafe**, churning out a wholesome Cuban breakfast followed by lunch on the pup-

friendly patio. Cooks on a mission collect routinely at ingredient-driven **Berkeley Bowl**, a grocery store-farmer's market hybrid, to scan their offering of fresh produce, cooked items, and health foods. Named after a region in Southwest India, **Udupi Palace** is equally revolutionary in concept, with cooking that is wildly popular for that same region's delicacies. Sample the likes of masala dosas, packed with spiced mashed potatoes and paired with pungent sambar, for an undoubtedly satisfying meal.

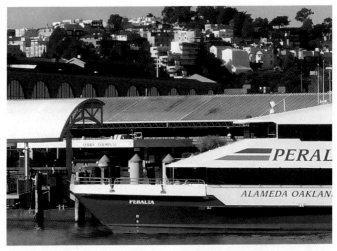

OAKLAND

Located across the bridge from the city, Oakland may not exude the same culinary flamboyance. Nevertheless, this earnest city has seen a resurgence of its own, thanks to an influx of businesses and residences. With panoramic views of the Bay, terrific restaurants, shops, and hopping nightlife, Jack London Square is not only a tourist draw but revered by locals as well for sun-soaked docks and a **Sunday Farmers' and Artisan Market**. Mornings are busy at **La Farine**, a European-style patisserie, proffering pastries, cakes, and buttery croissants. As noon sets in, downtown crowds nosh on po'boys from **Café 15**. But over in Temescal, **Bakesale Betty** caters to big appetites with bulky chicken sandwiches served atop ironing-board tables. Post-work revelry reaches epic status at **The Trappist**, pouring over 160 Belgian and other specialty beers. However, if dessert is the most divine way to end the day, then convene at **Fentons Creamery**, churning handmade ice creams for over 120 years. Not far behind, **Lush Gelato** spotlights homegrown ingredients like Cowgirl Creamery Fromage

Blanc in some of the city's most decadent flavors. **Tara's Organic Ice Cream** continues the craze with unique scoops like beet-balsamic served in compostable cups!

HOME IS WHERE THE HEART IS

Down-home Mexican food fans get their fiesta on at taco trucks parked along International Blvd. But local joints like **Taqueria Sinaloa** continue to flourish as the real deal for these treats. The Art & Soul Festival in August brings a buffet of world flavors; and the **Chinatown Streetfest** adds to the lure with curries and barbecue. Bonus bites await at **Rockridge Market Hall**, featuring **Hapuku Fish Shop** and **Highwire Coffee Roasters**. Set between Oakland and Berkeley, Rockridge boasts a plethora of quaint boutiques and tasty eateries—including **Oaktown Spice Shop** on Grand Avenue, which showcases excellent herbs and exotic spices, available in both small amounts and bulk bags.

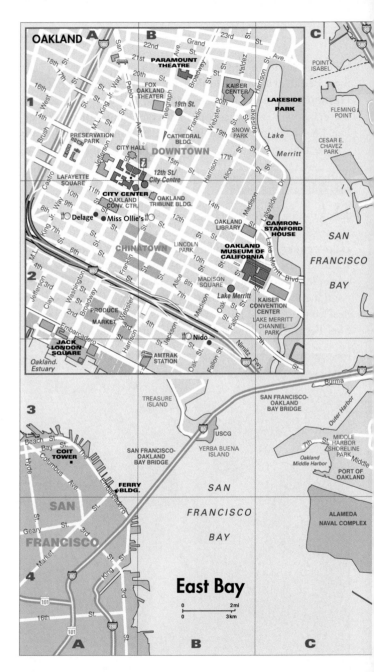

OAKLAND

A **B** **C**

22nd Grand 23rd St.
21st Ave.
18th St. 17th 980 20th **PARAMOUNT** Valdez Ave. POINT
16th St. San Broadway **THEATRE** St. ISABEL
St. Pablo **FOX** St. KAISER
14th King Jr. Way 19th St. Franklin OAKLAND Harrison CENTER FLEMING
West Telegraph **THEATER** St. 20th POINT
Brush Jefferson 19th St. Webster 19th **LAKESIDE**
Ave. **PRESERVATION CATHEDRAL** St. SNOW Lakeside **PARK** CESAR E.
Castro **PARK** BLDG. **PARK** CHAVEZ
11th **CITY HALL** **DOWNTOWN** 17th Lake PARK
LAFAYETTE 15th Alice Merritt
SQUARE 12th St/ Harrison St.
11th **City Centre** St.
King Jr. Way 10th **CITY CENTER** 14th Madison Lakeside
9th **OAKLAND** **OAKLAND** St. SAN
8th St. **CONV. CTR.** **TRIBUNE BLDG.** CAMRON-
ML 7th ⓘ**Delage** ⓘ**Miss Ollie's**ⓘ 12th **OAKLAND** STANFORD FRANCISCO
St. **LIBRARY** HOUSE
6th **CHINATOWN** LINCOLN **OAKLAND** Lake Merritt BAY
4th Franklin **PARK** 10th **MUSEUM OF** Blvd.
Jefferson 3rd **CALIFORNIA**
Clay Washington St. St. MADISON
2nd Broadway Webster 8th **SQUARE**
Embarcadero 880 Alice 7th Oak **Lake Merritt** KAISER
PRODUCE Madison St. **CONVENTION**
MARKET 3rd Fallon **CENTER**
4th Harrison Jackson St. LAKE MERRITT
JACK St. ⓘ**Nido** CHANNEL Nimitz
LONDON PARK Fwy.
Oakland **SQUARE** **AMTRAK** Oak 7th
Estuary **STATION** St. 880 St.

3

TREASURE SAN FRANCISCO- Burma 80
ISLAND OAKLAND
BAY BRIDGE Outer Harbor
Beach St. 80 USCG 7th MIDDLE
COIT The YERBA BUENA HARBOR
TOWER Embarcadero SAN FRANCISCO- ISLAND Oakland SHORELINE
Columbus Ave. OAKLAND Middle Harbor PARK
Hyde BAY BRIDGE SAN PORT OF
St. **FERRY** OAKLAND
BLDG. FRANCISCO
SAN ALAMEDA
4 Geary St. 3rd BAY NAVAL COMPLEX
FRANCISCO St.
80 Market
101 King St. **East Bay**
St.
16th St. 3rd 0   2mi
280 0   3km
101

A **B** **C**

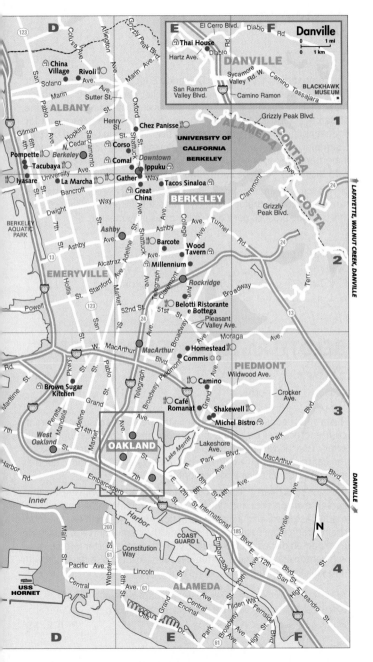

BARCOTE 🍴

Ethiopian

✗ | ♿ | ☂

The competition may be stiff in Oakland's Ethiopian restaurant row, but thanks to a warm and welcoming team of chef/owners as well as a menu that excels in weaving together the spices and seasonings, the cuisine at Barcote stands out and sparkles like no other. Whether you opt for a meaty plate of kitfo (spiced minced beef cooked in clarified butter); a sampler of vegetarian stews like spicy misir wot (lentils simmered in berbere sauce); or hearty atakilt (cabbage, potato, and carrot stew with turmeric); you'll be captivated by the layers of flavor.

The space is clean and simple, but friendly service and a tree-shaded front patio ensure that it's homey, not ho-hum. Don't come in a rush—this is a place to kick back and enjoy a leisurely meal.

▢ 6430 Telegraph Ave. (bet. Alcatraz Ave. & 65th St.), Oakland
☏ (510) 923-6181 — **WEB:** www.barcote.com
▢ Lunch & dinner daily   PRICE: 🍜

BELOTTI RISTORANTE E BOTTEGA 🍴

Italian

✗ | 🥂

Pasta aficionados will find paradiso in this petite and casual restaurant-cum-enoteca, set on a busy but bucolic stretch of Rockridge's main artery. Boasting an impressive passel of regulars, who frequently park at the bar to chat with the owner in Italian between bites, Belotti dabbles in the traditional cuisine of Piemonte.

Envision such hearty dishes as brasato—braised beef with mushrooms served over polenta and finished with a nebbiolo reduction. House-made pastas are also a major attraction here, including the heirloom grain spaghettini in a tomato sauce with creamy burrata. But more unexpected dishes excel as well: try the delicious butter lettuce salad with lemon and pine nuts, or the decadent tortino, a spinach flan with egg yolk and truffle.

▢ 5403 College Ave. (bet. Kales & Manila Aves.), Oakland
☏ (510) 788-7890 — **WEB:** www.belottirb.com
▢ Lunch & dinner Wed – Mon   PRICE: $$

BROWN SUGAR KITCHEN 😋
Southern

🍴 | ⛑ 🏠 🛋   **MAP:** D3

This tried-and-true Southern spot (open for breakfast and lunch only) may be far from any restaurant row, but visitors here will find plenty of company—mostly ahead of them in line. Over the years, Chef/owner Tanya Holland has built a loyal following, all of whom arrive early to avoid those long waits for her signature buttermilk fried chicken with a cornmeal waffle, decadent shrimp and grits, or hearty plate of gumbo. Others go for the juicy jerk chicken with a kick of heat, cooled by mashed yams and pineapple-red onion salsa. The vanilla-laden Bundt cake with "tears" of dark chocolate sauce is bound to leave one in...you guessed it...tears.

Casual and welcoming with a relaxed vibe and colorful look, BSK may be a crowd magnet, but it's earned the hype.

▨ 2534 Mandela Pkwy. (at 26th St.), Oakland
📞 (510) 839-7685 — **WEB:** www.brownsugarkitchen.com
▨ Lunch Tue – Sun   **PRICE:** 💰

CAFÉ ROMANAT 🍴
Ethiopian

🍴   **MAP:** E3

In a stretch of Oakland that teems with Ethiopian restaurants, Café Romanat is a standout, thanks to deliciously spiced dishes served in generous portions. Locals (including some Ethiopian families) fill the small room, set with traditional low stools and woven tables and featuring colorful fabric curtains and artwork.

Order up an Ethiopian beer, honey wine, or a nutty ground flax or sesame seed juice to pair with the sambussas, triangular pastries stuffed with piquant, chile-flecked ground beef. All the combo platters, served on spongy, slightly sour injera, are perfect for sharing. And the veggie combo, with dishes like sautéed collard greens, lentils in smoky berbere, and split peas with turmeric and ginger, will delight any crowd.

▨ 462 Santa Clara Ave. (near Grand Ave.), Oakland
📞 (510) 444-1800 — **WEB:** www.caferomanat.com
▨ Lunch Sat – Sun   Dinner Tue – Sun   **PRICE:** 💰

CAMINO 🍴
Californian

X | 🍸 ⚕ 🔥   **MAP:** E3

With its look of a medieval refectory and that central wood-burning hearth, Camino can seem like a trip to the days of yore—but the cool crowd, fun cocktails, and innovative food are decidedly modern. Take a seat under wrought-iron chandeliers at one of the long, communal tables (one of them is cut from a single redwood tree!) and expect to make some new friends.

Chef-owner Russell Moore worked at Chez Panisse for many years, and his food is appropriately hyper-seasonal. An egg baked in the wood oven, its yolk still velvety, is nestled in leeks, herbs, and cream, while slices of char-grilled sourdough provide the base for a sandwich of juicy pancetta and rustic sauerkraut. Moist, sticky Lardy cake is also grilled, and topped with rich ricotta and honey.

▨ 3917 Grand Ave. (bet. Jean St. & Sunnyslope Ave.), Oakland
✆ (510) 547-5035 — **WEB:** www.caminorestaurant.com
▨ Lunch Sat – Sun Dinner Wed – Mon   **PRICE: $$**

CHEZ PANISSE 🍴
Californian

XX | ⚕   **MAP:** E1

A legendary address among the foodie set, Alice Waters' Arts and Crafts bungalow continues to flourish as the Bay Area's temple of Californian cuisine. The talented team of chefs here work their magic in a gleaming open kitchen that is set at the very back of the dining room and served by an aromatic wood-burning oven.

Diners are privy to one nightly fixed menu of four rotating courses (three on Mondays). What they will get is a matter of chance, but rest assured it will feature only peak-season produce—from the fresh peas, asparagus, and black truffle in a spring risotto, to the sweet corn and squash blossoms served with a summer preparation of pork loin.

Seeking more freedom of choice? Head to the upstairs café, which offers meals á la carte.

▨ 1517 Shattuck Ave. (bet. Cedar & Vine Sts.), Berkeley
✆ (510) 548-5525 — **WEB:** www.chezpanisse.com
▨ Dinner Mon – Sat   **PRICE: $$$$**

CHINA VILLAGE 😶

Chinese

✗✗ | ⚐ ⚑

It takes a village to feed a big group, and this laid-back spot is a favorite with families. A stylish makeover featured a sleek front bar, contemporary chandeliers, and dramatic Chinese art, but one look at the scorching-hot menu options—think spicy Sichuan frog and flaky sautéed fish with pickled chili peppers—confirms the authenticity factor.

Skip the Hunan, Mandarin, and Cantonese offerings in favor of the Sichuan specialties, like dry-fried, bone-in chicken laced with ground chilies and numbing peppercorns. And be sure to order the five-spice hot and spicy pork shoulder. A house specialty, this mouthwatering dish is fork- (or chopstick) tender and rests atop a deliciously piquant chili-oil jus with baby bok choy, scallions, and garlic.

▨ 1335 Solano Ave. (at Ramona Ave.), Albany

✆ (510) 525-2285 — **WEB:** www.chinavillagealbany.com

▨ Lunch & dinner daily   PRICE: ⦾

COMAL 😶

Mexican

✗✗ | 🍸 ⚐ 🍄

For bold, zesty Mexican food crafted with pristine ingredients, Berkeleyites pack this industrial-chic hot spot, where an excellent cocktail program and an extensive tequila and mezcal selection keep things buzzing. The large flat tortilla griddles for which Comal is named are on full display in the open kitchen, while a covered, heated back patio draws locals for year-round outdoor dining

Fryer-fresh warm tortilla chips, paired with perfect, creamy guacamole, are irresistible; summon an order as you peruse options like the refreshing white shrimp ceviche and earthy hen-of-the-woods mushroom quesadilla. Just make sure the smoky wood-grilled rock cod tacos, with creamy avocado aïoli and spicy cabbage slaw, are on your must-order list.

▨ 2020 Shattuck Ave. (bet. Addison St. & University Ave.), Berkeley

✆ (510) 926-6300 — **WEB:** www.comalberkeley.com

▨ Dinner nightly   PRICE: $$

COMMIS ✿ ✿

Contemporary

XX | ♿

MAP: E3

Oakland continues to evolve and maintain its "destination" status thanks in large part to Commis and its hard-working troupe. This serene and sparse original from Chef/owner James Syhabout is still turning out a menu of measured, elegant and well-conceived dishes to a packed house every night.

Tucked into colorful, boutique-strewn Piedmont Avenue, the dining space is long and minimalist, with a smattering of tables up front; intimate banquette seating in the back; and a lively counter overlooking the humming kitchen. Soft music and a vibrant service staff set the mood—cool and contemporary; relaxed but never casual.

In the kitchen, Chef Syhabout pairs well-sourced, local ingredients with precise technique to create his sophisticated nightly tasting menu. Dinner might unveil a plate of silky scallops with tangy crème fraîche, poached asparagus, and charred lemon granité. Warm, roasted abalone with crispy fried artichoke may then be tailed by a chilled fava bean soup laced with green tomato gelée and smoked trout roe. Perfectly poached halibut with spring pea "porridge" and a fragrant ginger foam is another beautifully composed plate that reflects the kitchen's attention to detail.

▨ 3859 Piedmont Ave. (at Rio Vista Ave.), Oakland
☏ (510) 653-3902 — **WEB:** www.commisrestaurant.com
▨ Dinner Wed – Sun   **PRICE:** $$$$

CORSO 😋
Italian

✗ | ♿   **MAP:** E1

A Tuscan follow-up from the couple behind nearby Rivoli, Corso is every bit the equal of its big sister, thanks to generous, Florentine-inspired dishes like a roasted squid panzanella with torn flatbread, buttery white beans, and bright dashes of lemon juice and chili oil. Pasta fiends will swoon for house-made tagliatelle in a meaty beef and pork sugo, while butter-roasted chicken boasts juicy meat, golden-brown skin, as well as fresh peas and asparagus alongside.

Soul-warming in its hospitality, Corso is the kind of place where servers will bring complimentary pistachio biscotti simply because they're "so good when they're warm." It's no surprise that the tiny trattoria is a favorite among couples, so be sure to reserve in advance and come hungry.

▦ 1788 Shattuck Ave. (bet. Delaware & Francisco Sts.), Berkeley
℘ (510) 704-8004 — **WEB:** www.corsoberkeley.com
▦ Dinner nightly   **PRICE:** $$

DELAGE 🍴
Japanese

✗ | ♿   **MAP:** A2

The word is out about this tiny, omakase-only Japanese gem, located adjacent to Swan's Market in Old Oakland. It's a simple, casual space with a small counter and handful of tables, but it also provides a fine spotlight for a mixture of high-quality nigiri and kaiseki dishes.

Meals typically run about eight courses, with seasonal starters like a grilled apricot and mizuna salad; salmon sashimi adorned with a slice of Saturn peach; or garlic shoots enhancing seared Miyazaki beef.

Excellent nigiri, from tuna to mackerel to fluke, arrive at intervals alongside other captivating items, like seared duck breast with moro miso or scallops with shiso and umeboshi. The only downside is that reservations can be a challenge—so be sure to plan well ahead.

▦ 536 9th St. (bet. Clay & Washington Sts.), Oakland
℘ (510) 823-2050 — **WEB:** www.delageoakland.com
▦ Dinner Tue – Sat   **PRICE:** $$$

GATHER 🍴

Californian

✗ | ♿ 🍤 🛋️   **MAP:** E2

With its heavily Californian bill of fare, repurposed décor, and Berkeley clientele, Gather is a must for hordes of wholesome foodies of all ages. The aptly named hit serves busy professors during the bustling lunch hour before welcoming a more relaxed evening crowd, who come to sip at the bar and sup en plein air on the patio.

Pescatarians will delight in thick-cut toast spread with albacore tuna rillettes and topped with pan-fried broccoli de Ciccio, pickled radishes, and potatoes, while vegetarians will find it hard to resist a hefty portion of arugula salad tossed with goat cheese, almonds, pomegranate, and balsamic dressing. Be sure to try some dessert—specifically the luscious lime curd tart and its thick dollop of meringue. You won't be sorry.

🔲 2200 Oxford St. (at Allston Way), Berkeley
📞 (510) 809-0400 — **WEB:** www.gatherrestaurant.com
🔲 Lunch & dinner daily   **PRICE:** $$

GREAT CHINA 😊

Chinese

✗✗   **MAP:** E2

Chic enough for the style-savvy, cheap enough for students, and authentic enough for local Chinese families, Great China is one of the few Berkeley restaurants everyone can (and does) agree on. Spicehounds should look elsewhere, as the food is somewhat mild, but the ingredients are higher quality than the average Chinese spot.

Kick things off with an aromatic bowl of hot and sour soup or an order of vegetarian egg rolls, then sample generously portioned favorites like the sweet-and-spicy kung pao chicken; the beautifully lacquered tea-smoked duck; or the beloved "double skin"—a platter of mung bean noodles tossed with pork, mushrooms, squid, and a soy-mustard dressing. Only larger parties can reserve, so be aware there may be lines at peak hours.

🔲 2190 Bancroft Way (at Fulton St.), Berkeley
📞 (510) 843-7996 — **WEB:** www.greatchinaberkeley.com
🔲 Lunch & dinner Wed – Mon   **PRICE:** $$

HOMESTEAD ⅝○

American

✗✗ | ♿ 🗔   **MAP:** E3

If it wasn't housed in a beautiful Julia Morgan-designed building, this farm-to-table jewel would be defined by the enticing smells that engulf you upon entrance. It's a rustic space, full of large windows peering onto Piedmont Avenue, and the jars of dry ingredients, pickling vegetables, and cookbooks on the counter create an upscale country-kitchen demeanor.

The menu focuses on the best and freshest of local produce, such as yellowtail ceviche nestled in a tangy aguachile that is interspersed with bits of sweet corn and potato. Roasted duck breast boasts an intensely caramelized skin and is served in its own jus along with maitake mushrooms for a wonderfully woodsy touch. Craving a bright breakfast? Look no further than the homemade pastries or quiche.

■ 4029 Piedmont Ave. (bet. 40th & 41st Sts.), Oakland
℘ (510) 420-6962 — **WEB:** www.homesteadoakland.com
■ Dinner Tue – Sun   **PRICE:** $$$

IPPUKU 😀

Japanese

✗ | 🍶 ♿ 🍽   **MAP:** E1

Can't swing a ticket to Tokyo? Dinner at Ippuku is the next best thing. With its low Japanese-style tables, extensive woodwork, and enormous selection of sake and shochu, it feels like an authentic izakaya transplanted into a corner of downtown Berkeley. The low-profile entrance adds to the feeling that you've lucked upon a special dining secret—assuming you don't stroll right past it, that is.

Yakitori is the big draw here, with smoky, salty chicken thighs, necks, hearts, and gizzards arriving fresh off the binchotan.

Other excellent small plates include korokke, or golden-brown Dungeness crab croquettes, crisp on the outside and with a creamy interior, or yaki imo, caramelized white sweet potato with a sweet-and-salty glaze.

■ 2130 Center St. (bet. Oxford St. & Shattuck Ave.), Berkeley
℘ (510) 665-1969 — **WEB:** www.ippukuberkeley.com
■ Dinner Tue – Sun   **PRICE:** $$

IYASARE 🍴

Japanese

✗✗ | ♿ ☂   **MAP:** D2

Japanese techniques and Californian ingredients blend harmoniously at this charming Berkeley getaway, which flaunts a buzzing dining room and a delightful (heated) patio. Start the evening off right with an excellent (and reasonably priced) local wine on tap or a selection from the well-edited sake list. Then, order a variety of their exquisite small plates for sharing.

Every dish is a carefully crafted delight for the senses. Baby kale and mustard greens might not sound very Japanese, but they blend beautifully in a salad with Fuji apple and a sesame-miso dressing. The superb hamachi crudo is dusted with a sprinkle of wasabi snow and lemon-tamari oil, while fresh Manila clams arrive in an aromatic broth of sake, bacon, potatoes, and earthy shiitakes.

▪ 1830 4th St. (bet. Hearst Ave. & Virginia St.), Berkeley
☎ (510) 845-8100 — **WEB:** www.iyasare-berkeley.com
▪ Lunch & dinner daily   **PRICE:** $$$

LA MARCHA 🍴

Spanish

✗ | ♿   **MAP:** D2

This Spanish delight from the team behind acclaimed caterer Ñora Cocina Española does double duty as a mecca for both tapas and paella, offered in varieties from the traditional mixta (prawns, chicken, chorizo, garlic, peppers) to the inventive "tres cerditos" (three little pigs) featuring pork chorizo, shoulder, and belly. The classic tapas are also out in full force—from grilled head-on garlic shrimp and salt cod croquettes with nutty romesco, to tortilla Española.

Located on busy San Pablo Avenue, the lively space offers enticements for groups of all sizes: foursomes can make the most of the sizable paellas, while a duo of happy hours offer discounts on wine at the L-shaped bar and a selection of free tapas, perfect for solo diners or couples.

▪ 2026 San Pablo Ave. (bet. Addison St. & University Ave.), Berkeley
☎ (510) 269-7374 — **WEB:** www.lamarchaberkeley.com
▪ Dinner Tue – Sun   **PRICE:** $$

MICHEL BISTRO 😊

French

🍴 | ♿ 🛏

A slice of France on a prime block of Lakeshore Avenue, this bistro boasts a heavily Gallic waitstaff and clientele chatting away in their native tongue. With its exposed brick, soaring ceilings, and cute accents like an excerpt from a Marcel Pagnol play inscribed on the wall, it's a simple but pleasant spot to enjoy a delicious, low-key meal.

The food is authentic, with some modern touches like the green almonds in a trout amandine with Lyonnaise-style potato salad, or the bison tartare with a quail egg. Brunch is a highlight with a gourmet eggs Benedict over artisan levain and butter-basted asparagus that steals the show.

At either meal, the vanilla crème brûlée is a rich treasure—too often jumbled on other menus, it's perfectly rendered here.

▪ 3343 Lakeshore Ave. (at Trestle Glen Rd.), Oakland
📞 (510) 836-8737 — **WEB:** www.michelbistro.com
▪ Lunch Sun   Dinner nightly   PRICE: $$

MILLENNIUM 😊

Vegan

🍴🍴 | ♿ 🪑 🛏

After more than 20 years in San Francisco, this vegan paradise relocated to Oakland, where it's continuing to put out some of the most unique, delicious plant-based cuisine in the country. The rustic-chic new space is laid-back and unfussy, with lots of dark wood, a patio for alfresco dining, and a crowd of young families and professionals attended by welcoming servers.

While dedicated vegans are sure to swoon, even hardcore carnivores might reconsider the lifestyle after a dose of Chef/owner Eric Tucker's culinary creativity, showcased best on a five-course "Taste of Millennium" menu. Roasted pumpkin tamales with pumpkin seed pastor and a cashew nut crema are knockouts, as are the crunchy king trumpet fritters with chili-persimmon jam.

▪ 5912 College Ave. (bet. Chabot Rd. & Harwood Ave.), Oakland
📞 (510) 735-9459 — **WEB:** www.millenniumrestaurant.com
▪ Lunch Sun   Dinner nightly   PRICE: $$

MISS OLLIE'S 🍴
Caribbean

✗ | ♿

MAP: A2

Even on the coldest (a.k.a. 50-degree) Oakland day, the soul-warming Caribbean cuisine at this little cutie will transport you to the islands. Barbados-born Chef/owner Sarah Kirnon named her restaurant after her grandmother, and it now serves up many of her childhood favorites, including plump, sweet grilled shrimp in a jerk marinade and some of the best fried chicken in town—with a flaky golden-brown crust.

Housed in the historic Swan's Market building in Old Oakland, Miss Ollie's has a particularly loyal crowd of lunchtime regulars, who sip tart ginger limeade as they liberally dose their food with the excellent Scotch bonnet hot sauce. With colorful Afro-Caribbean art on the walls and a welcoming staff, it's a rustic slice of Caribbean soul.

■ 901 Washington St. (bet. 9th & 10th Sts.), Oakland
✆ (510) 285-6188 — **WEB:** www.realmissolliesoakland.com
■ Lunch & dinner Tue – Sat   **PRICE:** $$

NIDO 🍴
Mexican

✗ | ♿ 🛋

MAP: B3

The industrial area west of the I-880 freeway doesn't boast many good restaurants, but this hidden Mexican gem is an exception. Complete with hip reclaimed-wood décor and a local clientele of business people along with trendy foodies, it's definitely a cut above a taqueria in terms of quality and price, with fresher, lighter food in smaller—but by no means stingy—portions.

Lunchtime tacos feature handmade corn tortillas perhaps piled high with carnitas and salsa verde, chamoy-glazed grilled chicken, or braised beef with chile arbol salsa. Dinner might bring carne asada with black beans and salsa de chile cascabel, or pork pibil panuchos with pickled onion and sikil pak. With a truly relaxed vibe and home-cooked feel to the food, it's worth the extra effort to drop by.

■ 444 Oak St. (at 5th St.), Oakland
✆ (510) 444-6436 — **WEB:** www.nidooakland.com
■ Lunch Tue – Sun   Dinner Tue – Sat   **PRICE:** $$

POMPETTE ¶○

Californian

✗✗ | & 🕮 ⚑   **MAP:** D1

A newcomer to the 30-year home of Café Rouge, this neighborhood charmer has done an admirable job taking up its predecessor's mantle. Balanced on the edge of classic and contemporary, it draws a crowd seeking a respite from shopping on Fourth Street—especially on sunny days, where a front patio with pale-yellow umbrellas provides a lovely setting.

Chef/owner David Visick is an alum of Chez Panisse, and it's easy to tell by his daily menu, where ultra-fresh seasonal ingredients do the talking. Expect rustic, unadorned food, from pristine sweet corn soup to pesto-kissed bucatini, twirled with green beans, favas, and cherry tomatoes. The cloud-like angel food strawberry shortcake with a hint of citrus and macerated berries is a simple showstopper.

▨ 1782 4th St. (at Delaware St.), Berkeley
℘ (510) 356-4737 — **WEB:** www.pompetteberkeley.com
▨ Lunch daily Dinner Mon – Sat   **PRICE:** $$

RIVOLI ¶○

Californian

✗✗ | &   **MAP:** D1

Northern Californian cooking with a hint of regional Americana is the main draw at this lush charmer on the Albany-Berkeley border. It's popular with smartly dressed couples, who come here to savor items like an artfully presented arugula salad with winter citrus, Marcona almonds, and avocado, or a highbrow riff on gumbo with chicken confit and Andouille sausage perched atop Carolina rice. The excellent gâteau Basque, a caramelized wedge of creamy custard, is a must-order.

Set in an adorable cottage, Rivoli's dining room boasts enormous picture windows overlooking a lush "secret" garden blooming with tender fronds, camellias, and magnolia trees. Smartly serviced by an engaging waitstaff, the greenery is a nice contrast to the crisp, white-linen tables.

▨ 1539 Solano Ave. (bet. Neilson St. & Peralta Ave.), Berkeley
℘ (510) 526-2542 — **WEB:** www.rivolirestaurant.com
▨ Dinner nightly   **PRICE:** $$

SHAKEWELL ⍩⍥

Mediterranean

✗✗ | ♿ 🛋

MAP: E3

This trendy eatery, the brainchild of Top Chef alums Jen Biesty and Tim Nugent, was made for sipping and supping. Donning a bar up front and several dining nooks on either side of a central walkway, Shakewell keeps things Medi-chic with Moorish accents, reclaimed wood, and organic elements.

Service is particularly warm, and an even warmer teal-green wood-fired oven in the back turns out deliciously smoked items like crisp falafel served with romesco. A summer squash salad with heirloom tomatoes, fried bread, and feta offers an inspired blend of Greek and Tuscan flavors, and Bomba rice with braised fennel, piperade, chicken, and prawns is a fluffy take on paella. For a party in your mouth, finish with the caramel syrup-spiked crema Catalana.

▦ 3407 Lakeshore Ave. (bet. Longridge & Trestle Glen Rds.), Oakland
☏ (510) 251-0329 — **WEB:** www.shakewelloakland.com
▦ Lunch Wed – Sun   Dinner Tue – Sun

PRICE: $$

TACOS SINALOA ☺

Mexican

✗

MAP: E2

East Oakland's taco truck titans have finally put it in park with this outstanding Berkeley taqueria, which is quickly making its name as one of the best in the entire Bay Area. Sinaloa's logo is a smiling shrimp holding a taco, so your first choice may be the top-notch shrimp taco (full of plump, succulent, spice-rubbed shrimp), but there's more in store: smoky carnitas with fiery red chili salsa, tender roast chicken, and beautifully caramelized al pastor. For the adventurous eater, there's tripe, suadero, and pork stomach, too.

Like the truck, this operation is no-frills: pay at the counter, grab some plastic utensils, and seat yourself. But with food this good—and prices so low that even a penniless Cal student can afford to dine—who needs frills?

▦ 2384 Telegraph Ave. (bet. Channing Way & Durant Ave.), Berkeley
☏ (510) 665-7895 — **WEB:** N/A
▦ Lunch & dinner daily

PRICE: ⌾

TACUBAYA ⅃○

Mexican

✗ | ⅄ 🏠 🛋 　　　　　　　　　　　**MAP:** D1

Mega-popular Oakland Mexican restaurant Doña Tomás is reincarnated in taqueria form at this Berkeley shopping complex, where families grab a bite before or after errands. A line of people extends out the door from morning until night, ordering tangy limeade at the counter and claiming seats in the festive pink-and-orange dining room or on the sunny front patio.

The crowds come for chilaquiles and churros at breakfast, then transition into flavorful chorizo-and-potato sopes with black bean purée at lunch. Moist, well-seasoned beef enchiladas are doused in a smoky, tangy guajillo-tomatillo sauce and covered with melted cheese. Tamales de verdura are bested with zesty tomatillo salsa verde, drizzles of tangy crema, and fresh cilantro.

▨ 1788 4th St. (bet. Hearst Ave. & Virginia St.), Berkeley
𝒫 (510) 525-5160 — **WEB:** www.tacubaya.net
▨ Lunch & dinner daily 　　　　　　　　**PRICE:** ⌾

THAI HOUSE 😊

Thai

✗ | 🏠 🍽 　　　　　　　　　　　　**MAP:** E1

Many a warm evening has been spent on the garden patio of this fantastic Thai restaurant, where potted plants create a leafy retreat. Whether you're dining alfresco or tucked inside the tiny, colorful bungalow, you can be assured of a warm welcome and boldly flavorful food—a secret that's out with the locals, making this house a packed one from noon to night.

The consistently outstanding menu makes it hard to go wrong, but you can't miss with the creamy red pumpkin curry, full of tender scallops and prawns and perfectly balanced notes of sweet, spicy, salty, and sour. Other showstoppers may reveal pad prig khing, chicken in a spicy peanut-tamarind sauce, or the aromatic basil tofu, jam-packed with fresh vegetables, chili, and garlic.

▨ 254 Rose Ave. (bet. Diablo Rd. & Linda Mesa Ave.), Danville
𝒫 (925) 820-0635 — **WEB:** www.thaihousedanville.net
▨ Lunch Mon – Fri　Dinner nightly 　　　**PRICE:** $$

WOOD TAVERN

American

XX | ﹠

MAP: E2

There's always a crowd at this lively neighborhood standby, where groups of friends, parents on date night, and hip couples congregate for drinks at the copper-topped bar. Flanked by organic groceries, indie bookstores, and antique shops, its surroundings reek of peace, weaving a pleasantly bohemian spell that captivates both regulars and newcomers alike.

Rustic American food with a hint of Italian flair dominates the menu, and the local Belfiore burrata—served atop diced pears, honey-cashew cream, and peppery arugula—is a surefire hit. A bit of Calabrian chili adds a hint of heat to the otherwise earthy pan-roasted Maple Leaf duck breast, while the warm mini Bundt cake bursts with chocolate goodness.

▓ 6317 College Ave. (bet. Alcatraz Ave. & 63rd St.), Oakland

✆ (510) 654-6607 — **WEB:** www.woodtavern.net

▓ Lunch Mon – Sat   Dinner nightly   **PRICE:** $$

Remember, stars ✿
are awarded for cuisine only! Elements
such as service and décor are not a factor.

MARIN

MARIN

Meandering Marin is located north of the Golden Gate Bridge and draped along breathtaking Highway 1. Coastal climates shower this county with abounding agricultural advantages, which in turn become abundantly apparent as you snake your way through its food oases, always filled with fresh, luscious seafood, slurpable oysters, and cold beer. Farm-to-table cuisine is de rigueur in this liberal-leaning and affluent county, boasting an avalanche of local food suppliers. One of the most celebrated purveyors is the quaint and rustic **Cowgirl Creamery**, whose "cowgirl" employees are charged with churning out delicious, distinctive, and hand-crafted cheeses. By specializing in farmstead cheeses alone, they have refined the process of artisan cheese-making, and ergo, garnered national respect along the way. Continue exploring these fromageries at **Point Reyes Farmstead Cheese Co.**, a popular destination among

natives for the famously lush "Original Blue" and its heady flavor profile. Thanks to such driven, enterprising cheese-makers (who live by terroir or taste of the earth), surrounding restaurants follow the European standard by offering cheese before or in lieu of a dessert course. After so much savory goodness, get your candy crush going at **Munchies of Sausalito**; or opt for a more creamy scoop at **Noci Gelato**.

If cheese and meat are a match made in heaven, then North Bay must be a thriving intermediary with its myriad ranches. At the crest is **Marin Sun Farms**, a glorified and

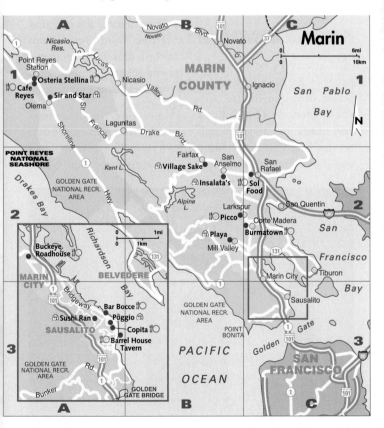

dedicated butcher shop whose heart and soul lies in the production of locally raised, natural-fed meats for fine restaurants, small-scale grocers, and everything in between. Championing local eating is **Mill Valley Market**, a can't-miss commitment among gourmands for top-quality foods, deli items, and other organic goods.

STOP, SIP & SAVOR

To gratify those inevitable pangs of hunger after miles of scenic driving complete with ocean breezes, **The Pelican Inn** makes for an ideal retreat. Serving hearty English country cooking along with a range of brews from their classic "bar," this nostalgic and ever-charming rest stop will leave you yearning for more. But forge ahead by strolling into **Spanish Table**, a shopper's paradise settled in Mill Valley, only to find foodies and locals alike reveling in unique Spanish cookbooks, cookware, specialty foods, and drool-worthy wines. Finally, peckish travelers with a sweet craving can also be found at **Three Twins Ice Cream** for their organically produced creamy treats that promise to leave an everlasting impression.

Waters off the coast here provide divers with exceptional hunting ground, and restaurants throughout Marin

count on supremely fresh oysters, briny clams, and meaty mussels. The difficulty in (legally) sourcing these large, savory mollusks makes red abalone a treasured species in area (Asian) establishments, though seafood does seem to be the accepted norm among restaurants in town. If fish doesn't float your boat, **Fred's Coffee Shop** in Sausalito is a no-frills find for fulfilling breakfast signatures like deep-fried French toast with a side of calorie-heavy, crazy-good caramelized "Millionaire's bacon." Carb addicts routinely pay their respects at **M.H. Bread & Butter**, said to be the best bakery around. Their crusty loaves make for fantastic sandwiches, but are equally divine just slathered with butter. If that's too tame for your tastes, enticing Puerto Rican flavors abound at **Sol Food**, settled in San Rafael. While this fertile county's natural ingredients may be sold in countless farmers' markets, many other celebrations of food and wine continue to pop

up throughout—during the spring and summer months. Given its culinary chops and panoramic views, Marin is one of the most sought-after counties for celebrities and visitors alike. True, some places here can seem touristy. But, these chefs and restaurants are lauded for good reason, and know how to make the most of their choice homegrown produce and food purveyors.

BAR BOCCE ¶○

Pizza

✗ | ♿ ☂   **MAP:** A3

This little bungalow on the bay draws big crowds for the harbor views from its covered patio, complete with a namesake bocce court. Equipped with beachside benches for watching youngsters at play and toasty fire pits for warding off the late-afternoon fog, it's often packed to the gills on weekend afternoons with locals lingering over a second (or fourth) glass of wine.

Should the buzz get too strong, there's hearty Italian fare to set you right, including wood-fired pizzas topped with pesto, ricotta, and kale; tender meatballs in a rich San Marzano tomato sauce; and rib-sticking eggplant parmesan dolloped with burrata. Perk yourself up for the ride home with a vanilla gelato affogato, drowned in espresso and sprinkled with Heath bar crumble.

▓ 1250 Bridgeway (bet. Pine & Turney Sts.), Sausalito
✆ (415) 331-0555 — **WEB:** www.barbocce.com
▓ Lunch & dinner daily   **PRICE:** $$

BARREL HOUSE TAVERN ¶○

Californian

✗✗ | ♿ ☂   **MAP:** A3

The former San Francisco-Sausalito ferry terminal has found new life as this lovely Californian restaurant, which gets its name from its barrel-like arched wood ceiling. A front lounge with a crackling fireplace and well-stocked bar is popular with locals, while tourists can't resist the expansive dining room and back deck, which boasts spectacular views of the Bay.

The cocktail and wine offerings are strong, as is the house-made soda program, which produces intriguing, never-too-sweet combinations like yellow peach, basil, and ginger. These pair beautifully with meaty Dungeness crab sliders coupled with watermelon-jicama slaw; though they might be too tasty to keep around by the time grilled swordfish and pork belly with white beans hit the table.

▓ 660 Bridgeway (at Princess St.), Sausalito
✆ (415) 729-9593 — **WEB:** www.barrelhousetavern.com
▓ Lunch & dinner daily   **PRICE:** $$

BUCKEYE ROADHOUSE 🍴

American

✗✗ | 🍹 ♿ 🍽 🛋 👐   **MAP:** A2

This hideout has welcomed generations of locals through its doors since 1937, even as its location on Highway 1 gave way to the more bustling 101. Enter the whitewashed craftsman building, and you'll be given your choice of dining—either at the clubby bar or the grand main room with wood-paneled walls and red leather banquettes.

The food here is classical but never dull, with a simple menu of salads, sandwiches, and grilled meats. Oysters bingo set over spinach and topped with garlic aïoli oozes with California panache, while succulent and crisp-skinned chili-lime brick chicken is just as delicious as its accompanying sides—think polenta sticks and cheese-stuffed pasilla peppers. Finish with a slice of pie—the s'mores version or Key lime are both winners.

▨ 15 Shoreline Hwy. (off Hwy. 101), Mill Valley
✆ (415) 331-2600 — **WEB:** www.buckeyeroadhouse.com
▨ Lunch & dinner daily   **PRICE:** $$

BURMATOWN 🍴

Burmese

✗   **MAP:** C2

Bypass the tired Asian-fusion offerings and head straight for the authentic Burmese dishes at this out-of-the-way cutie. A nutty, crunchy, and flavorful tea-leaf salad is the perfect answer to a hot summer day, while hearty potato-stuffed samosas and fresh, springy egg noodles tossed with barbecue pork and fried garlic chips will warm your soul in the cooler months.

Given the high quality of its food, it's no surprise that Burmatown is Corte Madera's most popular neighbor: it's big with local families from the surrounding residences, who pack every single table, attended to by warm servers. If you're willing to make a special trip to this charming bright-orange bungalow, the laid-back vibe will have you feeling right at home.

▨ 60 Corte Madera Ave. (bet. Bahr Ln. & Redwood Ave.), Corte Madera
✆ (415) 945-9096 — **WEB:** www.burmatown.com
▨ Dinner Tue – Sun   **PRICE:** $$

CAFE REYES ᵟ🍽

Pizza

✕ | 🎪   **MAP:** A1

This unassuming charmer in quaint Point Reyes Station is a perfect stop for day-trippers, who are sure to enjoy the many delicious dishes that emerge from its duo of wood-fired ovens. Pizza is the focus, with nine varieties ranging from a classic Margherita to more exotic combos of seasonal produce. But, there are also some delicious pies both savory (a spinach, egg, and cheese tortino with a salad of fresh greens) and sweet (a knockout berry version with a buttery crust). And every meal ends with a happy surprise—complimentary donut holes.

Given its cooking method, it's no surprise that Cafe Reyes is stacked high with wood, both against the walls and under the counter. The big, spacious, barn-like dining room is rustic and unfussy, perfect for groups.

▓ 11101 Shoreline Hwy. (at Mesa Rd.), Point Reyes Station
📞 (415) 663-9493 — **WEB:** N/A
▓ Lunch & dinner Wed – Sun   **PRICE:** $$

COPITA ᵟ🍽

Mexican

✕✕ | ♿ 🎪 🛶   **MAP:** A3

Set sail aboard the Sausalito ferry for dinner at this Mexican smash, just steps from the harbor's bobbing yachts. Colorful and casual, Copita's most coveted seats are on the sidewalk patio (complete with partial views of the water and the quaint downtown), but a spot at the exceptionally well-stocked tequila bar or in the brightly tiled dining room is no disappointment.

A light meal of tacos could include seared mahi mahi with pineapple pico de gallo and tomatillo salsa or tomato-accented chicken tinga with avocado and Mexican crema. Options abound for heartier appetites, like 24-hour carnitas and chicken mole enchiladas. And the lively surrounds are a hit with kids, who love sipping on the sweet house-made almond horchata.

▓ 739 Bridgeway (at Anchor St.), Sausalito
📞 (415) 331-7400 — **WEB:** www.copitarestaurant.com
▓ Lunch & dinner daily   **PRICE:** $$

INSALATA'S 😊
Mediterranean

XX | ♿ 🛌 🖐️   **MAP:** B2

San Anselmo restaurateur, Chef Heidi Krahling honors her late father, Italo Insalata, at this crowd-pleasing Marin hangout. The zucca-orange stucco exterior alludes to the Mediterranean air within. Insalata's upscale setting is framed by lemon-yellow walls hung with grand depictions of nature's bounty setting the scene for the array of fresh and flavorful cuisine to come.

Sparked by Middle Eastern flavors, Insalata's specialties include velvety smooth potato-leek soup made brilliantly green from watercress purée. Also sample grilled lamb skewers drizzled with cumin-yogurt atop crunchy salad and flatbread. The takeout area in the back is stocked with salads, sides, and sandwiches made with house-baked bread. Boxed lunches are a fun, tasty convenience.

▓ 120 Sir Francis Drake Blvd. (at Barber Ave.), San Anselmo
📞 (415) 457-7700 — **WEB:** www.insalatas.com
▓ Lunch & dinner daily   **PRICE:** $$

OSTERIA STELLINA 🍴
Italian

XX | ♿   **MAP:** A1

Its name is Italian for "little star," and this cutie does indeed shine in the heart of tiny Point Reyes Station, a one-horse clapboard town with little more than a filling station and a post office to its name. But the Wild West it's not: this frontier village is Marin-chic, and its saloon is a soothing retreat with soft sage walls, wide windows, and local produce on the menu.

You'll taste the difference in the pillowy house-made focaccia, the soothing chicken brodo, and the crisp salad of little gem lettuce with blue cheese, toasted walnuts, and honeycrisp apples. Organic, grass-fed beef stew is packed with spices and served over herbed polenta. Finish with a chocolate sponge cake with mocha mousse that's as unforgettable as the setting.

▓ 11285 Hwy. 1 (at 3rd St.), Point Reyes Station
📞 (415) 663-9988 — **WEB:** www.osteriastellina.com
▓ Lunch & dinner daily   **PRICE:** $$

PICCO 🍴
Italian

✕✕ | 🍸 🍹 ♿ 🎋 ⬚ 🖐

MAP: B2

Picco is Italian for "summit," and this charming Larkspur hilltop home has long been a beacon among Marin County diners. Chef/owner Bruce Hill is a true local-food devotee: his Italian-influenced fare heaps on Marin ingredients like the fresh turnips that dot his silky-smooth duck tortelli, or the Meyer lemon yogurt and beets that sit atop a nourishing kale salad. The "Marin Mondays" menu is a particular steal.

The precise staff moves ably through the busy dining room, carrying bowls of creamy risotto made on the half-hour. With a high ceiling and exposed brick walls, the vibe is graceful but never fussy, making this the perfect setting for couples and groups of friends who congregate here.

Also check out Pizzeria Picco next door.

🔲 320 Magnolia Ave. (at King St.), Larkspur
✆ (415) 924-0300 — **WEB:** www.restaurantpicco.com
🔲 Dinner nightly   **PRICE: $$$**

PLAYA 😋
Mexican

✕✕ | 🍹 ♿ 🎋

MAP: B2

The foggy beaches of Marin County may be a far cry from the sand and surf of Baja, but this lively spot keeps the vacation vibe alive with margaritas, mezcal, and madly delicious Mexican cooking. And while Playa feels upmarket with its colorful tiles, blown-glass lights, and walls of windows, its food is wonderfully authentic.

The menu makes for tough choices: opt for the outstanding al pastor tacos layered with sweet-spicy caramelized pineapple salsa, or the crispy empanadas stuffed with chorizo, currants, and green olives and drizzled with chimichurri. Whether you choose a cocktail and a mushroom-squash blossom quesadilla at the bar or bowls of chips and queso fundido with a big group on the sunny back patio, good times are guaranteed.

🔲 41 Throckmorton Ave. (bet. Blithedale & Miller Aves.), Mill Valley
✆ (415) 384-8871 — **WEB:** www.playamv.com
🔲 Lunch Tue – Sun   Dinner nightly   **PRICE: $$**

POGGIO 😊
Italian

XX | 🦽 🏠 ⛱ 🛥

A restaurant of Poggio's vintage could easily rest on its tourist-trap laurels—after all, its alfresco terrace has views of the Sausalito harbor that any starry-eyed visitor would long to savor. But this enduring favorite also provides plenty to enjoy on the plate, as well as a comfortable atmosphere, friendly service, and a solid Italian wine selection.

The menu takes some northern California detours, like the Dungeness crab salad with blood oranges and radishes. But even the most die-hard Italian would give a seal of approval to the homemade agnolotti, served in a succulent pork ragu with a dusting of parmigiano. Want something a little more special? In season, they're happy to give your pasta a hefty shaving of black or white truffles.

🔲 777 Bridgeway (at Bay St.), Sausalito
✆ (415) 332-7771 — **WEB:** www.poggiotrattoria.com
🔲 Lunch & dinner daily   **PRICE:** $$

SIR AND STAR 😊
Californian

XX | 🦽 🏠

This quirky roadhouse in the historic Olema Inn is one-of-a-kind, from the displays of branches in the light-flooded dining room to the poetic menu descriptions ("Softly Smoked Halibut Plucked From Surrounding Seas"). But in the hands of Chef/owners and longtime Marin fixtures Daniel DeLong and Margaret Gradé, you can always expect a fine meal made with painstakingly sourced local ingredients.

Sip a glass of Marin-made mead by the fire; then head to the dining room, where you'll sample dishes like Point Reyes Toma cheese "fondue," golden beet soup, and fluffy cardamom sugar beignets with local honey and strawberries—all accompanied by excellent crusty bread.

Saturday nights are dedicated to a pricier prix-fixe menu, so be sure to plan accordingly.

🔲 10000 Sir Francis Drake Blvd. (at Hwy. 1), Olema
✆ (415) 663-1034 — **WEB:** www.sirandstar.com
🔲 Dinner Wed – Sun   **PRICE:** $$

SOL FOOD ⚑○

Puerto Rican

✗ | ♿ 🏠 🗖

MAP: C2

You won't be able to miss this Puerto Rican favorite, recognizable by its grasshopper-green exterior and overflowing crowds of festive diners. In fact, Sol Food's comida criolla is so popular that it's taken over the block: a sister bodega does a booming takeout business, while gift store Conchita sells wares from San Juan and beyond.

Sol Food's soul food is hearty and abundant, from tamale-like pasteles of mashed plantain and taro stuffed with garlicky pork to fragrant sautéed shrimp loaded with tomato, onion, and spices. Outstanding daily specials, from arroz con pollo to pernil, are also big draws. Wash it all down with a delicious mango iced tea, and don't skip the decadent pineapple bread pudding, soaked in warm, buttery mango sauce, for dessert.

▨ 903 Lincoln Ave. (at 3rd St.), San Rafael
✆ (415) 451-4765 — **WEB:** www.solfoodrestaurant.com
▨ Lunch & dinner daily   **PRICE:** $$

SUSHI RAN 🅜

Japanese

✗✗ | � ♿ 🖵

MAP: A3

Chefs have come and gone at this Sausalito staple, but its Zen-like atmosphere and exquisite selection of raw fish remain unchanged—and that's just how the regulars like it. With its charming beachside-bungalow ambience, attentive service staff, and thoughtfully curated sake selection, Sushi Ran is as dependable as a restaurant can get.

Start off with a small bite like shrimp tempura over crisp veggies, tobiko, and asparagus, or a steamed red crab salad mingled with seaweed, cucumber, and a sweet soy dressing. Then move on to the main event: meticulously sourced, extraordinarily fresh hamachi, big-eye tuna, steamed blue prawns, and Santa Barbara uni. Whether you choose sashimi or nigiri, rest assured that these talented chefs will steer you right.

▨ 107 Caledonia St. (bet. Pine & Turney Sts.), Sausalito
✆ (415) 332-3620 — **WEB:** www.sushiran.com
▨ Lunch Mon – Fri   Dinner nightly   **PRICE:** $$

VILLAGE SAKE 😋

Japanese

✗ | ◊ �ċ ☂   **MAP:** B2

Set along a bustling stretch, Village Sake is a mighty hot and mod izakaya delivering authentic goods in the heart of quaint Fairfax. All the classic small plates are in full force here: crisp and creamy takoyaki (octopus croquettes), okonomiyaki, tataki (made with silky smoked hamachi), and coconut mochi cake complete with cardamom gelato. If you must have sushi, there's a small selection of excellent nigiri, too—make sure to sample the shima aji and kinmedai.

The look of the room suggests Tokyo, with closely spaced tables, an array of wood accents (including a live-edge wood counter), as well as a friendly staff, many of them Japanese natives. It's a popular spot that doesn't take reservations, so expect long lines, especially on weekends.

🔲 19 Bolinas Rd. (bet. Broadway Blvd. & Mono Ave.), Fairfax
✆ (415) 521-5790 — **WEB:** www.villagesake.com
🔲 Dinner Wed – Sun   **PRICE:** $$

Your opinions are important to us.
Please write to us directly at:
michelin.guides@us.michelin.com

PENINSULA

PENINSULA

A COLLISION OF CULTURES

Situated to the south of the city, the San Francisco Peninsula separates the Bay from the expansive Pacific Ocean. While it may not be known across the globe for stellar chefs and pioneering Californian cooking, the Peninsula boasts an incredibly diverse and rich Asian culture. Local eateries and numerous markets reflect this region's melting pot and continue to draw residents for authentic international cuisines. Those in need of a taste from the Far East should join Korean natives at **Kukje Super Market** as they scoop up fresh seafood, rolls of *gimbap*, and a host of other prepared delicacies. Alternatively, one may practice the art of chopstick wielding at one of the many Japanese sushi bars, ramen houses, and izakayas. Filipino foodies tickle their fancy with an impressive selection of traditional breads and pastries at **Valerio's Tropical Bakeshop** in Daly City. Fittingly set in a Filipino-

dominated quarter referred to as "**Little Manila**," Valerio's is famously revered as *the* best bakery around.

Beyond the Far East, sugar junkies of the Western variety savor classic Danish pastries at Burlingame's **Copenhagen Bakery & Cafe**, also applauded for their creamy special occasion cakes. Over in San Mateo, Italians can't miss a stop at **pasta pasta** for freshly made shapes, homemade sauces, and salads that are both fulfilling and easy to put together at home. If your domestic skills leave much to be desired, charming **La Biscotteria** has premium, hand-crafted Italian pastries and cookies on hand, including cannoli, amaretti, sfogliatelle, and biscotti in an assortment of flavors. This precious gem in Redwood City also sells beautiful hand-painted Deruta ceramics that are imported directly from Umbria.

The Peninsula is also known for its large Mexican-American population. Their taste for home can be gratified at such authentic taquerias as **El Grullense** in Redwood City; **El Palenque** in San Mateo; and **Mexcal Taqueria** in Menlo Park. Just as **Gabriel & Daniel's Mexican Grill** in the Burlingame Golf Center clubhouse is an ideal place to unwind after playing a round out on the plush course, dive-y **Back A Yard** in Menlo Park is eternally beloved among foodies yearning for flavorful Caribbean cuisine. Pescetarians know that **Barbara's Fishtrap** in Half Moon Bay is a sought-after "catch" for fish 'n chips by the harbor, whereas pig trumps fish at **Gorilla Barbeque**. Here, fat-frilled pork ribs are all the rage, especially when served out of an orange railroad car parked on Cabrillo Highway in Pacifica.

SUMMER'S BOUNTY

In addition to harboring some of the Bay Area's most authentic Cantonese dens and dim sum houses, Millbrae is a lovely spot to raise one last toast to summer. In fact, **The Millbrae Art & Wine Festival** is a profusion of wicked fairground eats—from meltingly tender cheesesteaks and Cajun-style corndogs, to fennel-infused sausages and everything in between. Motivated home chefs head to **Draeger's Market** in San Mateo to pick up some wine and cheese for dinner, and perhaps even sign up for cooking classes in a range of basic to highly specialized subjects. Finally, when hanging out in this 'hood, be sure to revel in a riot of Japanese goods at **Suruki Supermarket**.

Half Moon Bay is a coastal city big on sustainable produce; and in keeping with this philosophy, residents prepare for cozy evenings at home by loading up on a variety of local fruits and vegetables from one of the many roadside stands on Route 92. Find them also scanning the bounty at **Coastside Farmer's Market**, which has been known to unveil such Pescadero treasures as **Harley Farms** goat cheese as well as organic eggs from **Early Bird Ranch**.

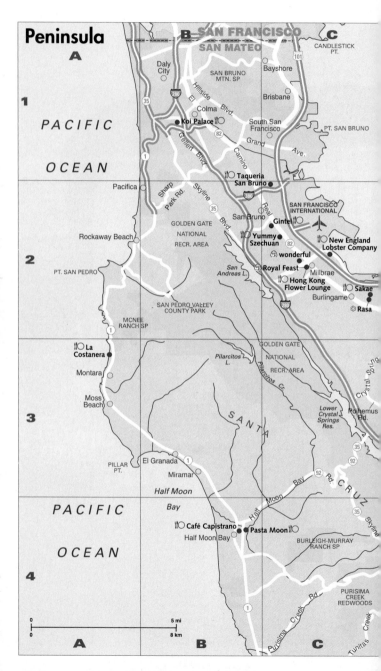

Peninsula

A

SAN FRANCISCO
SAN MATEO

B   **C**

CANDLESTICK PT.

PACIFIC

OCEAN

Daly City

SAN BRUNO MTN. SP

Bayshore

Brisbane

Colma

Koi Palace

South San Francisco

PT. SAN BRUNO

Pacifica

Taqueria San Bruno

SAN FRANCISCO INTERNATIONAL

Rockaway Beach

GOLDEN GATE NATIONAL RECR. AREA

San Bruno

Gintel

New England Lobster Company

Yummy Szechuan

wonderful

PT. SAN PEDRO

San Andreas L.

Royal Feast

Millbrae

Hong Kong Flower Lounge

Sakae

SAN PEDRO VALLEY COUNTY PARK

Burlingame

Rasa

MCNEE RANCH SP

La Costanera

Pilarcitos L.

GOLDEN GATE NATIONAL RECR. AREA

Montara

SANTA

Lower Crystal Springs Res.

Polhemus Rd.

Moss Beach

PILLAR PT.

El Granada

Miramar

Half Moon

CRUZ

Bay

PACIFIC

OCEAN

Café Capistrano

Pasta Moon

Half Moon Bay

BURLEIGH-MURRAY RANCH SP

PURISIMA CREEK REDWOODS

0   5 mi
0   8 km

A   **B**   **C**

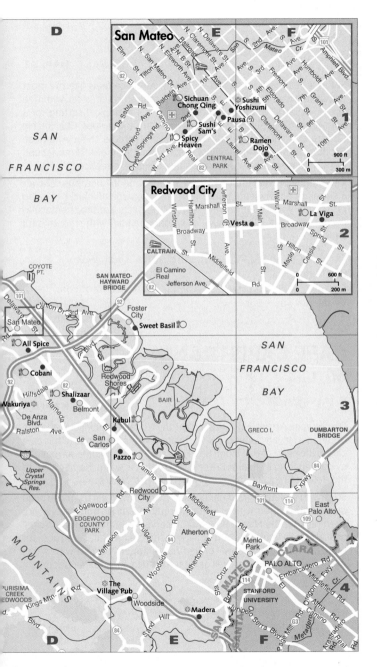

San Mateo

Elm St.
N. Claremont St.
N. Delaware St.
N. B St.
Railroad Ave.
N. Ellsworth Ave.
N. San Mateo Dr.
Tilton Ave.
1st Ave.
S. 2nd Ave.
S. Delaware St.
N. Fremont St.
S. B Ave.
S. 4th Ave.
El Camino Real
De Sabla Rd.
Baywood Ave.
Baldwin Ave.
2nd Ave.
S. Claremont St.
S. Fremont St.
S. Humboldt St.
S. Eldorado St.
S. 7th Ave.
S. Grant St.
S. 9th Ave.
S. 10th Ave.
Crystal Springs Rd.
W. 3rd Ave.
El Camino Real
Laurel Ave.
9th Ave.
N. 2nd Ave.
N. 3rd Ave.
Amphlett Blvd.
82
101

● Sichuan Chong Qing
● Sushi Yoshizumi
● Sushi Sam's
● Pausa
● Spicy Heaven
● Ramen Dojo

CENTRAL PARK
82

0   900 ft
0   300 m

Redwood City

Jefferson
Winslow
Hamilton
Marshall
St.
Main
St.
Walnut
St.
Marshall
St.

● La Viga
Broadway
● Vesta
Spring
Hilton
St.
Maple
St.
Cassia
St.

CALTRAIN St.
Broadway
El Camino Real
Middlefield
Jefferson Ave.
Rd.
82

0   600 ft
0   200 m

SAN FRANCISCO BAY

COYOTE PT.
Delaware
101
Clifton Dr.
3rd Ave.
San Mateo
92
SAN MATEO–HAYWARD BRIDGE
92
Foster City

● Sweet Basil

● All Spice

● Cobani
82
Hillsdale
● Shalizaar
Alameda
Belmont
Redwood Shores
BAIR I.
GRECO I.
DUMBARTON BRIDGE

●Wakuriya
De Anza Blvd.
Ralston Ave.
● Kabul
San Carlos
de
● Pazzo
Camino
las
Rd.
Redwood City
Upper Crystal Springs Res.
280
Edgewood
EDGEWOOD COUNTY PARK
Jefferson
Edgewood
Pulgas
Real
Middlefield
Rd.
101
Atherton
Atherton Ave.
Bayfront Expwy
84
East Palo Alto
114
109

SAN FRANCISCO BAY

Woodside
Rd.
Cruz
Sta.
Menlo Park
Santa
MATEO
CLARA

MOUNTAINS
PURISIMA CREEK REDWOODS
Kings Mtn. Rd.
Blvd.
84
Woodside
● The Village Pub
● Madera
Sand Hill Rd.
Junipero Serra Blvd.
STANFORD UNIVERSITY
PALO ALTO
Embarcadero Rd.
Middlefield
Oregon Expwy.
Alma St.
Page Mill Rd.
63
El Camino Real
Arastradero Rd.

187

ALL SPICE ¡⚬

International

XX

Set in a beautifully restored Victorian, All Spice feels like the most exquisite home in town. Each brightly colored room is set with fine linens, as large windows usher in light. It's a magical setting for a date, among a happy crowd that never seems too serious. Chef Sachin Chopra and wife, Shoshana Wolff, have created a "New American Exotic" cuisine with ingredients from around the globe. It may sound terribly conceptual, but fits the unique dining experience to a tee.

International tastes are on display with "tandoori" octopus set over a streak of earthy lentil purée with an Indian-spiced chickpea salad dressed in yogurt. Finish with tropical desserts like the spectacular coconut-pandan jellyroll cake, or cardamom kulfi with smooth dark chocolate.

▓ 1602 El Camino Real (bet. Barneson & Borel Aves.), San Mateo

𝒫 (650) 627-4303 — **WEB:** www.allspicerestaurant.com

▓ Dinner Tue – Sat   PRICE: $$$

CAFÉ CAPISTRANO ¡⚬

Mexican

X | ♿ ⌂ 🛋

Chef/owner Arturo Mul grew up on the Yucatán peninsula, and the traditional Mayan dishes of his youth are now the backbone of this cute café in the heart of Half Moon Bay. Housed in an older home surrounded by gardens and a small side deck, this retreat is warm, homey, and, to the delight of local families, off most tourists' radars.

Start with a plate of fried panuochos (stuffed with earthy black bean purée and topped with achiote-marinated tender pulled chicken). Then dig into the Mayan pork adobo served with fresh salsa, creamy guacamole, a lightly pickled coleslaw, and crema. But, save room for the true star of the show—grilled red snapper coupled with warm tortillas for wrapping as well as queso for rich and creamy goodness.

▓ 523 Church St. (at Miramontes St.), Half Moon Bay

𝒫 (650) 726-7699 — **WEB:** N/A

▓ Lunch & dinner daily   PRICE: ᴥ

COBANI ⅩO
Mediterranean

Ⅹ | ♿︎   **MAP:** D3

Just south of downtown San Mateo, this fast-casual Turkish spot is a favorite with the locals. Lunch hour brings a crowd—think nine-to-fivers and families with kids—and the modus operandi is simple: order at the counter, grab a number and utensils, and take a seat in the cheerful dining room, adorned with a colorful mural depicting a Turkish village.

The kitchen churns out a mix of Turkish, Mediterranean, and Middle Eastern items: you'll find an adana kebab—made of spicy, charbroiled minced lamb and beef—that's worthy of Istanbul. Then, look forward to shaved chicken gyros wrapped in lavash, followed by crispy falafel with baba ghanoush. And the skilled kitchen's take on künefe, a traditional dessert of mild white cheese broiled with syrupy pastry, is superlative.

▦ 8 W. 25th Ave. (bet. El Camino Real & Flores St.), San Mateo
℘ (650) 389-6861 — **WEB:** www.cobanigyro.com
▦ Lunch & dinner daily   **PRICE:** ⌘

GINTEI ⅩO
Japanese

ⅩⅩ | 🍶 ♿︎   **MAP:** C2

San Bruno's rep as a dining wasteland is due for a re-evaluation thanks to this sleek and stylish sushi spot, whose offerings can hang with the best in San Francisco. Bright and contemporary, with dramatic pressed-tin ceilings and a coveted eight-seat sushi counter, it's known as a reservations-required must for omakase enthusiasts, with deeply hospitable service.

Newbies to nigiri should make a beeline for the omakase, but the more experienced palate will revel in market specials like silky Hokkaido scallops, sweet and succulent live spot prawns (with the traditional deep-fried heads alongside), and firm yet tender octopus. Everything is minimally dressed—all the better to accentuate the fish's outstanding quality.

▦ 235 El Camino Real (bet. Crystal Springs Rd. & San Felipe Ave.), San Bruno
℘ (650) 636-4135 — **WEB:** www.gintei.co
▦ Lunch Tue – Fri   Dinner Tue – Sun   **PRICE:** $$

HONG KONG FLOWER LOUNGE 🍴

Chinese

XX | &. ⌂ ⚔ 🈴   **MAP:** C2

Generations of dim sum diehards have patronized this palace of pork buns, where a small army of servers will surround you with carts from the moment you take your seat. They bear innumerable delights: rich barbecue pork belly with crispy skin, pan-fried pork-and-chive wontons steamed to order and doused in oyster sauce, delicate vegetable dumplings, and a best-in-class baked egg custard bun. Evenings are a bit more sedate, emphasizing Cantonese seafood straight from the on-site tanks.

As with all dim sum spots, the early bird gets the best selection (and avoids the non-negligible weekend waits). Thankfully, the super-central Millbrae location, towering over El Camino Real, boasts plenty of parking—and a machine-like staff that knows how to pack them in.

▨ 51 Millbrae Ave. (at El Camino Real), Millbrae
📞 (650) 692-6666 — **WEB:** www.mayflower-seafood.com
▨ Lunch & dinner daily   PRICE: $$

KABUL 🍴

Afghan

XX | &.   **MAP:** E3

Fans of Afghan cuisine flock from miles around to this homestyle spot in San Carlos, tucked away in a deceptively large space within a modest shopping plaza. Kabul's walls are festooned with deep red tapestries and other Afghan embroidery, and even on weekday nights it fills up with local families. There's even a semi-private side dining room for big groups.

The friendly staff is happy to suggest favorite dishes, from smoky chicken and lamb kebabs over spiced basmati rice to sweet, fork-tender sautéed pumpkin served with a garlicky yogurt sauce and fluffy flatbread. And though everything comes in generous portions, you'll want to save room for the firnee, a gently sweet milk pudding flavored with cardamom and rosewater and topped with pistachios.

▨ 135 El Camino Real (bet. F & Holly Sts.), San Carlos
📞 (650) 594-2840 — **WEB:** www.kabul-cuisine.com
▨ Lunch Mon –Fri   Dinner nightly   PRICE: $$

KOI PALACE ⅃○

Chinese

✕✕ | ⅃ 🛆 ⌇

Long regarded as one of the Bay Area's best spots for dim sum, Koi Palace continues to earn its serious waits (guaranteed on weekends, and common at weekday lunch). The dining room is a step up from its competition, with shallow koi ponds weaving between tables, high ceilings, and huge tables to accommodate the Chinese-American families celebrating big occasions.

They come to share plates of perfectly lacquered, smoky-salty roasted suckling pig or sticky rice noodle rolls encasing plump shrimp, sesame oil, and minced ginger. Not far behind, find lotus leaves stuffed with glutinous rice, dried scallop, and roast pork, as well as big pots of jasmine tea. Save room for desserts like the fluffy almond cream steamed buns and flaky, caramelized custard tarts.

▨ 365 Gellert Blvd. (bet. Hickey & Serramonte Blvds.), Daly City
℘ (650) 992-9000 — **WEB:** www.koipalace.com
▨ Lunch & dinner daily   PRICE: $$

LA COSTANERA ⅃○

Peruvian

✕✕ | 🍸 ⅃ 🏠 🛆

Set atop one of the most beautiful perches in the entire Bay Area, this bungalow boasts a gorgeous patio and a dining room that's walled with windows.

While the panoramas are amazing—endless ocean, spectacular sunsets, and even frolicking dolphins if you're lucky—so are the boldly flavored plates produced by Chef Carlos Altamirano and his team. Cebiche pescado bathed in leche de tigre is perhaps the best way to experience Peru's national dish, while succulent langostino crocantes served over silky potatoes, or herb-marinated pollo salvaje accompanied by fried yuca are other treasures worth devouring.

Be sure to sample the creative cocktails. Alternatively, try a delicious and refreshing chicha morada, which is safer for the drive home.

▨ 8150 Cabrillo Hwy. (bet. 1st & 2nd Sts.), Montara
℘ (650) 728-1600 — **WEB:** www.lacostanerarestaurant.com
▨ Dinner Tue – Sun   PRICE: $$$

LA VIGA ⅈ◯

Mexican

⅄ | ♿   **MAP:** F2

Named after Mexico City's massive seafood market, La Viga is a Redwood City favorite for oceanic fare with a Latin twist. Wedged between an industrial area and downtown, the basic but cheerful dining room draws both blue- and white-collar workers for heaping tacos—soft white corn tortillas stuffed with fried snapper fillet, cabbage, and chipotle crema; or crisp prawns with tomatillo-garlic sauce and pico de gallo.

At the dinner hour, local residents stream in for the famed tallarines con mariscos, a sizable mound of al dente fideos studded with pristine seafood bathed in a spicy tomato sauce. With such fresh ingredients and bold flavors, the low prices and generous portions are particularly pleasing—be sure to allow room for a creamy, delicate flan to finish.

▓ 1772 Broadway (bet. Beech & Maple Sts.), Redwood City
✆ (650) 679-8141 — **WEB:** www.chefmanuelmartinez.com
▓ Lunch & dinner Tue – Sun   **PRICE:** $$

NEW ENGLAND LOBSTER COMPANY ⅈ◯

Seafood

⅄ | ♿ ☂   **MAP:** C2

You'll know your meal is fresh at this Peninsula palace of seafood, where flat-screen TVs showcase the bevy of crustaceans in their huge seawater holding tanks. Set in an industrial warehouse, NELC is both a fish market and a counter-service restaurant—complete with a nautical theme, picnic tables indoors and out, and a happy crowd of young and old diners donning lobster bibs.

Kick things off with the justifiably beloved lobster-corn chowder, thick with sweet, succulent meat in a rich and creamy—but not overly heavy—stock. (For dedicated fans, frozen to-go quarts are offered.) Then go for broke with the outstanding lobster roll, lightly dressed with mayo on a fluffy, buttery roll and accompanied by excellent house-made potato chips.

▓ 824 Cowan Rd. (off Old Bayshore Hwy.), Burlingame
✆ (650) 443-1559 — **WEB:** www.newenglandlobster.net
▓ Lunch & dinner daily   **PRICE:** $$

MADERA ✿
Contemporary

XxX | 🕸 ⅃ 🏠 ⛲ 📠 👞 🖐   **MAP:** E4

As evidenced by all those Teslas parked out front, this is a swanky spot for fine-dining in the Rosewood Sand Hill hotel. The grand open kitchen, roaring fireplace, and large outdoor patio complete with gorgeous views of the Santa Cruz mountains draw a moneyed crowd of local techies.

While its location inside a hotel may mean it is open for three meals a day, come for dinner to taste this kitchen's ambition and pure talent. The cuisine is contemporary, thoughtfully composed with seasonal ingredients, and even surprising at times. An excellent risotto sings with the flavors of roasted butternut squash, Perigord black truffles, airy Lacinato kale chips, and the unexpected, wondrous touch of finger lime. The kitchen also flaunts its dexterity in three preparations of guinea hen, including tender breast meat with crackling-crisp skin, sliced thigh, and excellent springy sausages accompanied by charred peaches bursting with sweetness, pickled chanterelles, toasted pecans, and green onion soubise.

Desserts are fun, delicious, and do not hold back, especially the insanely rich peanut butter and black sesame parfait, layered as fudgy brownie, ganache, mousse, and brittle in a glass goblet.

▨ 2825 Sand Hill Rd. (at I-280), Menlo Park
☏ (650) 561-1540 — **WEB:** www.maderasandhill.com
▨ Lunch & dinner daily   **PRICE: $$$$**

PASTA MOON ⭐🍴

Italian

XX | ♿ 🏠   **MAP:** B4

One of Half Moon Bay's most popular restaurants, Pasta Moon is always packed to the gills with locals and tourists filling up on massive portions of hearty Italian-American fare. With its vaulted ceilings, pops of bright red, and multiple intimate dining rooms, it's a hit with diners of all ages, especially those seated at tables with a view of the lovely side garden.

House-made pastas steal the show, with tempting options like the delicate 30-layer lasagna filled with ricotta, parmesan, and house Sicilian sausage. A grilled pork chop stuffed with peaches, pancetta, and caramelized onions arrives with mascarpone mashed potatoes. The butterscotch pudding (with shards of Ghirardelli chocolate, natch) is bound to send you over the moon.

▓ 315 Main St. (bet. Mill St. & Stone Pine Rd.), Half Moon Bay
✆ (650) 726-5125 — **WEB:** www.pastamoon.com
▓ Lunch & dinner daily   **PRICE:** $$

PAUSA 😋

Italian

XX | 🍸 🍺 ♿ 🏠   **MAP:** E1

Come to this San Mateo newbie for authentic Italian eats, where Chef/co-owner Andrea Giuliani dishes up the cuisine of his native Veneto. Thanks to the modern space and late hours (by San Mateo standards, at least), it's a big draw for the growing crowds of young tech types in town.

The dining room has a view of the charcuterie aging room and those enticing cured meats like delicate, fennel-flecked finocchiona or exceptional pork ciccioli terrine. The wood-fired Neapolitan pizzas are equally strong—try the porchetta variation, topped with gorgonzola and radicchio. And of course, the pasta doesn't disappoint either: seafood is a specialty of Veneto, and their perciatelli with a tomato-flecked shrimp and octopus ragù is downright perfect.

▓ 223 E. 4th Ave. (bet. B St. & Ellsworth Ave.), San Mateo
✆ (650) 375-0818 — **WEB:** www.pausasanmateo.com
▓ Lunch Mon – Fri   Dinner nightly   **PRICE:** $$

PAZZO ¶🍴

Pizza

XX | **MAP:** E3

New Haven transplants longing for the region's signature chewy, charred apizza will find a taste of home at this San Carlos jewel, which churns out authentically blistered pies. Keep it traditional with red sauce topped with house-made fennel sausage and crimini mushrooms. Or go slightly Californian with the garlicky asparagus pie, draped with creamy crescenza cheese.

Pazzo (Italian for "crazy") is anything but, thanks to a relaxed, family-friendly vibe. Kids of all ages will delight in the back counter, with a great view of the chef slipping pizzas into the cherry-red, wood-fired oven. And don't sleep through the house-made pastas: pillowy ricotta gnocchi, tucked into a lemony mascarpone and artichoke sauce, are good enough to steal the apizzas' show.

▦ 1179 Laurel St. (bet. Brittan & Greenwood Aves.), San Carlos
℘ (650) 591-1075 — **WEB:** www.pazzosancarlos.com
▦ Dinner Tue – Sat **PRICE: $$**

RAMEN DOJO ¶🍴

Japanese

X **MAP:** F1

The two-hour lines may have died down, but a 40-minute wait on the sidewalk is still standard at this noodle hot spot. The interior, when you finally reach it, is utterly spare—the better to showcase steaming bowls of tasty and satisfying soup. Customize your broth (soy sauce, garlic pork, soybean), spiciness, and toppings (like spicy cod roe and kikurage mushrooms), then dive in.

The ramen arrives in minutes, loaded with the standard fried garlic cloves, hard-boiled quail egg, scallion, chili, and two slices of roast pork. Your job is to slurp the chewy, delicious noodles (and maybe some seaweed salad or edamame), then hit the road—the hyper-efficient staff needs to keep the line moving, after all. But for one of the best bowls in town, it's worth it.

▦ 805 S. B St. (bet. 8th & 9th Aves.), San Mateo
℘ (650) 401-6568 — **WEB:** N/A
▦ Lunch & dinner Wed – Mon **PRICE:** ⊕

RASA ✿

Indian

✕✕ | ♿

In a bustling tech corridor that's also home to Indian expats with high culinary standards, Rasa has managed to find the perfect middle ground. No-joke dishes that aren't toned down for Western palates cater to both software execs and date-night couples, and though the bi-level space boasts a sleek, minimalist-mod décor with bright splashes of orange, stylish pendant lights, and dark wood fittings, the focus here is on food.

The elevated South Indian fare draws added elegance from superb ingredients and inventive presentations, like fluffy "Bombay slider" buns stuffed with well-seasoned crushed potatoes and drizzled with spicy, smoky "gunpowder" butter. The dosas are appropriately paper-thin and shatteringly crisp, while the uttapams topped with sweet peppers and ground masala lamb are earthy and delicate—but watch out for the punch from the accompanying ghost pepper chutney.

A fine meal could be made just out of Rasa's excellent small plates, but for bigger appetites, the flaky white fish moilee, stewed in a creamy coconut curry, is rich and satisfying. And no one should skip the cardamom brûlée for dessert: equal parts bread pudding and crème brûlée, it's dizzyingly delicious.

🟦 209 Park Rd. (bet. Burlingame & Howard Aves.), Burlingame
☎ (650) 340-7272 — **WEB:** www.rasaindian.com
🟦 Lunch & dinner daily   PRICE: $$

ROYAL FEAST 🐷

Chinese

✗ | ♿   **MAP:** C2

You'll dine like royalty at this Millbrae retreat, which offers an array of Chinese delicacies rarely seen outside banquet menus. Helmed by Chef Zongyi Liu, a onetime Chinese Bocuse d'Or competitor, the décor here is light on regal glamour, opting for a simple, spare interior with well-spaced tables. But the menu teems with sought-after items, from abalone to sea cucumber.

Dishes here run the gamut of China's eight great cuisines, with a special emphasis on spicy Sichuan food like white fish in a rich chili-laced broth, or steamed chicken dusted with Sichuan peppercorn and served in a pool of chili oil. For those seeking milder flavors, the shredded pork in a sweet garlic sauce, as well as fluffy pan-fried sesame cakes make for ideal choices.

▦ 148 El Camino Real (bet. Linden & Serra Aves.), Millbrae
✆ (650) 692-3388 — **WEB:** www.royalfeastmillbrae.com
▦ Lunch & dinner daily   **PRICE:** $$

SAKAE 🍴

Japanese

✗ | ♿   **MAP:** C2

Its glory days of crowds packed to the rafters have passed, but Sakae is still a solid option for elegant sushi and other Japanese specialties. Adjacent to downtown Burlingame and the Caltrain station, this is a sleek space clad in varying shades of wood, Japanese pottery, and fresh flowers. Local families enjoy sitting at the bar, where a friendly and engaging sushi chef is a hit with kids.

Skip the specialty rolls and stick to fresh and neat nigiri topped with the likes of albacore, yellowtail, crab, salmon, or daily featured fish. Otherwise, go for the whiteboard's changing specials like maitake mushroom tempura or grilled baby octopus. Be sure to order a pot of hojicha, a roasted green tea that nicely complements the impressive range of fish.

▦ 243 California Dr. (at Highland Ave.), Burlingame
✆ (650) 348-4064 — **WEB:** www.sakaesushi.com
▦ Lunch Mon – Sat   Dinner nightly   **PRICE:** $$$

SHALIZAAR ¶O

Persian

XX | & ⊡   **MAP:** D3

A perennial favorite for Persian flavors, Shalizaar is friendly, charming, and authentic. Lunchtime draws a large business crowd, while dinners cater to couples on dates. The upscale space features chandeliers, linen-topped tables, Persian carpets, and walls of framed windows that flood everything with light.

Meals here are always a pleasure, thanks to the high quality of every ingredient. Try the signature koobideh, smoky ground beef and chicken kebabs served with char-broiled whole tomatoes and rice. Or, tuck into baghali polo, a fork-tender lamb shank over bright green rice full of dill and young fava beans. For dessert, take the friendly servers' advice and order the zoolbia barnieh, sticky-crisp squiggles of fried cake soaked in rosewater syrup.

▓ 300 El Camino Real (bet. Anita & Belmont Aves.), Belmont
☏ (650) 596-9000 — **WEB:** www.shalizaar.com
▓ Lunch & dinner daily   **PRICE:** $$

SICHUAN CHONG QING ¶O

Chinese

X | &   **MAP:** E1

The medical staff at the Mills Health Center take plenty of heat in an average day, but that doesn't stop them from piling into this compact neighboring Sichuan restaurant for their fix of spicy chili oil and numbing peppercorns. Both ingredients are featured in the crispy Chong Qing chicken and shrimp, each laden with chili peppers (be sure to watch out for shards of bone in the cleaver-chopped chicken).

Skip the mild Mandarin dishes and stick to the house's fiery specialties, like the nutty, smoky cumin lamb with sliced onion and still more chilies and chili oil. Aside from a few contemporary touches, the décor isn't newsworthy and the staff is more efficient than engaging—but you'll likely be too busy enjoying the flavor-packed food to mind.

▓ 211 S. San Mateo Dr. (bet. 2nd & 3rd Aves.), San Mateo
☏ (650) 343-1144 — **WEB:** N/A
▓ Lunch & dinner Tue – Sun   **PRICE:** $$

SPICY HEAVEN 🍴○

Chinese

🍴

The surroundings are bare enough to qualify as purgatory, but for lovers of spicy Sichuan fare, this humble newcomer to downtown San Mateo is worthy of ascension into the astral plane. In an area with plenty of Sichuan dining options, the mostly Chinese-speaking crowd demands that the flavors are authentic and on point.

As is typical, most dishes here revolve around the interplay of tingling peppercorns, mouth-scorching dried chilies, and luscious chili oil, from the delicate pork wontons topped with crushed peanuts and scallions to the silky fish fillets and firm tofu swimming in a delectable bright-red chili oil bath. Calm your palate with bites of garlicky sautéed water spinach. Then dive in for another chopstick-full of the spicy, tangy chili pork.

▨ 35 E. 3rd Ave. (bet. El Camino Real & San Mateo Dr.), San Mateo

☏ (650) 781-3977 — **WEB:** N/A

▨ Lunch & dinner daily

PRICE: $$

SUSHI SAM'S 🍴○

Japanese

🍴 | ♿

San Mateo's sushi connoisseurs know that some of the region's best can be found at this tiny, no-frills joint, where waits are all but inevitable. Formica tables and chipped plates are part of the package, but with sushi this exceptional at a price this reasonable, that won't keep you from getting hooked.

Skip the average teriyaki, tempura, and udon in favor of an all-sushi experience; you can't go wrong with the exquisite nigiri, from wild king salmon with a touch of lemon juice and wasabi to silky medai with spicy minced daikon. The unusual battera roll, combining rich, oily mackerel with sweet-salty poached kelp, is a surprise success, as is the decadent dragon roll, a blend of buttery avocado, smoky unagi, and sweet shrimp tempura.

▨ 218 E. 3rd Ave. (bet. B St. & Ellsworth Ave.), San Mateo

☏ (650) 344-0888 — **WEB:** www.sushisams.com

▨ Lunch & dinner Tue – Sat

PRICE: $$

SUSHI YOSHIZUMI ✿

Japanese

✗ | ♿

MAP: E1

Plan ahead two months (to the day) before you'd like to dine here, then jump online for a reservation—Sushi Yoshizumi is worth the effort.

This is a place for Japanese expats yearning for a taste of home and sushi purists snapping iPhone shots faster than you can say "omakase." The setting is discreet in every way, with a tidy interior that consists of little more than eight seats, a cypress bar, as well as a chef's work station.

The menu is built around Edomae sushi, a style that Chef Akira Yoshizumi spent years perfecting in both Japan and New York. His training clearly pays off with food that is refined, delicate, and beautifully balanced. Employing wild seafood, mostly from Japan, to create an intimate omakase experience, Chef Yoshizumi offers detailed explanations and welcomes questions with his warm and open demeanor.

Clean flavors shine in each course; garnishes and sauces are kept to a minimum. A slice of wonderfully firm and surprisingly mild geoduck sashimi arrives with nothing more than fresh wasabi and a sprinkle of black sea salt. Still, the height of any meal here is the nigiri, with flavorful rice seasoned with akazu (red vinegar) and fish so fresh that its taste seems to name its species.

▨ 325 E. 4th Ave. (bet. B St. & Railroad Ave.), San Mateo
✆ (650) 437-2282 — **WEB:** www.sushiyoshizumi.com
▨ Dinner Wed – Sun

PRICE: $$$$

SWEET BASIL ♍️

Thai

✗✗ | ♿ 　　　　　　　　　　　　　　**MAP:** E2

Set near a charming bayside walking and biking trail on Foster City's perimeter, Sweet Basil makes for a great meal after a leisurely stroll or strenuous ride. The space is snazzy and contemporary-looking with bamboo floors and rustic tables, but the vibe is casual with the waitstaff hustling to serve the daytime rush of office workers as well as families (at night).

Though you may have to wait for a table, their signature kabocha pumpkin and beef in a flavorful red curry will merit patience. Other delights include moist and well-marinated chicken satay; tofu stir-fried with bell peppers and basil; or sticky rice topped with mango. You can choose your own spice level here, but watch out: when this kitchen says hot, they're not kidding around.

▨ 1473 Beach Park Blvd. (at Marlin Ave.), Foster City
☎ (650) 212-5788 — **WEB:** www.sweetbasilthai.net
▨ Lunch & dinner daily 　　　　　　　　　**PRICE:** $$

TAQUERIA SAN BRUNO ♍️

Mexican

✗ | 🍽️ 　　　　　　　　　　　　　　**MAP:** C2

If you're willing to forgive its divey, industrial location in San Bruno's auto-repair corridor, this taqueria will reward you with flavor-packed food that's worthy of the largely Mexican clientele that congregates here at lunchtime. Expect to sit elbow-to-elbow at communal tables, where options range from authentically Mexican to delightfully Americanized (hello, hefty super burritos).

Every type of taco served here is perfection—from fresh, plump marinated shrimp to sweet, caramelized al pastor. The superior chicken enchiladas sub smoky grilled chicken for the traditional boiled variety, then get added zest from a garlicky red chili sauce. Throw in warm, well-salted tortilla chips and piquant salsa, and you'll be a happy camper.

▨ 1045 San Mateo Ave. (bet. Hermosa & Scott Sts.), San Bruno
☎ (650) 873-1752 — **WEB:** N/A
▨ Lunch & dinner daily 　　　　　　　　　**PRICE:** ⊜

VESTA 😮

Pizza

XX | & ⊞   **MAP:** F2

Whether they're rolling in from their offices at lunch or their condos at dinner, Redwood City locals are always up for a wood-fired pie at this stylish downtown pizzeria. With an airy, mosaic-filled dining room extending into a large front patio, it's a relaxed, roomy space perfect for groups and families.

The menu is divided into red and white pies, and they're equally delicious: zesty tomato sauce enlivens a combo of peppery soppressata, smoked mozzarella, and spinach, while a white version with crumbled French feta, fresh slices of garlic, cherry tomatoes, and chopped applewood-smoked bacon is irresistible. Get your greens in with the arugula salad, tossed with shaved Parmigiano Reggiano, toasted hazelnuts, and a delicious apricot vinaigrette.

▪ 2022 Broadway St. (bet. Jefferson Ave. & Main St.), Redwood City
☏ (650) 362-5052 — **WEB:** www.vestarwc.com
▪ Lunch & dinner Tue – Sat   **PRICE:** $$

WONDERFUL 😮

Chinese

X | &   **MAP:** C2

Hunanese cuisine often takes a backseat to the Bay Area's bumper crop of Cantonese and Sichuanese restaurants, so it's no wonder that this hot spot has caught on with the area's Chinese transplants seeking Hunan dishes. Expect a wait at peak meal hours – especially for large parties, as the dining room is compact.

The boldly flavored dishes incorporate oodles of smoked, cured, and fermented ingredients—from the bacon-like pork wok-tossed with leeks, garlic, and soy, to the pungent pork, black bean, and pickled chili mixture that tops those spicy, chewy, hand-cut Godfather's noodles. The whole chili-braised fish, fresh and flaky in its bath of bright red mild chili sauce flecked with scallions and garlic, is an absolute must.

▪ 270 Broadway (bet. La Cruz & Victoria Aves.), Millbrae
☏ (650) 651-8888 — **WEB:** www.wonderful.restaurant
▪ Lunch & dinner Wed – Mon   **PRICE:** $$

THE VILLAGE PUB ⟨⟩

Gastropub

XxX | 🍸 🍺 ♿ ⛱ 💤 🍷

MAP: E4

Though it has the feel of a chichi private club, this attractive New American restaurant is open to all—provided they can live up to the style standards set by its fan base of tech tycoons and ladies-who-lunch. Draw your eyes away from those Teslas in the lot, and head inside for fine dining that exceeds this sophisticated restaurant's humble name.

Despite the glitz, the cuisine here is surprisingly approachable, from platters of house charcuterie served with fire-warmed artisan bread to the superb Pub burger, available in both the cozy front lounge and more formal main dining area. It's there that the kitchen shines its brightest, with more elaborate entrées like the almond wood-grilled pork loin, adorned with crispy shrimp-pork croquettes, pungent black garlic, and caramelized Brussels sprouts. The signature chocolate soufflé is an equally impressive display; its intense, not-too-sweet flavor cut by drizzles of crème anglaise infused with Earl Grey tea.

Given the clientele, the wine list is designed to court the deepest of pockets, with an outstanding selection of French vintages, particularly Bordeaux. On a budget? Aim for lunch, which is lighter not only in approach, but on the wallet.

▨ 2967 Woodside Rd. (off Whiskey Hill Rd.), Woodside
☏ (650) 851-9888 — **WEB:** www.thevillagepub.net
▨ Lunch Sun – Fri   Dinner nightly   **PRICE:** $$$

WAKURIYA ✿

Japanese

✗ | ⌒ ♿

MAP: D3

Innovative, serious, and very well-established, Wakuriya successfully combines a deep respect for kaiseki tradition with a contemporary touch. This is largely thanks to the lone chef behind the counter, Katsuhiro Yamasaki; his wife is the one so deftly managing and serving the dining room. The location is charmless, but there is a sober elegance here that is enhanced by the kitchen's quiet confidence. The room books a month in advance—set your alarm for midnight, phone them exactly 30 days ahead, and pray for a callback.

Each month brings a new, refined menu that combines the chef's personal style with superlative Japanese and Californian ingredients. Course after course arrives uniquely presented, perhaps on handcrafted ceramics or even a silver spoon, cradling chunks of poached lobster with intensely smoky dashi gelée, soft-boiled Jidori egg, crisp asparagus and fried kombu.

This may not be a sushi-ya, but the sashimi course is nonetheless excellent. Find that same level of talent in the yamaimo gratin with silky morsels of black cod and tender Brussels sprouts that are crisp, yet light as air and so delicious. The shirako tofu topped with Kabocha pumpkin tempura is beyond luxurious.

▮ 115 De Anza Blvd. (at Parrot Dr.), San Mateo
✆ (650) 286-0410 — **WEB:** www.wakuriya.com
▮ Dinner Wed – Sun   PRICE: $$$$

YUMMY SZECHUAN ⅋◯

Chinese

✗ | ♿   **MAP:** C2

Long waits for a great Chinese meal are common on the Peninsula, which makes this as yet line-free favorite doubly special. The space is no-frills, but the kitchen is all-thrills, knocking out classic dish after classic dish: crisp Chongqing-style fried chicken buried under a mound of dried chilies and numbing peppercorns, tender pork wontons swimming in gloriously mouth-searing chili oil, and chewy dan dan noodles tossed with ground pork, peanuts, and plenty of chili oil.

As with all Sichuan restaurants, those who can't stand the heat will have a hard go of it, but non-fiery options include a flaky rolled beef pancake and garlicky pea shoots. The moral of this story: while Yummy may not be anyone's idea of high style, the food assuredly lives up to its name.

▨ 1661 El Camino Real (bet. Park Blvd. & Park Pl.), Millbrae
✆ (650) 615-9648 — **WEB:** www.yummyszechuan.com
▨ Lunch & dinner daily   **PRICE:** $$

Avoid the search for
parking. Look for valet 🚗.

SOUTH BAY

SOUTH BAY

SILICON VALLEY

Silicon Valley has for long been revered as the tech capital of the world, but it's really so much more. Combine all that tech money with a diverse, international population and get an exceptionally dynamic culinary scene. If that doesn't sound like an outstanding (read: successful) formula on its own, think of the area's rich wine culture descending from the Santa Cruz Mountains, where a burgeoning vintner community takes great pride in its work, and realize that the South Bay may as well be sitting on a gold mine. Visitors should be sure to see everything the area has to offer, with a sojourn at **The Mountain Winery** in Saratoga—part-outdoor concert venue, part-event space, and part-winery—that offers stunning views of the vineyards and valley below.

FESTIVALS GALORE

The Valley is proud of its tech-minded reputation, but don't judge this book by its cover as South Bay locals definitely know how to party. In San Jose, celebrations kick off every May at the wildly popular **South Bay Greek Festival** featuring music, eats, drinks, and dance. Similarly and with little time to recover, buckets of cornhusks wait to be stuffed and sold at the **Story Road Tamale Festival**, also held every summer. Come July, **Japantown** breathes new life for the two-day **Obon**

Festival & Bazaar, and as August rolls around, the Italian-American Heritage Foundation celebrates its annual **Family Festa**. This is a year-long shindig, and **Santana Row** (a sleek shopping village housing numerous upscale restaurants and a fantastic farmer's market) plays a pivotal role in these festivities. One of San Jose's most notable destinations is **San Pedro Square Market**, whose four walls harbor a spectrum of artisanal merchants at historic Peralta Adobe downtown. Farmers and specialty markets are a way of life for South Bay residents and these locals cannot imagine living elsewhere.

CULTURAL DYNASTY

As further testimony to its international reputation, the capital of Silicon Valley is also a melting pot of global culinary influences. Neighborhood *pho* shops and *bánh mì* hangouts like **Huong Lan**, gratify the growing Vietnamese community. They can also be found gracing the intersection of King and Tully streets (home to some of the city's finest Vietnamese flavors) sampling decadent cream puffs at **Hong-Van Bakery** or crispy green waffles flavored with *pandan* paste at **Century Bakery**, just a few blocks away. **Lion Plaza** is yet another hub for bakeries, markets, and canteens paying homage to this eighth most populated Asian country. Neighboring Cambodia makes an appearance by way of delicious noodle soups at **Nam Vang Restaurant** or **F&D Yummy**. And Chinese food makes its formidable presence known at lofty **Dynasty Chinese Seafood Restaurant**. Located on Story Road, this is a popular arena for big parties and favored destination for dim sum. **Nijiya Market**, for instance, is a jewel with several locations, all of which sparkle with specialty goods, top ingredients, and other things Far East. Long before it was cool to be organic in America, Nijiya was focused on bringing the taste of Japan by way of high-quality, seasonal, and local ingredients to the California coast. Today, it continues to tantalize with some of the area's most pristine seafood and meat, as well as an array of tasty sushi and bento boxes.

Also available via their website are sumptuous, homespun recipes for a variety of noodle dishes, fried rice signatures, and other regional specialties. Encompassing the globe and traveling from this Eastern tip to South America, Mexican food enthusiasts in San Jose seem eternally smitten by the still-warm tortillas at **Tropicana**, as well as the surprisingly tasty tacos from one of the area's many **Mi Pueblo Food Centers**.

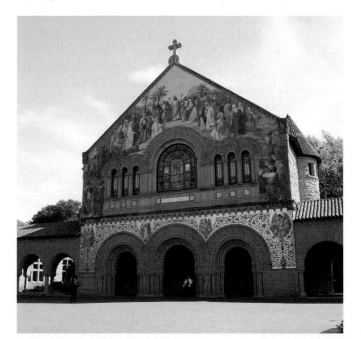

A STUDENT'S DREAM

And yet there is more to the South Bay than just San Jose. Los Gatos is home to prized patisseries like **Fleur de Cocoa** and such historic, continually operating, and specialized wineries like **Testarossa**. Meanwhile, cool and casual Palo Alto is home base for celebrated Stanford University, its countless students, and impressive faculty. Find locals lining up for homemade frozen yogurt at **Fraîche**. Others fulfill a Korean fantasy in Santa Clara, where these same settlers enjoy a range of authentic nibbles and tasty spreads at food court favorite—**Lawrence Plaza**. Just as foodies favor the soondubu jjigae at **SGD Tofu House**, more conservative palates have a field day over caramelized sweet potatoes at **Sweet Potato Stall**, just outside the Galleria. Fill your belly with impeccable produce along El Camino Real near the Lawrence Expressway intersection. Then treat your senses to a feast at Mountain View's **Milk Pail Market**, showcasing over 300 varieties of cheese. Have your pick

among such splendid choices as Camembert, Bleu d'Auvergne, Morbier, and Cabriquet, as well as imported Mamie Nova Yogurt. Despite the fast pace of technology in Silicon Valley, **Slow Food**—the grassroots movement dedicated to local food traditions—has a thriving South Bay chapter. Even Google in Mountain View feeds its massive staff three nourishing, square meals a day. For a wider range of delicacies, they may frequent surrounding eateries or stores selling ethnic eats. Residents of Los Altos also have their German food cravings covered between **Esther's German Bakery** and **Dittmer's**

Gourmet Meats & Wurst-Haus. In fact, Dittmer's sausages are made extra special when served on a salted pretzel roll from Esther's. **Los Gatos Meats & Smokehouse** is another stalwart serving these meat-loving mortals an embarrassment of riches. Think poultry, fish, and freshly butchered meat sandwiches served alongside savory beef jerky, prime rib roasts, pork loin, corned beef, and of course, bacon. But wait...did you want it regular, pepper, country-style, or Canadian? Pair all these salt licks with a sip from Mountain View's **Savvy Cellar Wine Bar & Wine Shop** only to discover

that it's a picnic in the making. Smokers looking to wind down in luxury may head to the handsome, upscale and members-only **Los Gatos Cigar Club**, where the choices are exceptional and conversation intriguing.

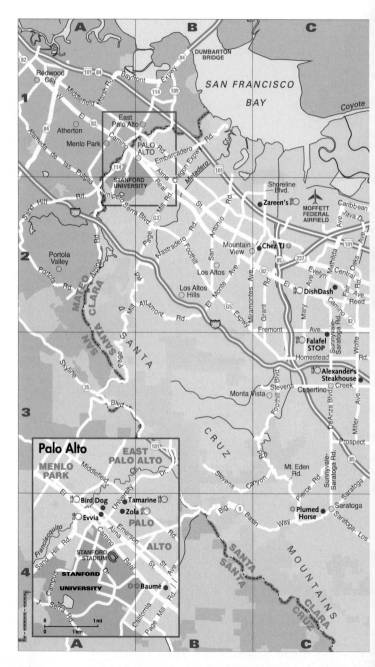

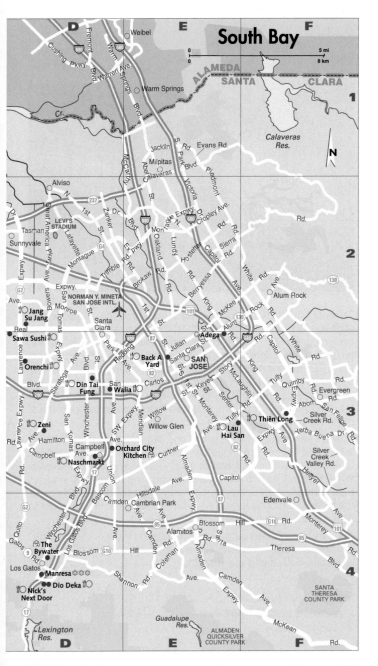

South Bay

0   5 mi
0   8 km

ALAMEDA
SANTA   CLARA

Calaveras
Res.

N

Weibel

Fremont

Cushling Pkwy.

Warm Springs Blvd.

Warren Ave.

Warm Springs

Cr.

Jacklin

Milpitas

Abel

Calaveras

Alviso

S. Park Rd.

Evans Rd.

Victoria

Piedmont

Rd.

McCarthy

Zanker St.

Montague Expwy.

Oakland Rd.

Cropley Ave.

N. 1st St.

Dr.

LEVI'S
STADIUM

Great America Pkwy.

Tasman

Sunnyvale

Lafayette

Montague

Lundy

Sierra

White Rd.

Alum Rock

Ave.

130

Expwy.

San Tomas

Bowers

Monroe St.

NORMAN Y. MINETA
SAN JOSE INTL.

Timble Rd.

Brokaw Rd.

Hostetter Rd.

Berryessa Rd.

Capitol Ave.

McKee Rd.

King Rd.

Rock Rd.

130

Ave.

Jang
Su Jang

Sawa Sushi

Real

Santa
Clara

1st St.

101

King St.

Alum Rock Rd.

Capitol

White Rd.

Orenchi

Lawrence Expwy.

Saratoga Ave.

Park Ave.

Hedding Ave.

87

82

Back A
Yard

San Julian St.

Santa Clara St.

SAN
JOSE

Adega

Story Rd.

McLaughlin Rd.

King Rd.

Capitol Expwy.

Din Tai
Fung

Walia

San Carlos St.

Keyes St.

Senter Rd.

Monterey Rd.

Tully Rd.

Quimby Rd.

Aborn Rd.

San Felipe Rd.

Evergreen

Rd.

Zeni

Hamilton Ave.

Winchester Blvd.

Meridian Ave.

SW Expwy.

Willow St.

Willow Glen

Ave.

Tully Rd.

Lau
Hai San

Thiên Long

Silver
Creek Rd.

Yerba Buena Dr.

Silver
Creek
Valley Rd.

Henyer Rd.

Campbell
Ave.

Naschmarkt

Orchard City
Kitchen

Union Ave.

Curtner

Almaden Expwy.

Capitol

82

Lawrence Expwy.

Quito Rd.

Los Gatos Blvd.

Campbell

San Tomas Expwy.

17

Bascom Ave.

Camden Ave.

Hillsdale

Cambrian Park

Camden Ave.

Ave.

85

Blossom Hill Rd.

Alamitos

Santa
Rd.

Almaden Expwy.

Coleman Rd.

87

Edenvale

G10 Rd.

Monterey Rd.

85

Theresa

101

G2

The
Bywater

9

Winchester Blvd.

Los Gatos
Gatos Rd.

Manresa

Blossom

Hill

G10

Shannon Rd.

Almaden Rd.

Camden Ave.

Camden Expwy.

SANTA
THERESA
COUNTY PARK

Dio Deka

Nick's
Next Door

17

Lexington
Res.

Guadalupe
Res.

ALMADEN
QUICKSILVER
COUNTY PARK

McKean Rd.

D   **E**   **F**

215

ADEGA ✿
Portuguese

XX | 🕸 ⚓ 🍽 🥾

MAP: E3

San Jose's "Little Portugal" may not be as thoroughly authentic as it once was, but this retreat has kept local tradition alive with its playful, contemporary riffs on the classics of this nation's cuisine. From rabbit terrine studded with pine nuts and drizzled with a luscious port reduction to tender roasted octopus atop fingerling potatoes and spinach, a meal here will win over both longtime fans of Portuguese fare and new converts. Many of them likely turned after one bite of the delicious arroz de pato, rice cooked with a smoky, savory blend of chouriço, bacon, and shredded roast duck.

Adega's environs are on the gritty side, but the space itself is lovely, with wood beams, brown leather banquettes, vintage winemaking tools on the walls, and a stunning glass-enclosed private dining room. Wine lovers will thrill to the stellar selection of more than 200 vintages from Portugal, many of them rarely or never found in the U.S. Of course, the friendly staff who largely hail from the same nation, are eager to help pick the perfect glass.

And finally, don't miss out on creative desserts like the "ovo de ovos," a whimsical "egg" of cream with a sweetened yolk filling, nested in cinnamon-dusted egg yolk threads.

■ 1614 Alum Rock Ave. (bet. 33rd & 34th Sts.), San Jose
☏ (408) 926-9075 — **WEB:** www.adegarest.com
■ Dinner Wed – Sun   **PRICE: $$$**

ALEXANDER'S STEAKHOUSE 🍴

Steakhouse

XxX | 🍴 🍷 ♿ 🎦 🧼   **MAP:** C3

Wealthy techies set down their smartphones and plug in face-to-face at this swank steakhouse, where a double-wide dining room, fireside lounge, and duo of exhibition kitchens aim to sate executives doing deals on the company tab. Pricey steaks emerge from the glass-enclosed aging room, while the bar is the place to go for high-dollar Napa cabernets and rare whiskeys.

The flash at Alexander's extends to the more-is-more menu, which often piles on overpowering ingredients to diminishing returns—and those with sensitive palates should order carefully. If you're not dining with a group, opt for the more sedate bar, which boasts friendlier, less-scripted service (you can skip the upsold hamachi shots) and a cast of interesting Silicon Valley characters.

▪ 10330 N. Wolfe Rd. (at I-280), Cupertino
☏ (408) 446-2222 — **WEB:** www.alexanderssteakhouse.com
▪ Lunch Tue – Sat   Dinner nightly   **PRICE: $$$$**

BACK A YARD 🍴

Caribbean

X | ♿   **MAP:** E3

Though this Caribbean spot is located in the heart of downtown San Jose, dining here feels like a vacation thanks to cheerful murals, a lively soundtrack, and hospitable servers. Unlike its Menlo Park predecessor, which mainly does to-go orders, this location boasts a capacious brick dining room.

Back A Yard is a Jamaican term meaning "the way things are done back home," and the food doesn't disappoint on that count. Specialties include smoky, spicy, and tender jerk chicken, flavorful curry goat, and vinegar-marinated escovitch fish fillets, all accompanied by coconut rice and red beans, a side salad, and caramelized fried plantains. Cool off your palate with a glass of coconut water, then order a slice of dense, flan-like sweet potato pudding.

▪ 80 N. Market St. (bet. Santa Clara & St. John Sts.), San Jose
☏ (408) 294-8626 — **WEB:** www.backayard.net
▪ Lunch & dinner Mon – Sat   **PRICE:** 🍜

BAUMÉ ✿ ✿
Contemporary

XxX | ♿

A bold and bright glass door in an otherwise nondescript building along Palo Alto's main thoroughfare marks the entrance to the mystical Baumé. Inside, find a dining room with a modernist sensibility that carries through orange-hued walls and fabric room dividers. The kitchen may do only one dinner seating a night, but tables are spaced widely for privacy and never rushed. Mrs. Chemel oversees this luxurious enclave, adding warmth, detailed knowledge, and clear enthusiasm for her husband's progressive (albeit pricey) cuisine.

Each contemporary dish is refined, balanced, and demonstrates an enormous attention to detail. The kitchen focuses on seasonal ingredients and coaxing flavor to profound levels. Morsels of sautéed black trumpet mushrooms are covered in thin slices of kohlrabi, then topped with a dollop of miso. Meals may reach their height of decadence with le boeuf, featuring a perfectly rosy slice of rib eye set beside two coins of braised and wonderfully juicy daikon.

Exquisite desserts include pear bavarois artfully crested with cassis jam and a frozen flower of grape sorbet. A bowl of chocolate rice pearls in passion fruit pulp is at once attractive and addictive.

■ 201 S. California Ave. (at Park Blvd.), Palo Alto
☎ (650) 328-8899 — **WEB:** www.maisonbaume.com
■ Lunch Thu – Sat   Dinner Wed – Sat   **PRICE: $$$$**

BIRD DOG 🍴○
Contemporary

XX | 🍸 ♿ 🖨️   **MAP:** A4

Anyone on the hunt for a happening scene in Palo Alto should follow the scent to Bird Dog, where the décor is sleek, the cocktails flow freely, and the diners sport head-to-toe designer duds. Boisterous and social, this is the kind of place where air kisses fly easily from the lips of Silicon Valley types who've scored must-have reservations. If you're hoping for a quiet meal, this is not your spot.

The food is as ambitious as the yuppie crowd, and while it may misstep here and there, it gets points for a modern approach. Delicious options include an exquisitely conceived tai crudo with chopped pecans and aji amarillo; green curry-breaded chicken thighs served over uni mousse; and finally, a chocolate crémeux enriched by ginger and white ale ice cream.

▓ 420 Ramona St. (bet. Lytton & University Aves.), Palo Alto
📞 (650) 656-8180 — **WEB:** www.birddogpa.com
▓ Lunch Mon –Fri   Dinner nightly   **PRICE:** $$

THE BYWATER 😊
Southern

X | ♿ 🏠 🛥️   **MAP:** D4

If dining at Manresa is like a weeklong stay at a luxury resort, this New Orleans-inspired little sib from Chef/owner David Kinch is more like a weekend of partying in the Big Easy. With its zinc bar, pressed ceilings, and open kitchen stacked with bottles of Crystal hot sauce, it might just fool you into thinking you're in Louisiana—right down to the zydeco and jazz playing on the stereo.

Reservations aren't accepted, so locals (some with kids in tow) line up early to get a taste of spicy, Andouille-flecked gumbo z'herbes, golden-brown hushpuppies, oyster po'boys, and other Cajun and Creole classics. For the finale, a luscious butterscotch pot de crème may sound less traditional, but rest assured that it tastes like heaven.

▓ 532 N. Santa Cruz Ave. (bet. Andrews St. & Roberts Rd.), Los Gatos
📞 (408) 560-9639 — **WEB:** www.thebywaterca.com
▓ Lunch & dinner Tue – Sun   **PRICE:** $$

CHEZ TJ ✿

Contemporary

XXX | ✿ ⌂

MAP: C2

Nestled into a charming 19th century Victorian in the heart of downtown Mountain View, Chez TJ likes to kick it old-school. After 35 years on the fine-dining scene, they know exactly what works: antique pictures and Venetian blown glass table lamps give the space a romantic feel, and the waitstaff is still formally suited.

This venerable restaurant has launched the career of many a culinary legend—the latest being the chef, Jarad Gallagher. He currently offers two menus: a ten-course seasonal option meant to highlight ingredients sourced from within 100 miles of the restaurant; and an extended chef's tasting menu (14+ courses) which explores international territory as well.

Dinner might begin with a delicately fried yuba skin beggar's purse, stuffed with plump Kumamoto oysters bobbing in spicy kimchi juice and served atop a porcelain soup spoon. Later, a delicate French onion soup, crowned with a Gruyère crostini and paired with homemade sourdough levain, makes its way to your table. Sashimi courses typically precede richer items, including a duo of veal, served beneath paper-thin shingles of turnip and slipped into a small crispy croquette set over sautéed Bloomsdale spinach.

938 Villa St. (bet. Bryant & Franklin Sts.), Mountain View
(650) 964-7466 — **WEB:** www.cheztj.com
Dinner Tue - Sat

PRICE: $$$$

DIN TAI FUNG 🍴○

Chinese

✗✗   MAP: D3

You'll need to wait (and wait, and wait) to get a taste of the much-coveted dumplings at the first Bay Area outpost of this acclaimed international chain, which has drawn crazy crowds to the Westfield Valley Fair mall since day one.

With only a handful of reservations taken a month in advance, expect to cool your heels for anywhere from 45 minutes to two hours. Is the wait worth it? Depends on how much you love xiao long bao, the Shanghai-style soup dumplings that are offered here in outstanding pork-crab and utterly decadent black truffle variations. Bring a crew so you can sample the non-dumpling offerings as well: delectably spicy wontons, top-flight barbecue pork buns, springy house-made noodles, and lightly sweetened black sesame buns for dessert.

▨ 2855 Stevens Creek Blvd. (bet. Monroe St. & Winchester Blvd.), Santa Clara
℘ (408) 248-1688 — **WEB:** www.dintaifungusa.com
▨ Lunch & dinner daily   PRICE: $$

DIO DEKA 🍴○

Greek

✗✗ | 🕸 ♿ 🏠 🖵 🗒   MAP: D4

Dio Deka may specialize in Greek food, but this is no typical taverna, as the stylish dining room (complete with a roaring fireplace) ably demonstrates. A wealthy, well-dressed Los Gatos crowd flocks to the front patio on warm evenings, dining and people-watching within the vine-covered walls of the Hotel Los Gatos. The bar also draws a brace of cheery regulars.

Skip the dull mesquite-grilled steaks and keep your order Greek: think stuffed grape leaves with tender braised beef cheek, or a bright pan-seared local salmon with roasted yellow peppers, potatoes, and artichokes. The adventurous shouldn't miss out on the fun offering of Greek wines, and sweet buffs should allow space for the crema me meli, a fantastic burnt-honey mousse with almond and lemon.

▨ 210 E. Main St. (bet. Jackson St. & Villa Ave.), Los Gatos
℘ (408) 354-7700 — **WEB:** www.diodeka.com
▨ Dinner nightly   PRICE: $$$

DISHDASH ⭐

Middle Eastern

XX | ♿ 🏠

MAP: C2

Dining on the run is certainly possible at this Mid-East gem on historic Murphy Avenue—just ask the techies who rush in to take food back to their desks. Families and groups congregate in the colorful dining room; and even though the space has expanded to include five outposts, you might want to linger in the front sidewalk patio— all the better to people-watch while savoring a bright, tangy tabbouleh, tender-crisp falafel, or baba ghanoush topped with black olives and roasted garlic cloves.

Served on griddled bread and enriched with a garlicky yogurt-parsley sauce, wraps like the incredibly smoky and juicy chicken shawarma are full-flavored and downright memorable. For dessert, go for the m'halabieh, a creamy and fragrant rosewater-and-pistachio pudding.

■ 190 S. Murphy Ave. (bet. Evelyn & Washington Aves.), Sunnyvale
☏ (408) 774-1889 — **WEB:** www.dishdash.com
■ Lunch & dinner Mon – Sat

PRICE: $$

EVVIA ⭐

Greek

XX | ♿ 🖐

MAP: A4

Inviting with its rustic wood beams, hanging copper pots, and roaring wood-burning fireplace, this central Palo Alto spot is a draw for Maserati-driving tech billionaires by day and couples in the evening. Dress to impress here, where the scene dictates high prices (though lunch features lighter dishes and more palatable pricing).

Much of the menu emerges from the wood-fired grill, including smoky, tender artichoke and eggplant skewers drizzled in olive oil and paired with garlicky Greek yogurt. The rustic, impossibly moist lamb souvlaki is nicely contrasted by a refreshing tomato, cucumber, and red onion salad. For dessert, pumpkin cheesecake is subtle, sweet, and accented with syrup-poached chunks of pumpkin.

■ 420 Emerson St. (bet. Lytton & University Aves.), Palo Alto
☏ (650) 326-0983 — **WEB:** www.evvia.net
■ Lunch Mon – Fri   Dinner nightly

PRICE: $$$

FALAFEL STOP ｮ◯

Israeli

✗ | 🏠   **MAP:** C3

It's little more than a bungalow with some picnic tables out front, but true falafel aficionados know that looks can be deceiving—and that Falafel STOP serves the most appetizing made-to-order falafel in town. It doesn't hurt that the accompaniments are also stellar: the hummus is insanely creamy and supremely smooth, with a hefty dose of nutty tahini, and the rounds of fresh-baked pita, served warm, are as fluffy as clouds. As an added bonus, prices and portions are both generous.

You'll want to choose your line before you order (those seeking a shawarma plate should get into the designated Grill STOP line). Then grab your food, seat yourself at a picnic table—they're tented in the winter months—and enjoy a transportive taste of the Middle East.

▓ 1325 Sunnyvale Saratoga Rd. (at Fremont Ave.), Sunnyvale
☏ (408) 735-7182 — **WEB:** www.falafelstop.biz
▓ Lunch & dinner daily   **PRICE:** ⊝

JANG SU JANG ｮ◯

Korean

✗✗ | ⌯ 🖵   **MAP:** D2

Smoky Korean barbecue, luscious soft tofu stews, and enormous seafood pancakes are among the standards at this Santa Clara classic and Koreatown jewel. Its strip-mall façade may not seem enticing, but the interior is classier than expected, thanks to granite tables equipped with grill tops and ventilation hoods, and a glass-enclosed exhibition kitchen located in the back.

This is fiery-flavored cuisine for gourmands who can stand the heat. A heavy-handed dose of kimchi flavors soft beef and pork dumplings, while the fierce red chili paste that slicks garlicky slices of marinated pork may actually cook the meat in daeji bulgogi. Cool down with mul naeng myun, a cold beef broth with tender, nutty buckwheat noodles, and a pot of bori cha.

▓ 3561 El Camino Real, Ste.10 (bet. Flora Vista Ave.
& Lawrence Expwy.), Santa Clara
☏ (408) 246-1212 — **WEB:** www.jangsujang.com
▓ Lunch & dinner daily   **PRICE:** $$

LAU HAI SAN ¥🍴

Vietnamese

✗

MAP: E3

Most Westerners don't think of hot pot when they're craving Vietnamese food, but it's actually a traditional favorite well worth sampling—and the proof is in this sunny spot. The overstuffed menu boasts 20 different variations on the theme, including a spicy seafood version with shrimp, mussels, squid, fish balls stuffed with salmon roe, and other aquatic delights. Dip them into the sour, tangy broth; twirl them with noodles; garnish with herbs—the choice is yours.

If hot pot isn't adventurous enough, bring a group to sample delicacies like chewy, flavorful curried coconut snails and crispy fried pork intestine. The diner-like space and strip-mall setting are nothing special, but the hot pot is so outstanding that lines are to be expected.

⬜ 2597 Senter Rd. (bet. Feldspar Dr. & Umbarger Rd.), San Jose
☎ (408) 938-0650 — **WEB:** N/A
⬜ Lunch & dinner Thu – Tue

PRICE: $$

NASCHMARKT ¥🍴

Austrian

✗✗ | ♿ 🏭

MAP: D3

A slice of Vienna in downtown Campbell, Naschmarkt scores high marks for its authentic flavors, inviting space, and friendly service. The cozy, brick-walled dining room is a favorite among couples, and solo diners will have a ball at the wraparound counter, which has a great view of the busy open kitchen.

Most of the menu is traditional: think bratwurst, kraut rouladen, and weiner schnitzel. The pan-roasted chicken breast, moist and juicy with a golden-brown seared crust, is served over a "napkin dumpling" made with compressed bread, tomato, and herbs. But, rest easy as there are a few items that have lighter Californian twists, like spätzle made with quark (a fresh white cheese) and tossed with smoked chicken, yellow corn, English peas, and wild mushrooms.

⬜ 384 E. Campbell Ave. (bet. Central & Railway Aves.), Campbell
☎ (408) 378-0335 — **WEB:** www.naschmarkt-restaurant.com
⬜ Dinner Tue – Sun

PRICE: $$

MANRESA ✤✤✤

Contemporary

XxX | 🍸 🍷 ♿ 🚪   **MAP:** D4

It may have a reputation for being one of the Bay Area's more intense restaurants, and yet Manresa is welcoming, distinctively stylish, and extraordinarily hospitable for a fine-dining operation. Sure, you might be seated next to a tech billionaire or celebrity chef, but there will be little fuss as everyone relaxes into a superb meal.

Chef David Kinch's nightly compositions are unknown until they arrive on the table (a souvenir copy of the menu will be handed to you at the end). The food is at once cerebral and luxurious, approachable and thoroughly delicious. Each course is likely to represent a moment within a season, beginning with savory petit fours that are an illusory play on the palate. Sample red-pepper pâtes de fruits, black olive madeleines, or green-garlic panisse with Meyer lemon curd and tahini. Chicken consommé containing buttery slices of local abalone is a surprising, clever, and cohesive dish, featuring sweet and earthy Okinawa black sugar dumplings, woodsy black truffle, roasted squash and allium blossoms.

Memorable desserts may include pumpkin purée with chocolate crémeux as well as sherry vinegar. Don't miss those excellent sea salt-caramels offered on your way out.

▧ 320 Village Ln. (bet. Santa Cruz & University Aves.), Los Gatos

✆ (408) 354-4330 — **WEB:** www.manresarestaurant.com

▧ Dinner Wed – Sun   **PRICE: $$$$**

NICK'S NEXT DOOR 🍴

American

✕✕ | 🍸 ⛄ 🏠

Though it originally opened as the sibling to Chef Difu's Nick's on Main, Nick's Next Door is now his sole restaurant—even more confusing given that it's actually across the street from his original spot and hidden behind a patio, in the shadow of a towering redwood tree. One fact is evident, though: the crowd here has ritzy tastes, often flocking in from the high-end cigar shop located merely steps away.

Upscale American bistro cooking is the focus, with such first-rate specialties as pan-fried abalone served with soft risotto and crispy Brussels sprouts, as well as meatloaf with potatoes and wild mushroom gravy. Whether you dine in the cozy and elegant dining room with its black-and-gray motif or outdoors, you'll receive a warm welcome—often from Nick himself.

■ 11 College Ave. (at Main St.), Los Gatos
☎ (408) 402-5053 — **WEB:** www.nicksnextdoor.com
■ Lunch & dinner Tue – Sat   PRICE: $$

ORCHARD CITY KITCHEN 😊

International

✕✕ | 🍸 ⛄ 🏠 🥢

Jeffrey Stout is at the helm of this international small-plates spot, which has been getting a level of buzz that radiates far beyond its humble shopping-center environs. Polished yet casual with a big front bar and patio, a meal here is best enjoyed with a group—so come prepared to max out the menu.

Kick things off with a cocktail, then get ready to savor a dizzying array of great dishes, including grilled artisanal bread spread with ricotta cheese and a mélange of wild mushrooms beneath a silky slow-poached egg. Then, slices of firm and fresh hamachi sashimi are arranged with shaved radishes and fuyu persimmon, finely diced avocado and a truffled ponzu sauce. Finally, toasted coconut takes rich butterscotch pot de crème to new heights.

■ 1875 S Bascom Ave., Ste. 190 (off Campisi Way), Campbell
☎ (408) 340-5285 — **WEB:** www.orchardcitykitchen.com
■ Lunch & dinner daily   PRICE: $$

ORENCHI ⅋○

Japanese

✗ | ♿   **MAP:** D3

Whether at lunch or dinner, this ramen specialist is known for its lines of waiting diners that curl like noodles outside its door. Even those who arrive before they open may face a long wait, so don't come if you're in a rush. Once inside, you'll be seated at a simple wood table or at the bar, collaged with Polaroid portraits of guests savoring their ramen.

The reason for the wait becomes clear when you're presented with a rich and utterly delicious bowl of tonkotsu ramen full of chewy noodles, roasted pork, and scallions. Shoyu ramen is equally delish, but make a point to show up early if you want to try the tsukemen (dipping noodles) as there is a limited number of servings available daily.

Orenchi Beyond is an equally busy younger sib in SF.

▮ 3540 Homestead Rd. (near Lawrence Expy.), Santa Clara
☏ (408) 246-2955 — **WEB:** www.orenchi-ramen.com
▮ Lunch & dinner daily   PRICE: 🍤

SAWA SUSHI ⅋○

Japanese

✗ | ♿   **MAP:** D3

Strict rules and big rewards unite at this zany, unusual and randomly located (in a mall) dive, where Chef Steve Sawa rules the roost. After going through the rigmarole of landing a reservation for his omakase-only affair, throw all caution to the wind and just go with the flow. Yes, the décor is nothing special; however, the food is anything but so-so, and the ad hoc prices are quite high.

So what draws such a host of regulars? Their pristine and very sublime fish, of course—from creamy Hokkaido sea scallops to delicious toro ribbons. Sawa is also an expert on sauces: imagine the likes of yuzu kosho topping kanpachi, or a sweet-spicy tamarind glaze on ocean trout. Accompany these with a top sake or cold beer and feel the joy seep in.

▮ 1042 E. El Camino Real (at Henderson Ave.), Sunnyvale
☏ (408) 241-7292 — **WEB:** www.sawasushi.net
▮ Dinner Mon – Sat   PRICE: $$$$

PLUMED HORSE ✿

Contemporary

XᵡX | 器 ᶜᴴ ⟷ ᵃ   **MAP:** C4

This cozy bungalow's small-town setting almost seems at odds with the luxury cars regularly parked out front. Tech money infuses the well-to-do suburb, making this a fine-dining favorite among locals. The surprisingly large interior features some specialized touches, like an iPad wine list and fiber-optic chandeliers, as a nod to the clientele. The vibe generally tilts towards classic luxury, thanks to the attentive staff and contemporary space with its enormous glass wine cellar and arched barrel ceiling.

The chef's table facing the kitchen has the best seats in the house—for those who reserve well in advance.

The fact that this kitchen showcases its own home-grown seasonal ingredients may not be entirely unique, but in the hands of such skilled cooks it translates into a noteworthy vegetarian tasting menu. More impressive is that they are equally adept with game meats, such as the supremely tender antelope loin served over farro and drizzled with tangy huckleberry sauce. Squab, with its beautifully lacquered skin and medium-rare meat, arrives with chive-flecked potato gnocchi and lightly fermented Brussels sprouts. For dessert, there may be no purer taste of chocolate than the Valrhona ganache.

▪ 14555 Big Basin Way (bet. 4th & 5th Sts.), Saratoga
℘ (408) 867-4711 — **WEB:** www.plumedhorse.com
▪ Dinner Mon – Sat   **PRICE:** $$$$

TAMARINE ⑪◯

Vietnamese

XX | 🍸 ♿ 🍽️   **MAP:** A4

Tamarine has long been a Palo Alto standby for its refined take on Vietnamese food that doesn't sacrifice authentic flavor. There's nearly always a corporate lunch happening in the private dining room, and techies, families, and couples alike fill the rest of its linen-topped tables.

Family-style sharing of dishes is encouraged, which is good because deciding on just one entrée is nearly impossible. To start, make like the regulars and order one of the "Tamarine Taste" appetizer platters with a round of tropical fruit-infused cocktails. Then move on to the fresh shrimp spring rolls, full of bean sprouts and mint; the springy ginger-chili seitan with steamed coconut rice; and curried long beans, sautéed with fragrant Makrut lime leaves and chili.

▓ 546 University Ave. (bet. Cowper & Webster Sts.), Palo Alto
✆ (650) 325-8500 — **WEB:** www.tamarinerestaurant.com
▓ Lunch Mon – Fri Dinner nightly   **PRICE: $$$**

THIÊN LONG ⑪◯

Vietnamese

X | ♿ 💵   **MAP:** F3

There are plenty of Vietnamese restaurants catering to the local expats in San Jose, but Thiên Long stands out for its pleasant dining room presenting delicious cooking—as the numerous families filling the large space will attest. Tile floors and rosewood-tinted chairs decorate the space, while walls hung with photos of Vietnamese dishes keep the focus on food.

Begin with sweet-salty barbecued prawns paired with smoky grilled pork and served atop rice noodles. But, it is really the pho with a broth of star anise, clove, and ginger, topped with perfectly rare beef that is a true gem—even the regular-sized portion is enormous. English is a challenge among the staff, but they are very friendly; plus the authentic flavors make up for any inadequacies.

▓ 3005 Silver Creek Rd., Ste.138 (bet. Aborn Rd. & Lexann Ave.), San Jose
✆ (408) 223-6188 — **WEB:** www.thienlongrestaurant.com
▓ Lunch & dinner daily   **PRICE:** 🍤

WALIA ⅋○

Ethiopian

✗ | ♿

MAP: D3

Authentic Ethiopian flavors are delivered without pretense at this easygoing, affordable restaurant, housed in a strip mall just off Bascom Avenue. Though the space is basic, the service is friendly and it's casual enough for kids in tow.

Start things off with an order of sambussas, fried dough triangles filled with lentil, onion, and chilies. Then choose from an all-meat, all-veggie, or mixed selection of tasty Ethiopian stews, like tibs firfir, featuring lamb in a garlicky berbere sauce dolloped on spongy injera. Vegetarians will particularly love dining here, as all of the plant-based options including alicha wot or split peas in turmeric sauce, shiro (spiced chickpeas), and gomen (wilted collard greens with onion and spices), are big winners.

▨ 2208 Business Cir. (at Bascom Ave.), San Jose
☏ (408) 645-5001 — **WEB:** www.waliaethiopian.com
▨ Lunch & dinner Wed – Mon   **PRICE:** ⌘

ZAREEN'S ⅋○

Indian

✗ | ♿

MAP: C2

Taking up residence just steps from the Googleplex, it's no surprise that this wholesome little South Asian restaurant is absolutely packed with tech employees seeking a taste of their homelands. But local families love Zareen's as well, perusing books from the lending library or doodling their heartfelt thanks on the wall. An added bonus: the space is set in a small shopping plaza with a big lot out front, making parking a non-issue.

The chicken Memoni samosas, supposedly made from a recipe known to only 23 grandmothers worldwide, are a must-order: crispy, well-spiced, and flavorful, they're so good they don't need chutney. Follow these with the outstanding chicken shami kababs, juicy and caramelized on their bed of fluffy basmati rice.

▨ 1477 Plymouth St. (off Shoreline Blvd.), Mountain View
☏ (650) 641-0335 — **WEB:** www.zareensrestaurant.com
▨ Lunch & dinner Tue – Sun   **PRICE:** ⌘

ZENI 🍴

Ethiopian

X | ♿   **MAP:** D3

From its home at the end of a shopping plaza, Zeni caters to expats, tech types, and families alike. The interior has a standard dining area decorated with colorful portraits and tapestries as well as traditional seating on low stools at woven tables. Either way, group dining is encouraged.

Relish the spongy, enticingly sour injera used to scoop up delicious yemisir wot (red lentils with spicy berbere); kik alitcha (yellow peas tinged with garlic and ginger); or beef kitfo (available raw or cooked) tossed with that aromatic spice blend, mitmita, and crowned by crumbled ayib cheese. Here, injera is your only utensil, but be assured as there's a sink in the back to tidy up. Balance the fiery food with cool honey wine, or opt for an after-dinner Ethiopian coffee.

▓ 1320 Saratoga Ave. (at Payne Ave.), San Jose
✆ (408) 615-8282 — **WEB:** www.zeniethiopianrestaurant.com
▓ Lunch & dinner Tue – Sun   **PRICE:** 💰

ZOLA 🍴

French

XX | ♿   **MAP:** A4

A Palo Alto sparkler, Zola charms its way into diners' hearts via a seductive French bistro menu with Californian flair. Whether you're spreading smoky salmon rillettes on toasted artisan levain, twirling pillowy caramelized ricotta gnocchi into the yolk of a soft-cooked egg in brown butter, or tucking into tender filet de boeuf with creamy sauce béarnaise and golden-brown fingerling potatoes, you're sure to fall hard for the food.

The stylish space updates a few classics (wood tables, bistro chairs, pressed ceilings) with a dark teal color scheme and enticingly low lighting, and the well-chosen wine list is equal parts Gallic and Golden State. Crème caramel for dessert may be traditional, but it's also perfectly executed and decadently rich.

▓ 565 Bryant St. (bet. Hamilton & University Aves.), Palo Alto
✆ (650) 521-0651 — **WEB:** www.zolapaloalto.com
▓ Dinner Tue – Sat   **PRICE:** $$

WINE COUNTRY

NAPA VALLEY

GRAPES GALORE

Revered as one of the most exalted wine growing regions in the world, Napa Valley is a 30 mile-long and luscious basin where wine is king. Given its grape-friendly climate and prime location (north from San Pablo Bay to Mount St. Helena, between the Mayacama and Vaca mountains), Napa ranks with California's most prestigious wineries. Here, powerfully hot summer days and cool nights provide the perfect environment for cabernet sauvignon grapes, a varietal for which the county is justifiably famous. But, it's not all about just *vino* here. Top chefs also have a buffet of exceptional ingredients to choose from, including a range of locally grown and pressed extra virgin olive oils. **The Brasswood Bakery**, a deli and culinary emporium, is primo for excursion essentials like market-driven salads, hearty sandwiches, flaky pastries, and so much more. Moving on to other savory spreads, culinary enthusiasts, cooks, and scientists make their annual expedition to the **Napa Truffle Festival**, a veritable shindig of all things earthy. Also on offer here are

cooking demos, seminars, and foraging. Among the region's many winemakers are names like **Robert Mondavi**, **Francis Ford Coppola**, and **Miljenko "Mike" Grgich**. Originally from Croatia, Grgich rose to fame as the winemaker at **Chateau Montelena** when his 1973 chardonnay took the top prize at the Judgment of Paris in 1976, outshining France's best white Burgundies. This triumph turned the wine world on its ear, and put California on the map as a bona fide producer. Since then, Napa's indisputable success with premium wines has fostered endless pride, country-wide. American Viticultural Areas (AVAs) currently regulate the boundaries for districts such as Calistoga, Stags Leap, Rutherford, and Los Carneros.

SPECIALTY FINDS

The Valley's wine-rich culture coupled with its illustrious restaurants that are destinations in themselves, make this region one of the world's most popular tourist attractions. Reclaimed

19th-century stone wineries and gorgeous Victorian homes punctuate the rolling landscape and serve as a constant reminder that there were some 140 wineries here prior to 1890. Up from a Prohibition-era low of perhaps a dozen, the area today boasts over 400 growers and producers. However, this is not to say that there aren't stellar alfresco dining spots and specialty stores situated along its picturesque streets. Gourmands never fail to make the trek to **Rancho Gordo**, headquartered here, for heirloom beans of the highest quality.

Serving as the main supplier to area chefs, it is also open to the public—who seem smitten by their divine selection. Looking for some inspiration? They can also instruct you on how best to cook them! Picnic supplies are the main draw at **Oakville Grocery**, the oldest operating store in town on Route 29; while **Model Bakery** in St. Helena or **Bouchon Bakery** in Yountville are wildly popular for fresh-baked breads and finger-licking pastries.

Napa's continued growth in wine production has spawned a special kind of food and wine tourism in this county,

and tasting rooms, tours, as well as farm-fresh cuisine are de rigueur here. **Olivier Napa Valley** is a quaint and historic retail shop in St. Helena that proffers oils, vinegars, and other local food products alongside beautiful handcrafted tableware and ceramics from Provence. Residents who aren't rejoicing over their wares may be found scouring the vendibles at **NapaStyle**, a lifestyle store from local celebrity chef, Michael Chiarello, that purveys everything from furniture and tabletop items, to kitchenware and pantry staples. Other megawatt personalities like Thomas Keller, Richard Reddington, Cindy Pawlcyn, and Philippe Jeanty also hail from around the way, and may be found rubbing elbows at the flagship location of gourmet grocer, **Dean & Deluca**.

SHOPPING TREATS

Visitors touring the Valley will spot fields of fennel, silvery olive trees, and rows of wild mustard that bloom between the grapevines in February and March. Mustard season kicks off each year with the **Napa Valley Mustard Festival** paying homage to the food, wine, art, and agricultural bounty of this region. Likewise, several towns host seasonal farmer's markets from May through October, including one in Napa (held near the **Oxbow Public Market** on Tuesdays and Saturdays); St. Helena (Fridays in Crane Park); and Calistoga (on Saturdays at Sharpsteen Museum Plaza on Washington Street). Launched in early 2008, the **Oxbow Public Market** is a block-long, 40,000-square-foot facility that is meant to rival the **Ferry Building Marketplace** that is housed across the Bay. Packed to the rafters with food artisans and wine vendors from within a 100-mile radius of the market, and cradled inside a barn-like building, Oxbow keeps fans returning for everything under the sun. Think cheese, charcuterie, and spices; or olive oils, organic ice cream, and specialty teas. Shoppers who work up an appetite while perusing these shelves can rest assured as there are numerous snacks also available to take home.

SIGHTS TO BEHOLD

Regional products such as **St. Helena Olive Oil** and **Woodhouse Chocolates** on Main Street, also in St. Helena, have similarly gained a large-scale nation-wide following. Three generations of one family run the latter, very charming chocolatier, which is most cherished for its handmade toffees. Just north of downtown St. Helena, the massive stone building that was erected in 1889 as Greystone Cellars, now inhabits the West Coast campus of the

renowned **Culinary Institute of America (CIA)**. Their intensive training and syllabus ensures a striking lineup of hot chefs in the making.

With all this going for the wine-rich valley, one thing is for certain—from the city of Napa (the county's largest population center) north to the town of Calistoga known for its mineral mud baths and clean, spa cuisine, this narrow yet noteworthy region is nothing less than pure nirvana for lovers of great food and fine wine.

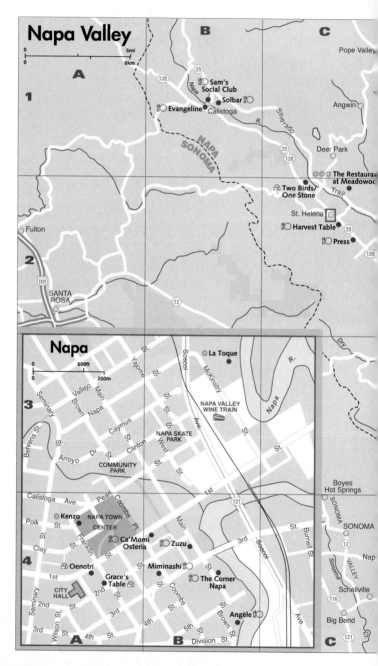

Napa Valley

0 — 5mi
0 — 8km

A

B

C

Pope Valley

128

29

○ Sam's
Social Club

Napa

Calistoga

Solbar ○

○ Evangeline

Silverado R.

Angwin ○

NAPA
SONOMA

29
128

Deer Park ○

※※※ The Restaura
at Meadowoc

Trail

St. Helena ○

○ Harvest Table

29

128

○ Press

Fulton ○

101

SANTA
ROSA

12

Dry

Napa

0 — 600ft
0 — 250m

※ La Toque

Sescol

McKinstry

Napa R.

3

Yajome
St.

Main St.

Vallejo St.

Brown St.

Seminary St.

Behrens St.

Napa St.

Caymus St.

Clinton St.

St.

St.

St.

Ave.

NAPA VALLEY
WINE TRAIN

NAPA SKATE
PARK

West St.

Dr.

Arroyo

COMMUNITY
PARK

St.

1st St.

Boyes
Hot Springs ○

Calistoga Ave.

Pearl St.

Coombs St.

121

SONOMA

SONOMA

※ Kenzo

NAPA TOWN
CENTER

Polk St.

Franklin St.

○ Ca'Momi
Osteria

○ Zuzu

Main St.

3rd St.

Sescol

Burnell St.

12

Clay St.

Sonoma

Nap

4

○ Oenotri

1st St.

St.

Miminashi ○

Grace's
Table ○

○ The Corner
Napa

VALLEY

Seminary St.

CITY
HALL

2nd St.

St.

Coombs St.

Brown St.

Ave.

116

Schellville ○

3rd St.

Wilson St.

St.

4th St.

5th St.

Angèle ○

Big Bend ○

121

A

B

Division St.

C

121

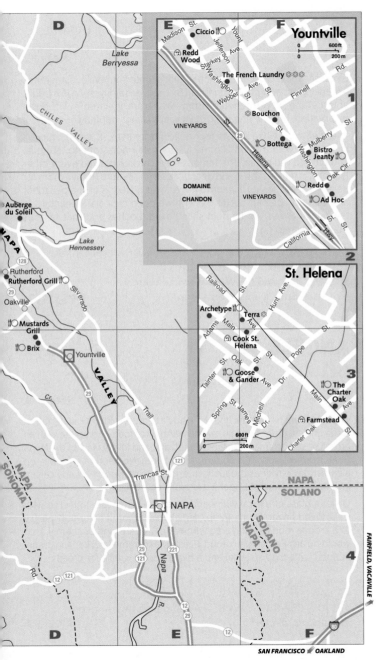

D

Lake
Berryessa

CHILES VALLEY

NAPA

Lake
Hennessey

(128)
Rutherford
Rutherford Grill ⁑◯
(29)
Oakville

⁑◯ **Mustards
Grill**

⁑◯ **Brix**

Silverado

⬜ Yountville

Cr.

(29)

VALLEY

Trail

(121)

Trancas St.

NAPA

(29)
(121)

(221)

Napa
R.

(12)
(25)

(12)

(121)

(12)

Rd.

**SONOMA
NAPA**

**NAPA
SONOMA**

**NAPA
SOLANO**

**SOLANO
NAPA**

Yountville
E   **F**

Madison St.
● **Ciccio** ⁑◯

Jefferson St.
Young St.
Starkey St.
Washington St.
Jefferson Ave.
Webber Ave.
Finnell Rd.

0   600ft
0   200m

⁑ **Redd
Wood**

The French Laundry ⚜⚜⚜

VINEYARDS

⚜ **Bouchon**

⁑◯ **Bottega**

Mulberry St.

**Bistro
Jeanty** ⁑◯

**DOMAINE

CHANDON**

VINEYARDS

Washington St.

Oak Cir.

⚜ **Redd**

⁑◯ **Ad Hoc**

Helena St.

California Hwy.

St.

1

2

St. Helena
Railroad St.

Hunt Ave.

⁑◯ **Archetype**

⚜ **Terra**

Adams St.

Main St.

St.

Pope St.

⚜ **Cook St.
Helena**

Tainter St.

Oak St.

Oak St.

Spring St.

St. James St.

Mitchell Dr.

⁑◯ **Goose
& Gander**

Main St.

⁑◯ **The
Charter
Oak**

Charter Oak Ave.

⚜ **Farmstead**

3

0   600ft
0   200m

4

⁑◯ **Auberge
du Soleil**

AD HOC ⑩

American

XX | ㄸ ㎓ ▨   **MAP:** F2

By far the most casual of Thomas Keller's three Yountville restaurants, Ad Hoc offers accessible American fare served family-style in a bright and inviting wood-paneled room. Waits are inevitable without a reservation, but the engaging staff keeps things hopping.

The breezy prix-fixe boasts four delicious courses (three at brunch), kicking off with a salad like the luscious heirloom tomato, arugula, and pickled red onion. The famous fried chicken, served every other Monday, is tender, spicy, and deeply flavorful. Be sure to save room for dessert, because you'll want to linger over a wedge of the decadent and custardy peanut butter pie with whipped chocolate Chantilly. In the back garden, Addendum sells boxed lunches and that famous fried chicken to go.

▦ 6476 Washington St. (bet. California Dr. & Oak Circle), Yountville
✆ (707) 944-2487 — **WEB:** www.adhocrestaurant.com
▦ Lunch Sun   Dinner Thu – Mon   **PRICE:** $$$

ANGÈLE ⑩

French

XX | ㄸ ㎓   **MAP:** B4

This airy French charmer, housed inside a century-old brick warehouse, is the perfect place to while away a warm afternoon—complete with an attentive staff, a chic Edith Piaf soundtrack, and lovely view of the Napa River from the spacious outdoor dining area. No need to shy away on a cooler day either as the rustic interior, with its wood A-frame ceiling and polished concrete floors, is equally compelling.

Order a glass of a local white and savor the bistro fare inflected with Californian flavor, from plump, garlicky escargot in flaky puff pastry to a croque monsieur, layered with ham, Gruyère, and béchamel, that would do any Frenchman proud. Finish with caramelized banana gratin, heaped with crisp streusel and a big scoop of vanilla ice cream.

▦ 540 Main St. (at 5th St.), Napa
✆ (707) 252-8115 — **WEB:** www.angelerestaurant.com
▦ Lunch & dinner daily   **PRICE:** $$

ARCHETYPE ⅋○

American

✗✗ | 🔥 🛏 🍴

MAP: E2

Even by the standards of luxuriously appointed Napa Valley restaurants, Archetype is quite the looker. Blending farmhouse comfort with luxurious modern touches, it's just as glamorous for an evening meal by the fireplace as it is for brunch on the covered, screened-in patio, strewn with climbing yellow rose bushes.

During the day, the menu focuses on comfort food like velvety artichoke soup with parmesan foam and flaky cheddar biscuits with sausage gravy. At night, things get more ambitious, with such satisfying plates as oak-grilled duck breast with scallion pancakes and gochujang; or curry-braised red snapper with crab dumplings. There are also plenty of fun theme nights for locals—from fish taco Thursdays to Sunday fried chicken and waffle nights.

🔲 1429 Main St. (bet. Adams & Pine Sts.), St. Helena
🔗 (707) 968-9200 — **WEB:** www.archetypenapa.com
🔲 Lunch & dinner Wed - Sun   **PRICE:** $$

BISTRO JEANTY ⅋○

French

✗✗ | 🔥 🛏

MAP: F1

Napa transforms into the French countryside via a meal at Bistro Jeanty, which serves rib-sticking favorites like coq au vin, boeuf Bourguignon, and a sinfully rich milk-fed veal chop with chanterelle mushrooms and Camembert sauce. But California's lighter side is here, too: a salad of silken smoked trout and frisée is garden-fresh, and daily specials highlight the best in local produce.

The classic bistro accoutrements (yellow walls, wooden tables, framed retro posters) are present and accounted for, but there's an element of quirky fun here as well—from the flower-bedecked bicycle out front to the porcelain hens and hogs that dot the dining room. Like the flaky, caramelized, and unmissable tarte Tatin, this is a gorgeous update on a classic.

🔲 6510 Washington St. (at Mulberry St.), Yountville
🔗 (707) 944-0103 — **WEB:** www.bistrojeanty.com
🔲 Lunch & dinner daily   **PRICE:** $$

AUBERGE DU SOLEIL ⍟

Californian

XxX | 🕸 🕴 🍴 🍽 🛋 🥂 🍷

MAP: D2

This is one of the first restaurants to elevate the Napa Valley to greatness. For the past decade, Chef Robert Curry has been ensuring its legacy with cooking that is the very definition of California cuisine: global flavors expressed through local, seasonal, and fresh ingredients. The kitchen's work is as impressive as the setting. Everything seems just a bit more beautiful from this extraordinary perch, overlooking the vineyards, mountains, and gardens. Those terrace tables have some of the best views in northern California.

Meals may be inspired by the comforting fall flavors of rosemary-enriched chicken jus, root vegetable purée, and intensely salty-sweet pancetta to complement a fillet of red snapper. Medallions of bacon-wrapped veal are cooked to a uniform blush, served alongside gnocchi interspersed with pearl onions and balsamic-braised radicchio for refreshing bitterness. For dessert, a buttery lemon cake is topped with faintly pine-scented ice cream, deep purple huckleberries, and lemon meringue.

Service is stylish, polite, and manages to refill your glass after each sip, without seeming intrusive. Their wine list is one of the most notable in the valley and proudly showcases local growers.

▦ 180 Rutherford Hill Rd. (off the Silverado Trail), Rutherford
✆ (707) 963-1211 — **WEB:** www.aubergedusoleil.com
▦ Lunch & dinner daily

PRICE: $$$$

BOTTEGA ¶○

Italian

✕✕ | ☖ ☖ ☖   **MAP:** F1

Michael Chiarello is one of the original celebrity chefs, and his higher-end Napa outpost draws fans from around the globe seeking a glimpse of the NapaStyle star. Hopefuls are indeed likely to see him in the kitchen, drizzling olive oil on plates of creamy, almost liquid fresh burrata and marinated mushrooms; or pouring persimmon purée across thick slices of yellowfin tuna crudo. Even the wine list features his house blends, which pair nicely with pastas like whole-wheat tagliarini tossed in a pitch-perfect Bolognese.

Large and boisterous, Bottega's autumn-hued dining room welcomes crowds with comfy banquettes; find lovely outdoor seating by the firepit. A well-made tiramisu and espresso offer a fine Italiano end to the festivities.

▦ 6525 Washington St. (near Yount St.), Yountville
☏ (707) 945-1050 — **WEB:** www.botteganapavalley.com
▦ Lunch Tue – Sun   Dinner nightly   **PRICE:** $$

BRIX ¶○

Californian

✕✕ | ☖ ☖ ☖ ☖ ☖   **MAP:** D3

This roadside treat overlooking the Mayacamas Mountains is almost as lauded for its 16-acre produce garden (which also provides many of the ingredients seen on your plate) and vineyard, as it is for its ultra-seasonal and eclectic-Californian cuisine. Dishes are wide-ranging and often refined as verified in ricotta gnocchi cooked to a gentle gold in rosemary-browned butter with creamy squash, plump Medjool dates, and almonds; or saffron and orange salmon that arrives firm and pink with quail eggs, dill aïoli, and potato salad. An extensive Sunday brunch buffet highlights offerings from the wood-fired oven and charcoal grill.

The interior feels like a mountain ranch with its stone walls, fireplaces, and chandeliers cleverly crafted from cutlery. Service is exceptional.

▦ 7377 St. Helena Hwy. (at Washington St.), Napa
☏ (707) 944-2749 — **WEB:** www.brix.com
▦ Lunch & dinner daily   **PRICE:** $$$

BOUCHON ❀

French

XX | ♿ 🏠 🛋

Timeless French food is recreated with great regard for quality and technique at Thomas Keller's exuberant brasserie, set down the street from his iconic The French Laundry. Complete with lush potted plants, shimmering brass accents, and enormous mirrors, this chic dining room is the spitting image of a Parisian bistro. A theatrical crowd uplifts the space with conviviality, and every lavish banquette or stool at the bustling bar is full. Always.

Thanks to the house bakery next door, the bread here is ace, so grab an extra hunk of the supremely fresh and crusty pain d'epi to slather with butter. The menu lists well-executed classics, including a rosy foie gras torchon with seasonal orange preserves and golden-brown toasted brioche. And thanks to the attentive staff, you may even get a second slice. Then, braised lamb demonstrates the power of rustic French cooking, set over polenta with grilled young leeks and carrots.

Desserts are quite literally the icing on the cake and often the very definition of decadence. Even the humble pie is elevated here, to be served as an almond-spiced pear, glazed with juice, and set over a tiny round of puff pastry matched with rich vanilla ice cream.

▧ 6534 Washington St. (at Yount St.), Yountville
✆ (707) 944-8037 — **WEB:** www.thomaskeller.com
▧ Lunch & dinner daily   PRICE: $$$

CA'MOMI OSTERIA 🍴

Italian

✕✕ | ♿ ⬚

A spinoff of the beloved Ca'Momi Enoteca kiosk in the nearby Oxbow Public Market, this stand-alone spot aims to promote buon gusto with its "heartcrafted" food (as indicated in a sign above the bar). Big and airy, with exposed brick and wooden beams, it is abuzz with pizzaiolos turning out Neapolitan pies from the wood-burning oven (note that the counter opposite the fire is the best seat in the house).

The massive menu is inspired by every region of Italy featuring crispy Piemontese sunchoke chips dusted with salt and fried parsley as well as Tuscan spinach-ricotta gnudi in creamy butter-and-sage sauce. There are also a variety of outstanding pizzas and the Campanian angioletti or fried pizza dough with hazelnut and chocolate, makes for a sinfully delicious finish.

▪ 1141 1st St. (bet. Coombs & Main Sts.), Napa
✆ (707) 224-6664 — **WEB:** www.camomiosteria.com
▪ Lunch Fri – Sun   Dinner Tue – Sun   **PRICE: $$**

THE CHARTER OAK 🍴

Californian

✕✕✕ | 🍸 🍹 ♿ ⛱ ⬚ 🥢   **MAP:** F3

Courtesy of The Restaurant at Meadowood team, this approachable retreat presents a rustic method to dining that centers on hearth-roasted fare. The beautifully restored room's design and large tables seem to promote sharing platters of roasted beef ribs or broccolini. And that hearth is indeed the heart of this kitchen, requiring intricate skill in cooking those same high quality ingredients from area farms and purveyors as found at Meadowood. Undoubtedly, the straightforward appearance of some of these dishes belie the work that went into their careful preparation. Keep this in mind when delving into roasted avocado with shaved rhubarb and ember oil.

The Charter Oak may be new, but its unique food is surely on the verge of becoming even more remarkable.

▪ 1050 Charter Oak Ave. (off St. Helena Hwy.), St. Helena
✆ (707) 302-6996 — **WEB:** www.thecharteroak.com
▪ Lunch & dinner daily   **PRICE: $$$**

CICCIO ™○

Italian

✗✗

MAP: E1

A pleasant contrast to the sleek new spots around town, Ciccio's country-style curtains and slatted front porch are a ticket to another era. Its location (a wood-framed 1916-era grocery) could pass as some John Wayne film set, but Ciccio is more of a spaghetti Western, thanks to the focused Italian-influenced menu featuring a mega-rich pasta accented with fresh uni, crisp breadcrumbs, and a generous dose of cream. Segue from carbs to the bone-in pork chop with fennel gratin, but don't miss the remarkable signature Ciccio sponge cake, soaked in citrus liqueur and topped with grapefruit and orange.

With turn-of-the-century square footage, tables are a hot ticket here. Expect a wait for even a lowly bar stool, happily passed with a glass of local pinot.

▓ 6770 Washington St. (bet. Madison & Pedroni Sts.), Yountville
✆ (707) 945-1000 — **WEB:** www.ciccionapavalley.com
▓ Dinner Wed – Sun

PRICE: $$

COOK ST. HELENA ☺

Italian

✗✗

MAP: F3

An artistically lit antelope head hangs in this Italian haven on St. Helena's main drag. Random? Not really, when one considers how rare solid cooking and sane prices can be in this tony burg. The cozy space has two seating options: a gleaming marble counter as well as tables that stretch from front to back (the ones up front are lighter, airier, and more preferable).

The food is thoughtful and refined with a daily rotating risotto, house-stretched mozzarella and burrata, and glorious pastas like ricotta fazoletti with a deeply flavored Bolognese. Grilled octopus salad with potatoes, olives, and tomato dressing is boosted by prime ingredients and careful seasoning. The wine list tempts at dinner, but bloody Marys are all the rage at brunch, served at Cook Tavern next door.

▓ 1310 Main St. (bet. Adams St. & Hunt Ave.), St. Helena
✆ (707) 963-7088 — **WEB:** www.cooksthelena.com
▓ Lunch Mon – Sat Dinner nightly

PRICE: $$

THE CORNER NAPA ⅋○

American

✕✕ | 🍸 🍹 ♿ 🏠 🖥 🛋

MAP: B4

With a library of 4,500 bottles, wine aficionados are sure to find something to love at this eco-chic retreat on the Napa River. And if they don't, there's also a terrific cocktail carte, featuring a similarly massive selection of whiskey and tequila. The modern, sleek décor is raw around the edges, with wood- and concrete-topped tables dotting the space.

Given the array of fine beverages, you'll want something good to eat. And with its wide-ranging menu that hits points both creative (sturgeon and avocado mousse with "everything"-spiced lavash) and comforting (a bone-in pork chop with roasted root vegetables), The Corner doesn't disappoint. Even the kitchen staff is here for a good time: for an extra $5, diners can ply them with a round of beers.

🔳 660 Main St. (bet. 3rd & 5th Sts.), Napa
📞 (707) 927-5552 — **WEB:** www.cornerbarnapa.com
🔳 Lunch Thu – Sun Dinner Tue – Sun   PRICE: $$

EVANGELINE ⅋○

American

✕✕ | ♿ 🏠 🛋

MAP: B1

Jazzy New Orleans flair infuses every inch of this Southern charmer, which adds just a hint of spice to the easy Californian charm of quaint Calistoga. A trellised garden patio (a must-visit on a warm day) blooms with fragrant jasmine, while the cozy indoor dining room provides an intimate retreat complete with midnight-blue banquettes.

A collection of French bistro- Californian- and Cajun-inspired dishes abound on the approachable menu. Rich, creamy duck rillettes arrive with toasted baguette and red pepper jelly; shrimp etouffee is spicy and complex, its thick, dark roux coating a heap of fluffy white rice; and melt-in-your-mouth tarte Tatin slathered with locally made Three Twins vanilla ice cream is as good as any beignet.

🔳 1226 Washington St. (bet. 1st St. & Lincoln Ave.), Calistoga
📞 (707) 341-3131 — **WEB:** www.evangelinenapa.com
🔳 Lunch Sat – Sun   Dinner nightly   PRICE: $$

WINE COUNTRY ▶ NAPA VALLEY

FARMSTEAD 🐷

Californian

✗✗ | ♿ 🏠 ⬛

For a down-home (but still Napa-chic) alternative to the Cal-Ital wine country grind, follow your nose to this Long Meadow Ranch-owned farmhouse, whose intoxicating smoker is parked right in the front yard. The cathedral ceiling, old-school country music, and boisterous locals give Farmstead a permanent buzz; for quieter dining, hit the front terrace.

Dishes are laden with ranch-grown products (from veggies to olive oil), utilized in outstanding preparations like a wood-grilled artichoke with sauce gribiche, meatballs with caramelized onions and tomato marmalade, or a smoked chicken sandwich with avocado, sweet onion rings, and a side of herb-fried potatoes. Try the ranch's own wine, or splurge on a fancy bottle at a shockingly reasonable markup.

🔲 738 Main St. (at Charter Oak Ave.), St. Helena
☎ (707) 963-9181 — **WEB:** www.longmeadowranch.com
🔲 Lunch & dinner daily   **PRICE:** $$

GOOSE & GANDER 🍴

American

✗✗ | 🍸 🏠 ⬛

With its mountain-lodge feel, this clubby retreat has been a favorite among Napa Valley diners since its bygone days as the Martini House. Those classic libations may have long since made way for elaborate concoctions from acclaimed mixologist Scott Beattie, but this gander retains all the charm of the goose—as well as the recipe for its justly famous mushroom soup, which could win over even the staunchest foe of fungi.

Elsewhere on the menu, you'll find hearty dishes like fettuccini carbonara, a bone marrow-topped burger, and fried chicken sandwich with charred jalapeño aïoli as well as duck-fat fries. Whether you're soaking up summer on the spacious patio or relaxing by the fireplace in the cavernous downstairs bar, you'll quickly feel at home here.

🔲 1245 Spring St. (at Oak Ave.), St. Helena
☎ (707) 967-8779 — **WEB:** www.goosegander.com
🔲 Lunch & dinner daily   **PRICE:** $$

THE FRENCH LAUNDRY ✿✿✿

Contemporary

XxxX | 🐝 ♿ ⬚

MAP: E1

Over 20 years old and topping every foodie's bucket list, Thomas Keller's legendary destination still doesn't miss a beat. The cuisine, staff, and a remodeled, state-of-the-art kitchen embedded with the chef's renowned sense of purpose and functionality continue to remain at their height. In fact this may be known as the greatest cooking space in America as every aspect of the setting is carefully determined—from the counter height to the flowing lines in the ceiling. It's a meeting point of the past, present, and future.

Chef Keller continues to pair incredibly classic French techniques with wildly fresh ingredients in a setting that is a perfect storm of restaurant greatness—we should all be so lucky to score a reservation here in our lifetime. Choose from two seasonal tasting menus, including a vegetarian option. Both feature products from boutique purveyors. Dinners may highlight signature oysters paired with white sturgeon caviar in a warm sabayon studded with tapioca pearls or golden striped bass with deconstructed deviled eggs.

Located along a shady, winding road, it is the very picture of bucolic charm, with ivy creeping up its stone exterior and a homey dining room with elegant everything.

▦ 6640 Washington St. (at Creek St.), Yountville
✆ (707) 944-2380 — **WEB:** www.thomaskeller.com
▦ Lunch Fri – Sun   Dinner nightly   **PRICE: $$$$**

GRACE'S TABLE 🐶
International

✖✖ | ⓩ 🍽 🗞

Around the world in four courses without leaving wine country? It's possible at this bright, contemporary downtown Napa space that balances fun with excellence. Only here can a top-notch tamale filled with chipotle pulled pork, green chile, and black beans be followed by cassoulet that would do any Frenchman proud—thanks to its decadent mélange of butter beans, duck confit, and two kinds of sausage.

With Italian and American staples in the mix as well, it might sound too eclectic for one meal, but Grace's Table earns its name with charming service and a thoughtful, well-priced wine list to bridge any gaps between cuisines. Don't miss the satiny, ganache-layered devil's food chocolate cake—a slice is big enough to split, and a winner in any tongue.

▨ 1400 2nd St. (at Franklin St.), Napa
℘ (707) 226-6200 — **WEB:** www.gracestable.net
▨ Lunch & dinner daily

PRICE: $$

HARVEST TABLE 🍴
Californian

✖✖ | ⓩ 🏠 🗞 🗏

Charlie Palmer's Harvest Inn is a culinary destination thanks to the thriving presence of Harvest Table. Its Californian menu relies on local purveyors and the Inn's own gardens for ingredients. Guests are encouraged to tour these grounds before or after meals. The space is simple and appealingly rustic thanks in part to the large fireplace. Two covered patios offer a comfy perch to enjoy the natural beauty of the inn.

Dark wood tables can be seen groaning under the weight of such enjoyable items as smoked Mt. Lassen trout with Meyer lemon gel. Scallops are then set atop savory cauliflower florets and sweet red grapes for a delightful balance in flavors; while a tropical fruit panna cotta with mango and roasted cashew praline should be relished at the end.

▨ 1 Main St. (bet. Lewelling Ln. & Sulphur Springs Ave.), St. Helena
℘ (707) 967-4695 — **WEB:** www.harvesttablenapa.com
▨ Lunch Wed – Sun   Dinner Tue – Sun

PRICE: $$$

KENZO ⌘

Japanese

XX | 🍷 ⚕ 🖭

MAP: A4

Kenzo Tsujimoto made his fortune developing thrilling video games like *Resident Evil* and *Street Fighter*, but his Napa temple of traditional Japanese cuisine is a place to hit pause and wash away worldly cares. Designed by Tsujimoto's wife Natsuko, this 25-seat arena is spare and minimal, incorporating traditional woods, maple trees, and river rocks to create a peaceful sanctuary.

Though Kenzo offers a handful of tables, the best seats are at the lengthy counter, where diners can chat with the chefs and see their sushi made firsthand. Two menus are offered under the guidance of acclaimed chef, Hiroyuki Kanda: one exclusively spotlights elegant kaiseki dishes like sea urchin chawanmushi and poached blue shrimp with asparagus, while the other also integrates a dozen pieces of nigiri, sourced directly from Tokyo's famed Tsukiji Fish Market. Exceptional servers thoughtfully explain more unusual dishes like shinjo, a gently poached dumpling made from egg whites and chopped scallops that is served in a delicate dashi.

There is an outstanding variety of sake showcased here, but adventurous diners may want to sample Kenzo's own California-grown estate wines, which are available by the flight.

🔳 1339 Pearl St. (at Franklin St.), Napa
📞 (707) 294-2049 — **WEB:** www.kenzonapa.com
🔳 Dinner Tue – Sun

PRICE: $$$$

LA TOQUE ❀
Contemporary

XxX | 🐝 ᫚ ⬜ 🍽

MAP: B3

You'll want to tip your own toque in appreciation after a meal at this downtown fine-dining palace in the Westin Verasa Napa, which blends a serious approach to cuisine and service that has just enough cheek to keep things lively.

La Toque may display an oversized inflatable chef's hat hanging above its walkway, but the interior is the soul of modern sophistication, with leather-topped tables, a fireplace, and an extensive wine list—proffered on an iPad. The cadre of staff is notable, and the well-trained, knowledgeable waiters move in synchronicity within the celebratory crowd.

Choose from a four- or five-course à la carte, beginning with exquisite canapés like perfectly seasoned tuna tartare, clams with apple vinaigrette, or crostini with a terrine of foie gras. Thin slices of beef loin carpaccio are lightly smoked, then artfully presented to resemble a flower, topped with creamy tuna sauce, sautéed wild mushroom, and dried tomato. Intense Lebanese spices come to life in wonderfully tender braised squid with dates, almond, cauliflower and a spoonful of Greek yogurt. Desserts like the triple-baked, butter-crunch cake with apple underscore the homey, glamorous, delicious character of the restaurant itself.

🔲 1314 McKinstry St. (at Soscol Ave.), Napa
📞 (707) 257-5157 — **WEB:** www.latoque.com
🔲 Dinner nightly

PRICE: $$$$

MIMINASHI 🍴

Japanese

✄ | ♿ **MAP:** B4

Izakaya fare gets Californian flair at this downtown Napa site, which has a distinctive and minimalist look inspired by several trips to Japan. A buzzy crowd of locals fills the wooden booths and tables, while an arrow-shaped bar is a major draw for solo diners.

A variety of skewered chicken parts grilled over the white-hot binchotan are the highlight of the menu—imagine the likes of succulent and smoky chicken thighs, or springy tsukune in an umami-rich tare glaze. A handful of seats at the narrow counter allow guests to chat with the grill cook. The rest of the menu emphasizes local produce, including rice and noodle bowls stuffed with seasonal vegetables; crunchy sweet corn fritters with Kewpie mayo; as well as gingery pan-fried chicken gyoza.

◼ 821 Coombs St. (bet. 2nd & 3rd Sts.), Napa
✆ (707) 254-9464 — **WEB:** www.miminashi.com
◼ Lunch Mon – Fri   Dinner nightly   **PRICE: $$**

MUSTARDS GRILL 🍴

American

✄✄ | 🐾 ♿   **MAP:** D3

At Cindy Pawlcyn's iconic roadhouse, it's a joy to eat your greens. Lettuces are freshly plucked from the restaurant's bountiful garden boxes and tossed with tasty dressings including a shallot- and Dijon mustard-spiked Banyuls vinaigrette. Fish of the day may unveil grilled halibut sauced with oxtail reduction and plated with silken leeks, fingerling potatoes, and baby carrots. But, save room as this is not the place to skip dessert, and the lemon-lime tart capped with brown sugar meringue that is fittingly described on the menu as "ridiculously tall," doesn't disappoint. It should come as no surprise that there's usually a wait for a table here. But no matter; use the time to take a stroll on the grounds for a preview of what the kitchen has in store.

◼ 7399 St. Helena Hwy. (at Hwy. 29), Yountville
✆ (707) 944-2424 — **WEB:** www.mustardsgrill.com
◼ Lunch & dinner daily   **PRICE: $$$**

OENOTRI 🐶
Italian

XX | & ⌂ ⛱

MAP: A4

There's no sweeter greeting than the aroma of wood smoke that beckons diners into this downtown standout. And with its Neapolitan pizza oven, sunny textiles, and exposed brick, Oenotri—from an ancient Italian word for "wine cultivator"—looks as good as it smells.

Chef/owner Tyler Rodde imbues the cooking of Southern Italy with a dash of Californian spirit and the resulting cuisine is nothing short of enticing. Options change with the season, but true fans know that pizza is a must. Mixed chicory salad with mozzarella di bufala, pickled red chilies, and house-cured salametto is also a crowd-pleaser. Not far behind is the torchio, or corkscrew pasta, presented with diced roasted winter squash, toasted pine nuts, fried sage, and a drizzle of brown butter.

▤ 1425 1st St. (bet. Franklin & School Sts.), Napa
☏ (707) 252-1022 — **WEB:** www.oenotri.com
▤ Lunch Sat – Sun   Dinner nightly   **PRICE: $$**

PRESS ⅋O
Steakhouse

XXX | 🍸 & ⌂ ▢

MAP: C2

The classic steakhouse gets a wine country twist at this standby, where the G&Ts are designed to specifications and the dry-aged USDA Prime steaks hold equal standing with the "vegetable cocktail"—a stunning edible still life of local produce. But indulgence is still the name of the game, from a take on the classic wedge salad made with local Pt. Reyes blue cheese to a decadent mashed potato pancake.

With a bucolic location off Highway 29, Press combines traditional dark wood, cozy booths, and a flickering fireplace with lofty and soaring ceilings. The well-to-do crowd marvels at decorative wonders like a massive ceramic clock sourced from a bygone New York train station, all the while sipping full-bodied Napa reds that pair perfectly with the rich food.

▤ 587 St. Helena Hwy. (near Inglewood Ave.), St. Helena
☏ (707) 967-0550 — **WEB:** www.presssthelena.com
▤ Dinner Wed – Mon   **PRICE: $$$$**

REDD ⅋○

Contemporary

✗✗ | ⚬ 🍸 ♿ 🏠 🛶

In this quaint hamlet, Redd stands out both for its modern look and contemporary approach to cuisine, with flavors from around the globe. A meal here might begin with Chinese-style lettuce cups filled with succulent chicken, stir-fried eggplant, and fresh herbs; then veer into India and Spain simultaneously via a Petrale sole fillet with coconut-jasmine rice, curry-saffron broth, and salty-spicy chorizo. And any Londoner would be proud of the buttery sticky toffee pudding, with tart crème fraîche ice cream and huckleberries. The sleek, modernist décor attracts a sedate crowd, attended to by professional servers.

On nice days, be sure not to miss the serene outdoor patio, which begs to be savored with a glass of Joseph George sauvignon blanc from Yountville.

▨ 6480 Washington St. (at Oak Circle), Yountville
☏ (707) 944-2222 — **WEB:** www.reddnapavalley.com
▨ Lunch Fri – Sun Dinner nightly   **PRICE:** $$$$

REDD WOOD ⊛

Italian

✗✗ | ♿ 🏠 🖵

Napa Valley's answer to the hip Cal-Ital hot spots of San Francisco, Redd Wood boasts an edgy indie soundtrack and a parade of bearded, tattooed waiters. But unlike some cityside establishments, the waitstaff here is personable and enthusiastic, and there's plenty of breathing room (including a private area that's popular for events).

Artisan pizzas are the main attraction of this kitchen and sometimes simplest is best—like the fresh mozzarella, basil, and tomato. Another topped with pancetta, asiago, taleggio and black garlic is equally enticing. But, don't let that limit your choices. The house-cured salumi, fresh pastas, and appealing antipasti are also winners. However, just be sure to save some room for their outstanding toffee cannoli.

▨ 6755 Washington St. (bet. Madison & Pedroni Sts.), Yountville
☏ (707) 299-5030 — **WEB:** www.redd-wood.com
▨ Lunch & dinner daily   **PRICE:** $$

THE RESTAURANT AT MEADOWOOD ✿ ✿ ✿

Contemporary

XxxX | 🍇 🍸 ♿ 🧼

MAP: C2

With its elusive balance of rustic luxury, this is the kind of property that will floor you with its understated, olive tree-lined beauty. Everything here exudes California-style wealth and comfort, from those cottages dotting the Napa hills to the front lounge's stone fireplace and shelves lined with Chef Kostow's debut cookbook. Beyond this, the dining room is a sophisticated barn of sorts, decked in polished stone tables, wood columns, and rural splendor.

This all makes for an elegant backdrop for romantic evenings or family celebrations, as long as everyone is willing to splurge. Servers are impeccable, professional, and know how to keep their guests happy and at ease.

The cooking never ceases to better itself through innovation and purity. The soft, saline flavors of cauliflower custard topped with caviar nearly explode in the mouth. Tableside preparations add to the night's entertainment and pleasure, like the plump lamb chop with roasted pluot, finished before your eyes with a copper pot of marigold-coriander jus. A mesmerizing presentation of eggplant Foster, which cleverly substitutes a vegetable for the traditional banana, would not be possible without such beautiful produce.

▨ 900 Meadowood Ln. (off Silverado Trail), St. Helena
✆ (707) 967-1205 — **WEB:** www.therestaurantatmeadowood.com
▨ Dinner Tue – Sat

PRICE: $$$$

RUTHERFORD GRILL 🍴

American

XX | ♿ 🏕

As the crowds filter out of neighboring Beaulieu Vineyards and other Highway 29 wineries, they head straight to this upscale chain, which boasts long lines at even the earliest hours. Kudos to the amiable host staff for handling them smoothly. The dark wood interior is clubby yet accommodating, and a large patio offers drinks for waiting diners.

Every portion here can easily serve two, beginning with a seasonal vegetable platter boasting buttery Brussels sprouts, a wild rice salad, and braised red cabbage. For those looking to stave off tasting-induced hangovers, the steak and enchilada platter is the ticket with plenty of juicy tri-tip, yellow and red escabeche sauce, and a poached egg. A wedge of classic banana cream pie delivers the knockout punch.

■ 1180 Rutherford Rd. (at Hwy. 29), Rutherford
𝒞 (707) 963-1792 — **WEB:** www.hillstone.com
■ Lunch & dinner daily

PRICE: $$

SAM'S SOCIAL CLUB 🍴

American

XX | ♿ 🏕 🛍 ⚑

MAP: B1

Lauded as the main restaurant for the Indian Springs resort, Sam's Social Club is a supremely beloved destination, thanks in large part to its Spanish colonial look and soothing, bucolic vibe. Named for resort founder Samuel Brannan, this Mission Revival dining room boasts lofty ceilings, plush couches, bright murals, and a big patio complete with a geyser-fed water feature.

The unpretentious atmosphere extends to the plates, from grilled octopus endowed with a peppy Romesco sauce and crispy new potatoes. Specials may include pan-seared duck served with bright green broccoli rabe and sweetly acidic piquillo. Tourists have already caught on: you'll find them happily sharing bottles of wine and digging into plates of strawberry-rhubarb crisp.

■ 1712 Lincoln Ave. (at Indian Springs Resort), Calistoga
𝒞 (707) 942-4969 — **WEB:** www.samssocialclub.com
■ Lunch & dinner daily

PRICE: $$

SOLBAR 🍴
Californian

✕✕ | 🍸 ⛓ 🏠 🖵 📱 💼 🛋 🍽

MAP: B1

It may take a few twists and turns around the palatial Solage Calistoga property to locate this bijou, but once inside, you'll find a romantic dining room decked with banquettes and a contemporary fireplace. Well-heeled tourists flock to the patio to dine on a four-course à la carte menu under the twinkling lights, while regulars may opt for the glassed-in Chef's Atrium.

With the arrival of a new chef, the cuisine here has tilted slightly towards Europe. But, its Californian spirit is still very much alive and well, like in the inventive Chandler strawberry gazpacho garnished with duck prosciutto. Gently seared salmon bathed in tzatziki and harissa tailed by a citrus pavlova also reflect this kitchen's global inspirations.

◼ 755 Silverado Trail (at Rosedale Rd.), Calistoga
☎ (707) 226-0860 — **WEB:** solage.aubergeresorts.com
◼ Lunch & dinner daily

PRICE: $$$

TWO BIRDS/ONE STONE 😊
Fusion

✕✕ | ⛓ 🏠 🖵

MAP: C2

Acclaimed Chefs Douglas Keane and Sang Yoon join forces at this hip aviary, located within the striking Freemark Abbey Winery. The space blends the original stone walls with steel trusses, overhead skylights, as well as a spacious patio— reflecting the menu's Californian take on traditional Japanese kushiyaki.

Meals start with seasonal small plates like "Ham & Eggs" featuring a small stone jar filled with savory egg custard, topped with smoked duck ham, onsen jidori egg, and shaved scallions. Then shift into a selection of meats, like Ibérico de bellota—tender, rosy pork shoulder glazed with spiced Vietnamese caramel and grouped with kimchi. Pair one of their wines with sweet Pepony grapes accompanied by shattered white miso custard for an exclusive finish.

◼ 3020 St. Helena Hwy. (bet. Ehlers & Lodi Lns.), St. Helena
☎ (707) 302-3777 — **WEB:** www.twobirdsonestonenapa.com
◼ Dinner Thu – Mon

PRICE: $$

TERRA ✿
Contemporary

XxX | 🐝 ♿

MAP: F2

Serious and mature yet understated, Terra is quaintly tucked into a 19th-century building known as The Hatchery (because it really was a chicken hatchery). The décor embraces its rustic past with an eye on luxury, through floor-to-ceiling wine racks, exposed stone, and chunky wood beams. The result looks decidedly more old-world European than 21st-century wine country—nothing here changes and that is a nice thing.

The kitchen's distinct personality is evident in each seasonally driven menu, ranging from four to six courses of Japanese- and Mediterranean-influenced cuisine. Begin with broiled and marinated black cod served in a clear shellfish broth floating a dumpling stuffed with minced shrimp. A fine, delicate hand is clear in the light and airy chawan mushi filled with remarkably tender lobster meat finished with a few snips of chives. Rosy duck breast is served atop creamy polenta scattered with chanterelles and foie gras-duck jus.

Classic desserts promise wonderful balance of flavors. Find evidence of this in the tartlet filled with huckleberries that are none too sweet, deliciously tart, and a perfect contrast to the crispy oatmeal crumble on top, as well as the crème fraîche ice cream on the side.

▨ 1345 Railroad Ave. (bet. Adams St. & Hunt Ave.), St. Helena
☎ (707) 963-8931 — **WEB:** www.terrarestaurant.com
▨ Dinner Thu – Mon   **PRICE: $$$$**

ZUZU ╫◯

Spanish

▤ | ♿

MAP: B4

This Mediterranean-inspired cutie was dishing out small plates long before it was cool, and its rustic bi-level space still draws a steady crowd of local regulars. Spanish-style tile floors, a pressed-tin ceiling, and honey-colored walls give Zuzu an enchanting old-world vibe, setting the scene for sharing the more than two dozen tapas, both frio and caliente.

They include the popular boquerónes, grilled bread heaped with aïoli, hard-boiled eggs, and cured anchovies, as well as the outstanding pork cheek—its rich, caramelized flavor balanced by a tart sherry gastrique. In the evening, killer wood-fired paellas are worth saving a slot for.

For similar cuisine in a more modern atmosphere, sister restaurant La Taberna is also worth a visit.

▤ 829 Main St. (bet. 2nd & 3rd Sts.), Napa
✆ (707) 224-8555 — **WEB:** www.zuzunapa.com
▤ Lunch Mon – Fri   Dinner nightly

PRICE: $$

Look for our symbol 🍸
spotlighting restaurants
with a serious cocktail list.

SONOMA COUNTY

Bordering the North Bay, Sonoma County boasts around 76 miles of Pacific coastline and over 400 wineries. Eclipsed as a wine region by neighboring Napa Valley, this county's wineries know how to take full advantage of some of California's best grape-growing conditions. Today, 17 distinct wine appellations (AVAs) have been assigned in this area, which is slightly larger than the state of Rhode Island itself, and produce a groundbreaking range of fine varietals. This region however is also cherished for its culinary destinations starting with **The Naked Pig**, an amazing pit-stop for brunch or lunch. Reinforcing the wine country's ethos of farm-to-table dining, the items on offer here ooze with all things local and sustainable—maybe bacon waffles with Santa Rosa wildflower honey? But, there are plenty of big and bold bites

to be had in town. **Bar-B-Que Smokehouse** in Sebastopol is quite literally award-winning, as their 'cue took home the crown at the **Sonoma County Harvest Fair** in 2010. Other premium pleasures include **Screamin' Mimi's**, a local but nationally known ice cream shop that has been preparing its 300-plus recipes since 1995, as well as **Moustache Baked Goods**, a boutique operation churning out exceptional, all-American baked goods with quirky names. In fact, cupcakes (like The Outlaw or even The Vintner) have been known to cultivate a sizable following. The North American headquarters of the South American energy-boosting beverage line,

Guayaki Yerba Mate Cafe, is also settled here as a café-cum-community center, while **The National Heirloom Exposition** is commended among epicureans for its sustainable farming and healthy food practices. Along Highway 12 heading north, byroads lead to isolated wineries, each of which puts its own unique stamp on the business of winemaking. Named after the river that enabled Russian trading outposts along the coast, **The Russian River Valley** is one of the coolest growing regions in Sonoma, largely due to the river basin that acts as a conduit for coastal climates. At the upper end of the Russian River,

Dry Creek Valley yields excellent sauvignon blanc, chardonnay, and pinot noir. This region is also justifiably famous for zinfandel—a grape that does especially well in the valley's rock-strewn soil. And for snacks to go with these notable sips, Sonoma's eight-acre plaza is occupied by restaurants, shops, and other such stops. Of epicurean note is building contractor Chuck Williams who bought a hardware store here in 1956. He gradually converted its stock to a selection of exceptionally unique French cookware and kitchen tools, and today, **Williams-Sonoma** has over 600 stores nationwide. Following in his footsteps, **Bram** is similarly beloved for their handmade earthenware, that is inspired by the Egyptian clay pots of yore. And located on the same square, **Sign of the Bear** is yet another specialty shop (as well as an essential stop) for all types of table- and cook-ware.

BEST IN LIFE

Throughout scenic and bucolic Sonoma County (also known locally as SoCo), vineyards rub shoulders with orchards and farms. The words "sustainable" and "organic" headline these local farmers' markets, where one may find every item imaginable— from just-picked heirloom vegetables to uni so fresh that it still appears to be moving. Of course, freshness comes first at **Amy's Drive Thru**, where organic veggie burgers and the plant-covered "living rooftop" are well-worth a visit. In business since 2010, **Petaluma Pie Company** keeps picky palates sated and happy with both sweet and savory pies crafted from organic ingredients. And over on Petaluma Blvd., find a cult of carb fans at **Della Fattoria**—drooling over their lineup of just-baked bread.

This very fertile territory also has more than just a fair share of great seafood. In fact, some of the best oysters can be found off the Sonoma coast and enthusiasts drive along Highway 1 to sample as many varieties as possible— from **Tomales Bay Oyster Company** and **The Marshall Store**, to **Hog Island Oyster Co**. Naturally there are much more than just mollusks to be relished here. Start your day right with a serious breakfast at **The Fremont Diner** where the **Bellwether Farms'** ricotta pancakes are light, fluffy, and... you guessed it...regionally sourced. Devour these hearty eats at local sensation **Bear Republic Brewing Company Pub & Restaurant**—a family-owned Healdsburg hot spot favored for unique, award-winning brews and tours (by appointment only); or over a top-notch IPA, which are all

the rage at **Lagunitas Brewing Company**—a taproom for the Petaluma-based brewery. For a different kind of buzz, coffee shops are fast becoming the new tasting room in these parts, featuring ethically sourced beans from the world's best growing regions that are roasted locally and expertly brewed to order. **Acre Coffee** and **Flying Goat Coffee** are two such highly regarded options with outposts locasted throughout this county.

Numerous ethnic food stands bring global cuisines to this wine-centric community, with offerings that have their roots as close as Mexico and far off as India and Afghanistan. Thanks to Sonoma County's natural bounty, farm-to-table cuisine takes on new heights in many of its surrounding restaurants and some chefs need go no farther than their own on-site gardens for delicious fruits, vegetables, and aromatic herbs. With such easy access to local products like Dungeness crab from Bodega Bay, poultry from Petaluma, and cheeses from the **Sonoma Cheese Factory**, it's no wonder that the cooking

in this town has attracted such high levels of national attention. Serious home gardeners should make sure to scour the shelves of **Petaluma Seed Bank**, located in the historic Sonoma County Bank Building, as it happily counts motivated farmers among its clientele. Find them along with a host of other visitors rejoicing at the Bank's selection of over 1500 heirloom seeds, after which a luscious scoop or slice from stylish **Noble Folk Ice Cream & Pie Bar** seems perfectly in order.

Finally, both area residents as well as tourists in town can't seem to get enough of the local and handcrafted bounty found inside the original **Powell's Sweet Shoppe** in Windsor. This old-fashioned candy store carries an impressive spectrum of old-world classics, modern (gluten-free) items, and "sweet gift boxes" that are big during the holidays. All you have to do is walk in, pick up a pail, and start filling up! If that doesn't result in a sugar rush, there's no going wrong with a scoop of creamy gelato.

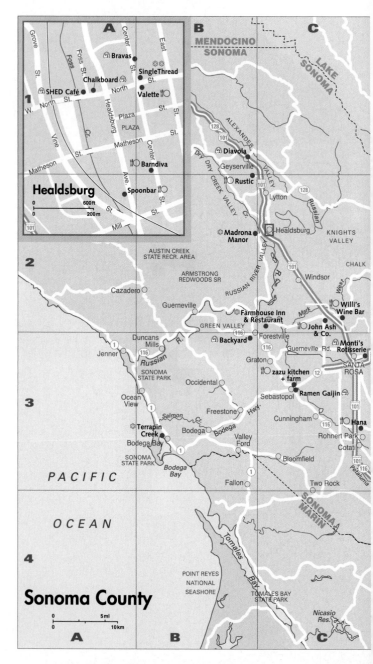

Healdsburg

A
🍴 Bravas
🍴 Chalkboard
☸ SingleThread
SHED Café
🍴 Valette

B

Center St.
East St.
Foss St.
Foss
W. North St.
North St.
Healdsburg
Plaza
PLAZA
Matheson St.
Matheson St.
Vine St.
Center St.
🍴 Barndiva
Spoonbar 🍴
Ave.
St.
Mill St.
101

0   600ft
0   200m

Sonoma County

MENDOCINO
SONOMA

LAKE SONOMA

ALEXANDER VALLEY
128
101

DRY CREEK VALLEY
DRY CREEK

🍴 Diavola
Geyserville
🍴 Rustic
Lytton
128
Russian

101
Healdsburg
KNIGHTS VALLEY

☸ Madrona Manor
RUSSIAN RIVER VALLEY
R. de.

AUSTIN CREEK STATE RECR. AREA

CHALK
101
Windsor
West

ARMSTRONG REDWOODS SR

Cazadero ○

Guerneville
☸ Farmhouse Inn & Restaurant
GREEN VALLEY
116
Forestville
116
🍴 Willi's Wine Bar
Mark
🍴 John Ash & Co.

Duncans Mills
Russian R.
🍴 Backyard
Guerneville Rd.
🍴 Monti's Rotisserie
SANTA ROSA

Jenner
1
SONOMA STATE PARK
Graton ○
🍴 zazu kitchen + farm
12

Ocean View
Occidental ○
Sebastopol
🍴 Ramen Gaijin
101

Salmon Cr.
Freestone ○
Hwy.

☸ Terrapin Creek
Bodega
Bodega
Cunningham ○
116
🍴 Hana
Rohnert Park

Bodega Bay
SONOMA STATE PARK
Valley Ford
Cotati
101
116
Petaluma

PACIFIC

Bodega Bay
Bloomfield ○

Fallon ○
Two Rock

OCEAN
SONOMA
MARIN

POINT REYES NATIONAL SEASHORE
Tomales Bay
TOMALES BAY STATE PARK
Nicasio Res.

0   5mi
0   10km

A   **B**   **C**

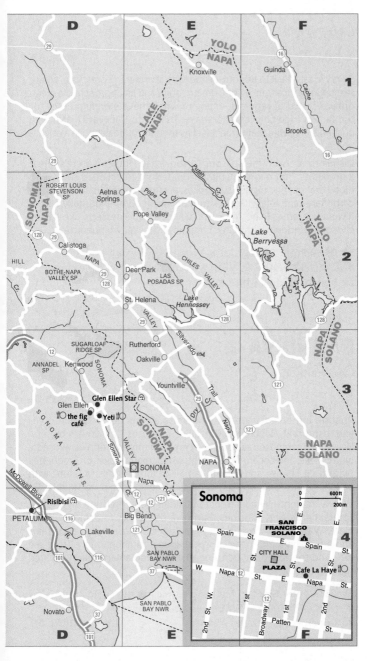

BACKYARD 😳

Californian

✗ | 🚹 ⛺ 🛋   **MAP:** B3

Savvy locals flock to this out-of-the-way charmer in Forestville, where reasonable prices, an inviting dining room, and an approachable menu draw a crowd of regulars—many of whom have standing dates for the famed fried chicken Thursdays. Thanks to Backyard's attentive husband-and-wife team, you'll feel as though you're eating in a private home.

Dishes rotate with the seasons to showcase Mother Nature's finest ingredients. You might encounter tender grilled calamari salad with blood oranges and pickled sunchokes; or creamy house-made pasta à la carbonara complete with black trumpet mushrooms and smoky bacon. It would be remiss to not try one of their delectable desserts, like velvety chocolate pudding with salted caramel and sweet whipped cream.

🔳 6566 Front St. (bet. 1st & 2nd Sts.), Forestville
📞 (707) 820-8445 — **WEB:** www.backyardforestville.com
🔳 Lunch & dinner Thu – Mon   **PRICE:** $$

BARNDIVA 🍴

Californian

✗✗ | 🍸 🚹 ⛺ 🛋   **MAP:** B1

Pristine ingredients are the real stars at this decidedly un-diva-like restaurant, which thoughtfully showcases California's bounty. Beautifully composed salads, like a combo of romaine, apples, avocado, blue cheese, and bacon, shine bright; while creative takes on croquettes (with goat cheese and tomato jam) and lobster rolls (a "club" with bacon, tomato, and arugula) don't sacrifice balance or technique.

With a thoughtfully constructed cocktail menu boasting an array of spirits, herbs, and infusions, Barndiva offers lots to explore off the plate. Witty decorative touches like two-story green velvet curtains and a wall-hanging made of wood shoe stretchers only add to the fun. And for post-meal perusing, there's even an art gallery located right next door.

🔳 231 Center St. (bet. Matheson & Mills Sts.), Healdsburg
📞 (707) 431-0100 — **WEB:** www.barndiva.com
🔳 Lunch & dinner Wed – Sun   **PRICE:** $$

BRAVAS 😊
Spanish

XX | 🏠   **MAP:** A1

"Jamón in" says the cheeky neon sign at this lively tapas bar, set in a former home full of sunny accents and '70s psychedelic posters. While there's a small bar inside, most visitors make a beeline to the huge backyard with its outdoor porch and garden. Thanks to a welcoming cocktail-party vibe, this is the kind of place where big groups of tourists and locals can be found in abundance.

Whether you like your tapas traditional or with a little added flair, there's plenty to sample and share, from plancha-seared sea scallops with creamy romesco to a classic tortilla Española. Lighter appetites will enjoy the chilled tuna belly salad packed with crisp fennel and buttery green olives—it's practically made for washing down with a glass of cava-spiked sangria.

▦ 420 Center St. (bet. North & Piper Sts.), Healdsburg
℘ (707) 433-7700 — **WEB:** www.starkrestaurants.com
▦ Lunch & dinner daily   **PRICE:** $$

CAFE LA HAYE 🍴
Californian

XX | ♿   **MAP:** F4

For years, Cafe La Haye has been a standby off the square in downtown Sonoma. One bite of its luscious burrata, surrounded with Early Girl tomatoes and crispy squash blossoms in the summer, or vinaigrette-dressed pea shoots in spring, proves it hasn't aged a day. The small, modern space is still charming, with large windows and lots of mirrors. Stunning local artwork for sale decorates the walls.

The food spans cultural influences, including a delicate risotto with pine nuts in a cauliflower broth, or soy-sesame glazed halibut atop whipped potatoes and braised kale. A postage stamp-sized bar pours glasses of Sonoma chardonnay and cabernet, perfect with rich strozzapreti tossed with braised pork ragù, Grana Padano, and toasted breadcrumbs.

▦ 140 E. Napa St. (bet. 1st & 2nd Sts.), Sonoma
℘ (707) 935-5994 — **WEB:** www.cafelahaye.com
▦ Dinner Tue – Sat   **PRICE:** $$

CHALKBOARD 😋

American

XX | ♿ ⌷   **MAP:** A1

Located in the luxury boutique Hotel Les Mars, Chalkboard is a surprisingly laid-back boîte, with a casual vibe and a buzzing bar that offer a refreshing counterpoint to a day of wine tasting. The dining room's low vaulted ceilings and marble tables might feel a touch austere if not for the rustic wooden chairs, open kitchen, and warm, easygoing service.

The menu of small plates spans every cuisine and appetite—from whitefish crudo with blood orange and sesame seeds to fried chicken and sunchoke-black truffle soup.

Be sure to sample at least one of the homemade pastas, including tiny shells with SarVecchio cheese, spicy pork sausage, and braised greens. Of course, be sure to leave room for the sticky toffee cake, finished with tart green apple foam.

▨ 29 North St. (bet. Foss St. & Healdsburg Ave.), Healdsburg
☏ (707) 473-8030 — **WEB:** www.chalkboardhealdsburg.com
▨ Lunch Sat – Sun   Dinner nightly   **PRICE: $$**

DIAVOLA 😋

Italian

Ⅹ | ♿ ⌂   **MAP:** B1

Its home in downtown Geyserville may look like the Wild West, but this devilishly good Italian restaurant can hold its own with any city slicker. Festooned with statues of saints, boar tusks, and stacks of cookbooks, it has a playful yet smart vibe.

Excellent pizzas, like the signature combo of spicy meatballs, red peppers, provolone, pine nuts, and raisins, are the reason why crowds pack this spot. And top-notch house ingredients like salumi, lardo, and cured olives elevate each and every dish. But, that's not to count out their exquisite pastas, including linguine tossed with baby octopus, bone marrow, zucchini, and bottarga. Desserts, like the chocolate pistachio semifreddo paired with a perfectly pulled Blue Bottle espresso, are yet another delight.

▨ 21021 Geyserville Ave. (at Hwy. 128), Geyserville
☏ (707) 814-0111 — **WEB:** www.diavolapizzeria.com
▨ Lunch & dinner daily   **PRICE: $$**

FARMHOUSE INN & RESTAURANT ✿
Californian

XxX | 🎀 ♿

MAP: C2

Urbanites seeking an escape from the fray head to this charming inn, nestled in a quiet, woodsy corner of Sonoma, for fine cooking, upscale accommodations, or both. Dinner guests will find themselves charmed by the dining room's soothing colors, rustic-elegant décor, crackling fireplace, and numerous intimate nooks—including an enclosed patio.

The protein-centric menu reads like an ode to California's purveyors, and a focus on seasonality is in keeping with the area's ethos. Not surprisingly, the results are often rewarding: succulent, perfectly balanced heirloom tomatoes are twirled with crunchy seaweed, briny clams, and mirin dressing, while flaky halibut arrives atop a richly flavored fennel-tomato beurre blanc, dotted with corn and huitlacoche pudding. The signature "rabbit, rabbit, rabbit" showcases the kitchen's creativity, bringing together a confit rabbit leg, an applewood-smoked bacon-wrapped loin, and a minuscule rack of chops rounded out with Yukon potatoes and whole grain mustard-cream sauce.

Pair your meal with a bottle from the impressive list of local and European wines. Then complete the seduction with an airy soufflé concealing a treasure of Blenheim apricot preserves.

▧ 7871 River Rd. (at Wohler Rd.), Forestville
☎ (707) 887-3300 — **WEB:** www.farmhouseinn.com
▧ Dinner Thu – Mon   **PRICE:** $$$$

GLEN ELLEN STAR 🙂

Californian

🍴 | ♿

MAP: D3

The country charm of this quaint cottage belies the level of culinary chops that will impress even a hardened city slicker. With knotty pine tables, well-worn plank floors, and a wood-burning oven, the space is delightful. A perch at the chef's counter affords a great view of the action.

Here, Chef Ari Weiswasser showcases his signature style via the use of Mediterranean and Middle Eastern ingredients. Imagine wood-roasted asparagus with lavash crackers and shaved radish over a tangy hen egg emulsion; or chicken cooked under a brick with coconut curry and sticky rice. Daily pizzas like the tomato-cream pie with Turkish chilies are also a thrill. Save room for house-made ice cream in flavors like vanilla maple Bourbon, salted peanut butter, or peach verbena.

🔲 13648 Arnold Dr. (at Warm Springs Rd.), Glen Ellen
📞 (707) 343-1384 — **WEB:** www.glenellenstar.com
🔲 Dinner nightly   **PRICE:** $$

HANA 🍴⭕

Japanese

🍴🍴 | 🍷 ♿

MAP: C3

Rohnert Park denizens continue their love affair with this spacious gem featuring semi-private nooks and a lounge. Tucked in a hotel plaza next to the 101, Hana is run by affable Chef/owner Ken Tominaga, who sees to his guests' every whim. For the full experience, park it at the bar where the obliging chefs can steer you through the best offerings of the day. Top quality fish flown in from Tsukiji Market (ask for the daily specials), traditional sushi and small plates are the secret to their success, though mains like pan-seared pork loin with ginger-soy jus also hit the spot.

The omakase is a fine way to go—six pieces of nigiri which may include toro, hamachi belly, kampachi, tai, halibut with ponzu sauce, or sardine sprinkled with Hawaiian lava salt.

🔲 101 Golf Course Dr. (at Roberts Lake Rd.), Rohnert Park
📞 (707) 586-0270 — **WEB:** www.hanajapanese.com
🔲 Lunch Mon – Sat   Dinner nightly   **PRICE:** $$

JOHN ASH & CO. 🍴

Californian

XX | 🎴 ♿ 🏕️

MAP: C2

A pioneer in farm-to-table dining, this stalwart in the Vintners Inn (owned by Ferrari-Carano) is 35+ years strong and still serving the region's best, much of it grown in the on-site gardens. The rustic Front Room is a popular happy-hour spot with its menu of bar snacks, while the Tuscan-inspired dining room boasts plush booths, a stone fireplace, and Italian landscapes on the walls.

Chef Tom Schmidt has broadened the restaurant's focus, incorporating Latin touches like a halibut ceviche with aji amarillo and creamy sweet potato. But there are still indulgent classics aplenty, like the dry-aged beef filet, cooked to a buttery medium rare and accompanied by decadent Point Reyes blue cheese mashed potatoes, or the rich chocolate truffle cake for dessert.

▓ 4330 Barnes Rd. (off River Rd.), Santa Rosa
☎ (707) 527-7687 — **WEB:** www.vintnersinn.com
▓ Dinner nightly   **PRICE: $$$**

MONTI'S ROTISSERIE 😊

American

XX | ♿ 🏕️ 🍷

MAP: C3

With the scent of wood smoke hanging in the air, it seems impossible to resist ordering the day's offering hot off the rotisserie. Those smoked prime ribs or pomegranate-glazed pork ribs do not disappoint, either. But the oak-roasted chicken is a perennial favorite and deserves a visit on its own. Succulent auburn skin, seasoned flesh, heirloom carrots, smashed fingerling potatoes, and crisped pancetta, render this dish a thing of beauty. End your meal over baby lettuces with Point Reyes blue cheese and candied walnuts; or butterscotch pudding for lip-smacking comfort food—Monti's-style.

Set within Santa Rosa's Montgomery Village, this is your quintessential wine country hangout, dressed with rustic tables and centered around a roaring fireplace—natch.

▓ 714 Village Court (at Sonoma Ave.), Santa Rosa
☎ (707) 568-4404 — **WEB:** www.starkrestaurants.com
▓ Lunch & dinner daily   **PRICE: $$**

MADRONA MANOR ❀

Contemporary

XxX | 🕸 ⚙ ☂ 🖵

MAP: B2

This romantic Victorian mansion is the unexpected home of a forward-looking kitchen. It's the kind of place that makes one want to dress up—at least a little bit—to fully engage in the art of dining. Arrive early to enjoy a sunset drink out on the terrace. You can either stay there to dine, or head inside to settle into one of several timelessly elegant dining rooms cloaked in sleek marble, plush silk, and old-world grandeur.

The showmanship here extends to the artistic, often theatrical plates that make the most of herbs and flowers to create novel and very focused flavors throughout the menus. Expect a separate amuse for each new dish to prepare the palate, so bread with mustard-lardo cream arrives as a prelude to kohlrabi cooked al forno, then topped with shallots and cress. The kitchen is also particularly adept with raw vegetables, as may be found in the roasted quail that is cut and served with raw and olive oil-fried chard with onion soubise.

A green profiterole stuffed with apple mousse leads to a "morning breakfast dessert" of Turkish figs, apple sorbet, thin and crunchy melba toast, as well as a host of garnishes like chocolate, jelly, raisins, and corn caramels.

■ 1001 Westside Rd. (at W. Dry Creek Rd.), Healdsburg
✆ (707) 433-4231 — **WEB:** www.madronamanor.com
■ Dinner Wed – Sun

PRICE: $$$$

RAMEN GAIJIN 😀

Japanese

🍴 | ♿ 🏠   **MAP:** C3

"Gaijin" is the none-too-polite Japanese term for a foreigner, but the American chefs of this clandestine noodle joint clearly take pride in their outsider status, fusing local ingredients with traditional technique. This is an expansive restaurant that retains a friendly and casual vibe.

The best seats are at the counter, where you can chat with the chef as he assembles bowls of light, fresh shoyu ramen filled with thick house-made rye noodles and caramelized pork belly chashu. Appetizers are also notable, like a surprisingly elegant salad of smoked cod and baby gem lettuces. Don't miss such creative and delicious desserts as black-sesame ice cream with miso caramel. After 3:30, the menu goes on to offer izakaya fare, like gyoza and okonomiyaki.

🔲 6948 Sebastopol Ave. (bet. Main St. & Petaluma Ave.), Sebastopol
✆ (707) 827-3609 — **WEB:** www.ramengaijin.com
🔲 Lunch & dinner Tues – Sat   **PRICE:** $$

RISIBISI 😀

Italian

🍴🍴 | ♿ 🏠 ⊡   **MAP:** D4

Though it's named for a comforting dish of rice and peas, Risibisi's seafood-heavy take on Italian cuisine is a bit more sophisticated. A meal at this Petaluma treasure might begin with a chilled slice of veal roast topped with creamy tuna sauce and dried capers. Also try the pesce di giorno, perhaps featuring beautifully grilled swordfish served alongside cheesy potatoes and green beans in olive-lemon sauce. End with their house-made tiramisu or cannoli with bits of candied fruit, caramel, and strawberry sauce.

A makeshift picture gallery constructed out of salvaged Tuscan chestnut window frames, wine barrels, and wagon wheels bring character to this inviting brick-walled dining room. A back patio offers views of the river and old train tracks.

🔲 154 Petaluma Blvd. N. (bet. Washington St. & Western Ave.), Petaluma
✆ (707) 766-7600 — **WEB:** www.risibisirestaurant.com
🔲 Lunch & dinner daily   **PRICE:** $$

RUSTIC ⵍO

Italian

XX | & 🏠   **MAP:** B2

Those Godfather Oscars certainly could have funded a posh restaurant for Francis Ford Coppola, but the director has kept it relatively simple at his enormous Geyserville eatery, offering Italian classics from his childhood. Savory pettole doughnuts in a paper bag kick off the meal, followed by crispy chicken al mattone sautéed in olive oil with strips of red pepper. Coppola's personality is a big part of Rustic's appeal, and these walls are covered with his film memorabilia as well as his own wines. Although the real reason for the crowds is the Italian-American music, games, and nostalgia that define Coppola's past as well as those of his customers.

Come on Tuesdays to find a special prix fixe, as well as the sociable staff donning vintage garb.

▦ 300 Via Archimedes (off Independence Ln.), Geyserville
℘ (707) 857-1485 — **WEB:** www.franciscoppolawinery.com
▦ Lunch & dinner daily   **PRICE:** $$

SHED CAFÉ 😳

Californian

X | & 🏠 📖 🍽   **MAP:** A1

Despite its humble "café" moniker, this is the jewel in the crown of the ambitious Healdsburg SHED complex, a foodie wonderland with an in-house market, coffee bar, housewares shop, and even its own farm. The eatery's location is a bit odd—it's in the rear of the complex with little barrier to those milling about shopping for gadgets—but the food is good enough that you might not notice.

The well-arranged, generously portioned plates vary with the seasons, but you might find yellowtail sashimi with seaweed and kimchi powder; roasted potatoes with green garlic and chicharrónes; as well as the luscious braised pork cheeks, dusted with fennel pollen and served over thyme spätzle. For dessert, the Meyer lemon pavlova is a crunchy, creamy delight.

▦ 25 North St. (at Foss St.), Healdsburg
℘ (707) 431-7433 — **WEB:** www.healdsburgshed.com
▦ Lunch daily   Dinner Wed – Mon   **PRICE:** $$

SINGLETHREAD ✿✿

Contemporary

XxxX | 🍸 ♿

MAP: B1

The single thread for which this luxurious newcomer is named is the humble onion—the only item that can be grown year-round on the five-acre farm that supplies it. Everything else in its dizzying array of plates is carefully modulated with the seasons: a foie gras dish, for example, comes draped with sweet persimmon coulis and crushed hickory nuts in the fall, transitioning to earthy Chioggia beets and pear by mid-winter.

Chef Kyle Connaughton cooked for years in Japan, and displays a skill and affinity for donabe cooking. The pots line the walls and arrive at tables bearing tender, buttery steamed cod over crisp brassicas and silky Mt. Lassen trout smoked over cherry blossom wood. Other dishes utilize the hearth, as in a finale of whole miso-glazed sweet potato dusted with cream and cocoa, and topped with chicory ice cream.

Each element of the experience is treated with utmost precision, from the swank rooftop garden where diners enjoy champagne and canapés to the plush rooms at the adjoining inn, where many bed down after the meal. Yet the experience is always warm: staff contribute to the décor, chat merrily with guests, and add to the overall feeling of a rich, regional celebration of place.

▦ 131 North St. (at Center St.), Healdsburg
℘ (707) 723-4646 — **WEB:** www.singlethreadfarms.com
▦ Lunch Sat – Sun   Dinner Tue – Sun   **PRICE: $$$$**

SPOONBAR 🍴

Contemporary

✗✗ | 🍸   ♿   🏠   **MAP:** A2

Seeking a modern departure from wine country's faux-rustic aesthetic? This restaurant in the eco-chic h2hotel will fit the bill with reclaimed wood tables and 3-D artwork. Its bar is a local haunt, with wine-weary tasters arriving to palate-cleanse via an extensive list of cocktails. In the kitchen, a husband-and-wife chef team successfully guides the menu in a sophisticated, vegetable-driven direction. Find such inventive dishes as Meyer lemon ricotta gnudi in a parmesan-mushroom broth; or seared scallops with roasted and pickled brassicas and black garlic purée.

Should you order a dessert, like the honey crème fraîche panna cotta, don't be surprised if a second arrives gratis— the chef likes to test out her latest experiments on an all-too-willing public.

▨ 219 Healdsburg Ave. (bet. Matheson & Mill Sts.), Healdsburg
✆ (707) 433-7222 — **WEB:** www.spoonbar.com
▨ Dinner nightly   **PRICE:** $$

THE FIG CAFÉ 🍴

Californian

✗✗ | ♿   🛋   **MAP:** D3

Sondra Bernstein's Cal-Med café takes on a more modern look with communal tables, orange bar stools, and geometric lighting. But pilgrims to this sleepy address shouldn't fret: Rhone-style wines (a house specialty) remain on the shelves, and inviting horseshoe-shaped booths are still the best seats in the house. The nightly prix-fixe—displayed on butcher paper—is as great a deal as ever, and approachable faves like fried olives and a burger are out in force. Start with a salad like grill-charred romaine Caesar with anchovy-spiked dressing; then segue to a seasonal entrée like trout with wild rice, caramelized onions, and green beans.

For like-minded cuisine, visit the girl & the fig in Sonoma's main square.

▨ 13690 Arnold Dr. (at O'Donnell Ln.), Glen Ellen
✆ (707) 938-2130 — **WEB:** www.thefigcafe.com
▨ Lunch Sun   Dinner nightly   **PRICE:** $$

TERRAPIN CREEK ✿

Californian

XX

MAP: B3

Terrapin Creek isn't easy to find, but those who persevere will be rewarded with a delightful little hideaway bearing delicious cuisine. Dramatically situated above picturesque Bodega Bay, this lovely retreat is just steps from the water. (During the January-March whale-watching season, you might even catch a glimpse of these gentle giants bobbing in the Pacific.)

The upbeat, sun-filled dining room, done in orange and yellow and filled with big, bold paintings, is clean and unfussy. The small-town staff is every bit as warm as the space, and treats everyone like a regular. A meal might begin with a mixed-green salad topped with goat cheese, persimmon, prosciutto, and a tart cherry vinaigrette. Then segue into three coins of ravioli filled with kabocha squash and floating in a fragrant black truffle-and-butter sauce. Tender duck breast with deliciously seasoned and crisped skin is then cooked to pink perfection and coupled with a sauté of cabbage, shiitakes, and fingerling potatoes. Paired with a Napa red blend, it's equal parts modern and classic.

Desserts promise to please, but for a powerful—never heavy—finish, opt for the dark chocolate pot de crème topped with slices of sweet banana.

■ 1580 Eastshore Rd. (off Hwy. 1), Bodega Bay
✆ (707) 875-2700 — **WEB:** www.terrapincreekcafe.com
■ Dinner Thu – Mon　　　　　　　　　　　　**PRICE:** $$

VALETTE ⅋O

Californian

XX |

Housed in the former Zin space, this contemporary darling is actually a full-circle comeback for Chef Dustin Valette and his brother/General Manager Aaron Garzini, whose grandfather owned the building in the 1940s. Its current look, however, is as cutting-edge as ever thanks to dandelion-like light fixtures, concrete walls, and horseshoe-shaped banquettes. The bill of fare is modern American with a few French twists. Scallops arrive beneath squid ink puff pastry, into which a server pours caviar-flecked champagne-beurre blanc. Then, Peking-spiced duck breast set atop hearty forbidden rice is taken to the next level with a touch of tamarind sauce.

For a happy ending, dig into the smooth, creamy block of chocolate mousse with a luscious salted caramel center.

🔲 344 Center St. (at North St.), Healdsburg
℘ (707) 473-0946 — **WEB:** www.valettehealdsburg.com
🔲 Dinner nightly   **PRICE:** $$$

WILLI'S WINE BAR ⅋O

International

XX | ♿ 🏠

Don't be fooled by the roadhouse vibe at Mark and Terri Stark's flagship spot, which actually boasts an extremely well-traveled menu. The eclectic dishes are meant to be shared—and paired with local wine, naturally—and the clean, comfortable environs, rich with dark wood, create an ideal setting for a fun evening out with friends.

Willi's wide-ranging menu isn't afraid to take inspiration from wherever it comes—whether adding pancetta and sherry vinegar butter to scallop dumplings; or piling Dungeness crab, baby artichokes, and crescenza cheese on a puffy flatbread. To really indulge, opt for the warm spinach salad with goat cheese and dates, before digging into the Meyer lemon pudding cake, with its airy top and delightful lemon curd.

🔲 4404 Old Redwood Hwy. (at Ursuline Rd.), Santa Rosa
℘ (707) 526-3096 — **WEB:** www.starkrestaurants.com
🔲 Lunch Tue – Sat   Dinner nightly   **PRICE:** $$

YETI ♨️🍴

Nepali

✕✕ | 🏠

Its sleepy location may be unusual, but with a creekside view and friendly service, Yeti makes for a pleasant getaway from the wine country grind. Inside the sunken dining room, soft folk music, Tibetan artwork, and a blisteringly hot tandoor set an authentic scene.

Though this food may hail from the Himalayan frontier, many dishes are from both India's north (think grilled meats and biryanis) as well as southern coastal regions (fish curries and coconut sauces). Try the lamb chops coated in garam masala and served over a bed of charred onion and bell pepper. Vegetable momos (steamed dumplings stuffed with cabbage, carrots, beans, and green onion) served with spicy sambal, cilantro, and sweet tamarind dipping sauces are a party in your mouth.

🔲 14301 Arnold Dr., Ste. 19 (in Jack London Village), Glen Ellen
📞 (707) 996-9930 — **WEB:** www.yetirestaurant.com
🔲 Lunch & dinner daily   **PRICE:** $$

ZAZU KITCHEN + FARM 🍴

American

✕✕ | ♿ 🏠 🛍️

A fun change from the rustic décor seen in much of wine country, this big and bright industrial space is practically translucent, thanks in large part to its garage-like doors and glossy cement floors. Natural wood tables and huge wildflower arrangements keep it from feeling chilly, as do surprisingly great acoustics—you won't struggle to be heard, even if the massive 20-seat family table is full.

Pork is the priority here, as evidenced by the sharp, spicy, and addictive Cuban sandwich with house-made mortadella.

Vegetarians will delight in the tart tomato soup with an oozing Carmody grilled cheese, or the black beans with baked eggs. But the real key for carnivores is to bring home the bacon; it's a little bit pricey, but worth every penny.

🔲 6770 McKinley St., Ste. 150 (bet. Brown & Morris Sts.), Sebastopol
📞 (707) 523-4814 — **WEB:** www.zazukitchen.com
🔲 Lunch Fri – Sun   Dinner Wed – Mon   **PRICE:** $$

MICHELIN IS CONTINUALLY INNOVATING FOR SAFER, CLEANER, MORE ECONOMICAL, MORE CONNECTED AND BETTER ALL AROUND MOBILITY.

Tires wear more quickly on short urban journeys.

TRUE!

You tend to accelerate and brake more often when driving around town so your tires work harder!
If you are stuck in traffic, keep calm and drive slowly.

Tire pressure only affects your car's safety.

FALSE!

Driving with underinflated tires (0.5 below recommended pressure) doesn't just impact handling and fuel consumption, it will take 8,000 km off tire lifespan.
Make sure you check tire pressure about once a month and before you go on vacation or a long journey.

*If you only encounter **winter weather from time to time** - sudden showers, snowfall or black ice - **one type of tire** will do the job.*

TRUE!

The revolutionary **MICHELIN CrossClimate** - the very first summer tire with winter certification - is a practical solution to keep you on the road whatever the weather.

Fitting **2 winter tires** on my car guarantees maximum safety.

?

FALSE!

In the winter, especially when temperatures drop below 44.5°F, to ensure better road grip, all four tires should be identical and fitted at the same time.

2 WINTER TIRES ONLY =
risk of compromised road grip.

4 WINTER TIRES =
safer handling when cornering, driving downhill and braking.

If you regularly encounter rain, snow or black ice, choose a **MICHELIN Alpin tire**. This range offers you sharp handling plus a comfortable ride to safely face the challenge of winter driving.

MICHELIN

MICHELIN
IS COMMITTED

▶ MICHELIN IS THE **GLOBAL LEADER IN FUEL-EFFICIENT TIRES** FOR LIGHT VEHICLES.

▶ **EDUCATING YOUNGSTERS ON ROAD SAFETY FOR BIKES,** NOT FORGETTING TWO-WHEELERS. LOCAL ROAD SAFETY CAMPAIGNS WERE RUN IN **16 COUNTRIES** IN 2015.

QUIZ

1 TIRES ARE BLACK SO WHY IS THE MICHELIN MAN WHITE?

Back in 1898 when the Michelin Man was first created from a stack of tires, they were made of natural rubber, cotton and sulphur and were therefore light-colored. The composition of tires did not change until after the First World War when carbon black was introduced. But the Michelin Man kept his color!

2 HOW LONG HAS MICHELIN BEEN GUIDING TRAVELERS?

Since 1900. When the MICHELIN guide was published at the turn of the century, it was claimed that it would last for a hundred years. It's still around today and remains a reference with new editions and online restaurant listings in a number of countries.

3 WHEN WAS THE "BIB GOURMAND" INTRODUCED IN THE MICHELIN GUIDE?

The symbol was created in 1997 but as early as 1954 the MICHELIN guide was recommending "exceptional good food at moderate prices." Today, it features on the MICHELIN Restaurants website and app.

If you want to enjoy a fun day out and find out more about Michelin, why not visit the l'Aventure Michelin museum and shop in Clermont-Ferrand, France:
www.laventuremichelin.com

INDEXES

ALPHABETICAL LIST OF RESTAURANTS

A

B

U

V

W

Y

Z

RESTAURANTS BY CUISINE

EASTERN EUROPEAN

ETHIOPIAN

FRENCH

FUSION

GASTROPUB

JAPANESE

KOREAN

MEDITERRANEAN

MEXICAN

MIDDLE EASTERN

MOROCCAN

NEPALI

PERSIAN

PERUVIAN

PIZZA

PORTUGUESE

PUERTO RICAN

SEAFOOD

SOUTHERN

SPANISH

Bellota ⅋◯	128
Bravas ⍟	273
Coqueta ⍟	40
La Marcha ⅋◯	158
Zuzu ⅋◯	262

SRI LANKAN

1601 Bar & Kitchen ⍟	140

STEAKHOUSE

Alexander's Steakhouse ⅋◯	217
Press ⅋◯	256

THAI

Farmhouse Kitchen Thai ⍟	75
Kin Khao ❀	43
Sweet Basil ⅋◯	201
Thai House ⍟	163

VEGAN

Millennium ⍟	159
Shizen ⅋◯	82

VEGETARIAN

Greens ⅋◯	56

VIETNAMESE

Khai ⅋◯	133
Lau Hai San ⅋◯	224
Slanted Door (The) ⅋◯	46
Tamarine ⅋◯	229
Thiên Long ⅋◯	229

CUISINES BY NEIGHBORHOOD

SAN FRANCISCO

CASTRO

Californian

CIVIC CENTER

American

EAST BAY

PENINSULA

SOUTH BAY

WINE COUNTRY

NAPA VALLEY

STARRED RESTAURANTS

✿ ✿ ✿

✿ ✿

✿

BIB GOURMAND

UNDER $25

Tell us what you think about our products.

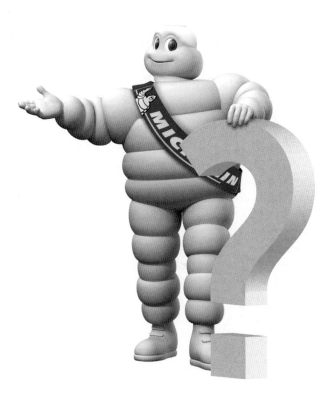

Give us your opinion
satisfaction.michelin.com

CREDITS

All images © 2017 Michelin North America.

MICHELIN TRAVEL PARTNER

Société par actions simplifiées au capital de 11 288 880 EUR
27 Cours de l'Ile Seguin - 92100 Boulogne Billancourt (France)
R.C.S. Nanterre 433 677 721

Impression et Finition : Transcontinental (Canada)

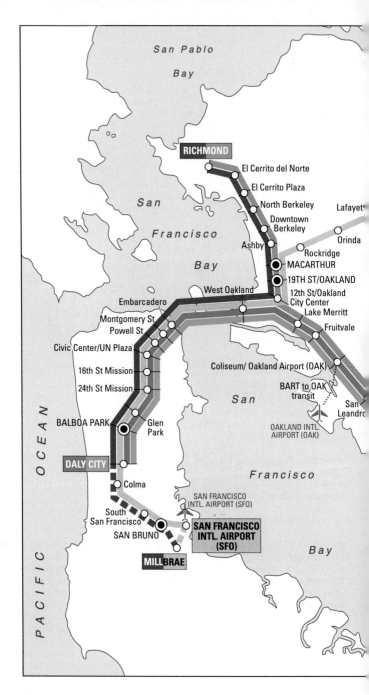